Poetical Dust

Poetical Dust

Poets' Corner and the Making of Britain

Thomas A. Prendergast

PENN

UNIVERSITY OF PENNSYLVANIA PRESS

PHILADELPHIA

A volume in the Haney Foundation Series, established in 1961
with the generous support of Dr. John Louis Haney.

Published by
University of Pennsylvania Press
Philadelphia, Pennsylvania 19104-4112
www.upenn.edu/pennpress

Printed in the United States of America on acid-free paper
1 3 5 7 9 10 8 6 4 2

Library of Congress Cataloging-in-Publication Data
Prendergast, Thomas A., author.
   Poetical dust : Poets' Corner and the making of Britain /
Thomas A. Prendergast.
      pages cm. — (Haney Foundation series)
   Includes bibliographical references and index.
   ISBN 978-0-8122-4750-3 (alk. paper)
   1. Poets' Corner (Westminster Abbey)—History.
   2. Literary landmarks—England—London—History.
   3. Literature and society—Great Britain—History.
   4. Authors and readers—Great Britain—History.   5. Poets,
English—Tombs.   6. Authors, English—Tombs.   I. Title.
II. Series: Haney Foundation series.
   PR110.L6P74 2015
   820.9'9421—dc23
                                             2015016154

For Terry and Charles

I passed some time in Poet's Corner [*sic*], which occupies an end of one of the transepts or cross aisles of the abbey. The monuments are generally simple, for the lives of literary men afford no striking themes for the sculptor. Shakespeare and Addison have statues erected to their memories, but the greater part have busts, medallions, and sometimes mere inscriptions. Notwithstanding the simplicity of these memorials, I have always observed that the visitors to the abbey remained longest about them. A kinder and fonder feeling takes the place of that cold curiosity or vague admiration with which they gaze on the splendid monuments of the great and the heroic. They linger about these as about the tombs of friends and companions, for indeed there is something of companionship between the author and the reader.

—Washington Irving, *The Sketchbook of Geoffrey Crayon*

CONTENTS

Sometime in the 1850s Nathaniel Hawthorne visited Poets' Corner in West-minster Abbey for the first time and remarked on the impression that he had been there before. Yet, far from feeling that weird sense of dread that usually accompanies the *Unheimliche*, or uncanny, he remarks on the hominess of the space.

> It seemed to me that I had always been familiar with the spot. Enjoying a humble intimacy—and how much of my life had else been a dreary solitude!—with many of its inhabitants, I could not feel myself a stranger there. It was delightful to be among them. There was a genial awe, mingled with a sense of kind and friendly presences about me; and I was glad, moreover, at finding so many of them there together, in fit companionship, mutually recognized and duly honored, all reconciled now, whatever distant generations, whatever personal hostility or other miserable impediment, had divided them far asunder while they lived. I have never felt a similar interest in any other tombstones, nor have I ever been deeply moved by the imaginary presence of other famous dead people. A poet's ghost is the only one that survives for his fellow mortals, after his bones are in the dust,—and he not ghostly, but cherishing many hearts with his own warmth in the chillest atmosphere of life. What other fame is worth aspiring for?[1]

Of course, Hawthorne, as a writer, has a special kinship with those ghosts who inhabit Poets' Corner, but, like his countryman Washington Irving (who provides the epigraph for this book), he extends this feeling to the larger public—creating what might be called spiritual communion with those writers who have gone before. In so doing, Hawthorne and Irving oppose the cold marmoreal presence of dead heroes and kings with the warmth, one might say vitality, of dead writers. Indeed, invoking a tradition that goes back to the Roman author Horace, Hawthorne will go on to claim that it is, in fact, poets who are responsible for the continuing fame of statesmen and heroes. Immortality is thus produced by poets, and this immortality, in turn, seems to warm and enliven the space in the Abbey that is inhabited by so many poetical corpses—to make it a "home" for all.

I begin this book about a profoundly English space with two American writers because I want to convey the temporal and geographical reach of Poets' Corner. Though both writers visit Poets' Corner as members of an English-speaking fraternity, their sense of kinship is born not out of a desire to be immortalized within the walls of Westminster Abbey but out of a recognition that the space elicits a certain kind of feeling from them.[2] We might expect these writers to feel a "companionship" with their fellow writers, which they do, but both also move from their personal experience to a larger public feeling about the particular aspects of the writer in his or her afterlife. The writer is, as Hawthorne notes, a ghost—but not ghostly—because of the warmth he possesses and engenders in the visitor. Both Irving and Hawthorne, in other words, use their visits to Poets' Corner to enlarge on the relationship between "the author and the reader" and both contrast the experience in the Corner with the experience one has when one encounters other monuments or gravestones. Poets' Corner becomes a place that reminds them of the bond between reader and writer that remains long after the writer has died.

In this way, Poets' Corner might be seen as a classic *lieu de mémoire*—a place that, as Pierre Nora puts it, embodies "a memorial consciousness that has barely survived in a historical age."[3] It stands as a place that not only commemorates literature but also keeps the memory of writers alive. History penetrates and petrifies these authors, rendering them as traces of what they once were. In Nora's evocative metaphor, they are no longer alive, but neither are they dead, "like shells on the shore when the sea of living memory has receded."[4] Poets' Corner functions as a kind of memory activator. Like the tombs of kings and heroes, the monuments of Poets' Corner stand as palpable reminders of the memory that we are about to lose.

But as long as we focus solely on the monuments' commemorative functions, we remain locked into a reading of the space as exclusively melancholic—an attempt to maintain a connection with what we have lost. Given that so much poetry seems obsessed with loss, it is not surprising that Poets' Corner seems to invite reactions that emphasize loss and memorial recuperation. As

Andreas Huyssen puts it, "Memory . . . was a topic for the poets and their visions of a golden past, or conversely, for their tales about the hauntings of a restless past."[5] But to treat the statues and plaques in Poets' Corner merely as lithic traces of the poetical past is to fail to distinguish between the place of Poets' Corner and the larger space of Westminster Abbey. It is to suggest that the graves of poets and the tombs of what Irving calls "the great and heroic" perform much the same function—to consolidate a feeling of belonging that lends itself to a national consciousness. But Poets' Corner is different from the rest of the Abbey in that its commemorative function seems at odds with that which makes literature worth commemorating. One of the primary claims of literary culture (made by Horace, Shakespeare, Milton, and others) was that the truest, most immortal monuments were literary, while material monuments could fall into decay and thus were evanescent reminders of mortal transience. And, in fact, it is this permanency that enabled "literature . . . to mediate religious, ethnic and class conflicts within [the] nation."[6] At best, the monuments in Poets' Corner would seem extraneous—an impermanent duplication of the literary works that already guarantee the immortality of the poet.

So what is it that Poets' Corner does? What does it try to immortalize? I would argue that we need to ask not only what this site of culture did for the visitor, but what Poets' Corner did *to* the visitor. The "reminding" that Poets' Corner seems to engage in is not merely the spurring of abstract recollections of great literary men and women that would render "cold curiosity or vague admiration," but an "uncovering" of affect in the visitor. What does it mean to employ a metaphor of excavation in relation to affect? It suggests that if visitors to Poets' Corner come in order to exhume (both figuratively and literally) the bodies of the poets, Poets' Corner requires that the visitor unearth his or her emotions vis-à-vis these writers. Insofar as it calls forth or even demands something from the visitor, Poets' Corner has agency. This is not so strange a statement as it may appear. The Corner is very old and is the product of a series of discrete actions over five hundred years. The Corner contains all of these actions, yet all of these actions do not encompass the Corner. This is not to say that those who erected statues, lobbied for burial, or wrote about the Corner did not wish to use the Corner to accomplish various political, ethical, or poetical goals. Poets, politicians, and even merchants all understood the significance of the Corner and attempted to use it to their own purposes. But the larger sensibility created by all of these acts often led the Corner to affect its visitors in very different ways.

Poets' Corner is not merely a space in which various interests are realized, for it also becomes an unacknowledged (because unrecognized) actor in
the cultural and political sphere of England. Its insistent ideology, if we can
call it that, is wrapped up in its own *sui generis* nature and, by extension, the
incommensurability of art. As we will see, claims about the incomparable
nature of art were not universally accepted. Even as politicians and civil society laid claim to the power of the place, they also attempted to use the
boundaries of Poets' Corner to circumscribe the power of literature and, in
a contradictory move, claim that the space—essentially a graveyard—was
commensurate with other spaces in the Abbey. Hence the corpses of poets,
kings, and commoners all mixed together in the undifferentiated space under
the masonry became the occasion for a familiar but potent warning that
death treated all exactly the same. This corporeal leveling, aimed at the material basis for the power of the Corner, was meant to assert that corpses of
poets were no different from the dead bodies of politicians, rulers, and merchants. The implication is that poetry had no special claim to immortality but
was as subject to the ravages of time as politics or patronage. But the paradoxical logic of the Corner operated differently than the commemorative
logic of the rest of the Abbey.

If Poets' Corner "acts" on the visitor, what kind of agency can we attri-
bute to the space? It helps to think about the Corner as the material representation of a kind of text. Using the idea of the "plot" of a text here might seem
contrived, but the word "plot" was, in fact, originally connected with space.
As Lorna Hutson has argued, the word "plat" (the most common early modern variant) meant "a piece of ground used for some purpose" and, by extension, a conceptual scheme or plan of a space.[7] This connection with space led
writers like Philip Sidney to extend what had been a material idea to a more
abstract realm. Thus, in *A Defense of Poetry*, he makes the case that poets
build their works out of "an imaginative ground plot of a profitable invention."[8] For Hutson, emplotment here, like the plan of a plot of land, is ultimately valuable insofar as it alerts the "reader to the *uses* of narrative as a
method for the emplotment or reinterpretaton of circumstances in the interests of a fortunate end."[9] I treat Poets' Corner as a kind of text which indeed
constantly calls attention to its own plot in both senses of the word. It is,
admittedly, a peculiar kind of narrative whose lapidary prose and poetry con-
tinually draws attention to its own construction. And the sheer number of
"authors" involved in the construction of the Corner might seem to compli-
cate claims for a single guiding consciousness behind this place. But I argue

that it is precisely the variousness of the actors involved in Poets' Corner that gives it a kind of authorial consciousness that at once inhabits the present and the past.

As a cemetery, the Corner operates within time as a place where people can gather, and yet it is not quite in time because its purpose is to defeat the predations of history. As a place that is seemingly both within and outside of time, it operates in much the same way as what Michel Foucault calls a heterotopia or "other space." Foucault describes this peculiar space as "most often linked to slices in time—which is to say that they open onto what might be termed, for the sake of symmetry, heterochronies. The heterotopia begins to function at full capacity when men arrive at a sort of absolute break with their traditional time. This situation shows us that the cemetery is indeed a highly heterotopic place since, for the individual, the cemetery begins with this strange heterochrony, the loss of life, and with this quasi-eternity in which her permanent lot is dissolution and disappearance."[10]

Unlike Foucault's notion, of course, this space in Poets' Corner is no mere cemetery, but something that moves beyond the graveyard. Its plot is defined by presence (Geoffrey Chaucer) and absence (William Shakespeare). It is a space that looks to the losses of the past, but also offers the potential for imagining the nation in the future. And it does this by acting as a text that calls forth a certain affective response from its visitor—akin to the affective response that literature calls forth from the reader.

Introduction

The Significance(s) of Poets' Corner

Like any story, the plot of Poets' Corner has a beginning, middle, and end. And it is part of the object of this book to explore how Poets' Corner came to be and what made it important. Yet before we begin to recover the plot of this peculiar place, it is important to acknowledge that the story seems less compelling than it once was. By this I don't mean to suggest that the space in the South Transept of Westminster Abbey doesn't retain cultural significance. Indeed, the model of Westminster's space inspired the cathedral of the Episcopal Diocese of New York, St. John the Divine, to open up an American Poets' Corner in 1984. A Scottish Poets' Corner (Makar's Court) was created in Edinburgh in 1999. Canada and even Texas boast their own Poets' Corners. The name itself seems to retain a certain kind of resonance, as there are a number of websites, housing developments, and even pubs that use the name. (The Old Poets' Corner in Ashover, England, was, for instance, recently runner-up in the nationwide search for best local pub.) Yet the original space seems to have lost some of the energy, one might even say the vitality, that had characterized it since the burial of the poet Edmund Spenser in 1599. I am not certain, in other words, that very many people would now agree with Washington Irving that pilgrims to the Abbey remain longest in the South Transept. If they do, it's only because the marshals have urged them to move briskly along the royal tombs in order to alleviate crowding at the north door. Tourists continue to visit the South Transept, yet in the 1840s Poets' Corner was so popular that Parliament had to pass legislation ensuring that entry would be free to all who wished to enter.[1] What has changed?

Part of the answer is that poetry no longer plays the same role in culture that it once did. This state of affairs is perhaps most obvious if we look back to Thomas Carlyle's influential 1840 lecture "The Hero as Poet," in which he identifies the exemplar of literature, Shakespeare, as hero and even prophet.

He cites the writing on the scroll of the Shakespeare statue in Poets' Corner (a somewhat mangled quotation from *The Tempest*) as evidence that the playwright is "divine . . . the still more melodious Priest of a true Catholicism, the 'Universal Church' of the Future and of all times."[2] In Carlyle's reading, Shakespeare is the poet who not merely lends cultural unity to England but through a kind of cultural sovereignty will unify all Anglophone nations: "Here, I say, is an English King, whom no time or chance, Parliament or combination of Parliaments, can dethrone! This King Shakespeare, does not he shine, in crowned sovereignty, over us all, as the noblest, gentlest, yet strongest of rallying-signs; indestructible; really more valuable in that point of view than any other means or appliance whatsoever? We can fancy him as radiant aloft over all the Nations of Englishmen, a thousand years hence."[3] Shakespeare, then, belongs in what is often called the burial ground of kings because he himself is a king. Like those other English kings, his function is to knit together the English people, but, unlike those kings, his reign cannot be interrupted by mere political considerations, or, it seems, death.

While Carlyle clearly meant to exalt the place of literature in his elevation of Shakespeare to king, his suggestion that Shakespeare provided a form of cultural and political unity (or as Carlyle put it, spoke "forth melodiously what the heart of it [the nation] means") in some sense subordinated art to the needs of the nation.[4] And his observation, that the place where we can "hear" his voice is the same place where we can view "that scroll in Westminster Abbey, which . . . is of the depth of any Seer," indicates a fundamental change in the way writers themselves described Poets' Corner.[5] Previously they had resisted the analogy between sovereign power and poetry, or, more specifically, the analogy between the political and poetical body. But Carlyle now contends that Shakespeare is important insofar as he is a "rallying-sign", and, by extension, poetry is important because it guarantees empire. This suggestion that the political and the poetical are in some sense commensurate certainly seems to rely on the affective power of poetry, but it also narrows that power. Poetry is tied to the material vagaries of politics and is powerful only insofar as it can be utilized. Few, now, would look to poets, even Shakespeare, as guarantors of empire, divine prophets, or kings, but in the nineteenth century, such a claim seemed plausible and also seemed to signal the great power that poetry had in the polis. But once poetry's worth was tied to its political utility, its loss of utility led to its loss of power. And with this loss of power came a corresponding lack of need for a space in which the power of poetry could be marshaled (as by Carlyle) for the national good.

The change in the nature of this power can be seen in the change in the experience of the place itself. One of the most famous reveries about the Abbey and the Corner, by the eighteenth-century poet, playwright, and essayist Joseph Addison, captures something of the quieter mood of pre-twenty-first-century Westminster: "WHEN I am in a serious humour, I very often walk by myself in Westminster Abbey; where the gloominess of the place, and the use to which it is applied, with the solemnity of the building, and the condition of the people who lie in it, are apt to fill the mind with a kind of melancholy, or rather thoughtfulness, that is not disagreeable."[6] This sense of melancholy is difficult to find in the modern Abbey—not because it has become less popular, but because it has become too popular. Indeed, before a scheme to reduce the calamitous noise was put into place, the sheer number of people (up to sixteen thousand a day) led one of the canons to characterize the noise in the Abbey as "rather like a railway station concourse."[7] Given the hubbub in the surrounding Abbey, it is difficult to see how a twenty-first-century Irving could reenact the "companionship between author and reader" that is seemingly akin to the solitary reading experience. The Abbey has become a destination for tour buses—more a space to disembark than a space to meditate on the relationship between poet and audience, art and life, life and death. One would not want to fall into a simplistic dismissal of the modern tourist "tramping through Gothic cathedrals" as someone who merely wishes to "appropriate otherness," but the meditation and melancholia that governed Irving's and Addison's visits to the space were clearly different from what Michael Harkin has characterized as the "contiguous" visits of contemporary tourists.[8]

Part of the difference between Carlyle's or Addison's experiences in Poets' Corner might well also be the result of fundamental differences in the burial protocols of the South Transept. Unlike the various versions of Poets' Corner in other countries that merely commemorate poets, the one in Westminster is a poetical burial ground as well. Since Geoffrey Chaucer was buried near the east wall, it has served as a place of honor for poets and writers from Edmund Spenser (1599) to John Masefield (1967). Here, however, the line of poetical burials abruptly stops because the South Transept has seemingly run out of room. This state of affairs, while hardly unprecedented (cemeteries in the nineteenth century were often declared full and retrenched), has created problems for the idea of Poets' Corner. Unlike nineteenth-century sextons, the current guardians of Poets' Corner (the Dean and Chapter of the Abbey) cannot simply retrench this poetical graveyard. Indeed, only one poet has been exhumed from the Abbey and placed elsewhere—Thomas May, who was thrown into a pit behind St. Margaret's because of his ties to Oliver Cromwell.[9] So the Corner has reached something of a state of stasis. No one else can be buried in the South Transept. And no one (not even the least well known) can be dug up to make room for new corpses. Does this stasis mark the end of Poets' Corner? Can we claim that the relevance of the Corner is in proportion to the possibilities of new burials?

Body and Monument: The Making of Place

The inability to make room for even the best-known writers would seem to create problems for the continuing relevance of the space. In a poem that uses the term "Poets' Corner" for the first time (1733), Thomas Fitzgerald claims that the "reliques of the tuneful train [the bodies of the poets] / . . . beneath the hallow'd Pavement" bring a "juster reverence to the Abbey."[10] So, too, Thomas Fuller (1655) asserts that the bodies of Chaucer, Spenser, and Drayton are enough "to make passengers' feet to move metrically, who go over the place where so much *Poetical dust* is interred."[11] In general terms, the power of these poetical corpses is an extension of the more general symbolic meaning of the dead body. Katherine Verdery has spoken to the efficacy of the corpse as symbolically effective because it is "indisputably there . . . it has the advantage of concreteness that nonetheless transcends time, making past immediately present."[12] The corpse seems to establish a kind of presence in this space that, despite the ephemeral nature of the body, actually endures.

The model for this kind of place is, of course, the idea of sacred space that, in Christianity at least, is built on the notion of the body. The bodily disappearance of Christ from his tomb, far from deemphasizing the body, actually made the body more important. We can see the effect of this importance in the numerous relics that made their way throughout the East and West. Indeed, it was the body, or parts of the body, that identified specific civic or monastic institutions as those that were worthy of pilgrimage. Canterbury and Compostela existed as pilgrimage centers because of the presence of Saint Thomas and Saint James, respectively. Even in the more mundane designation of sacred space, the Church used bodies; each church altar was to contain a relic.[13] Such a shrine, as Peter Brown has pointed out, was "very often called quite simply, 'the place': *loca sanctorum, ὁ τόπος*. It was a place where the normal laws of the grave were held to be suspended. In a relic, the chilling anonymity of human remains could be thought to be still heavy with the fullness of a beloved person."[14] In this sacred formulation, the place of the body is a locus where heaven and earth come together.[15] It is no accident that the Corner is located in a place that had not only institutional, or state significance, but was a place of religious worship. This religious aspect ultimately aided in the formation of the Corner, even if its most important inhabitants were not always the most religious of people themselves.

Yet the dead body's connection with transcendence was not unproblematic. After all, a good deal of the English Reformation had to do with the denial of what was considered the dangerously "magical" qualities of the corpse.[16] The religious quality of the relic, in fact, was one of the main points of contention within the post-Reformation English church. English suspicions of "Catholic" monumental remembrance were realized in the mid part of the sixteenth century when iconoclastic Protestants destroyed funerary monuments in places like Old St. Paul's and Christ Church Greyfriars, seeking to erase what was seen as the idolatrous worship of the dead.

It is, therefore, no accident that the founding moment of Poets' Corner takes place during the temporary resurgence of Catholicism in England in the sixteenth century. It was in the third year of Queen Mary's reign that the corpse of Geoffrey Chaucer was exhumed from its medieval grave by Nicholas Brigham (1556) and reburied in the tomb that currently stands against the east wall of the South Transept. This translation of Chaucer's bones was most likely an attempt to "re-Catholicize" a poet who had been appropriated as a proto-Protestant after Henry VIII's break with Rome.[17] If so, it also seems to have had the effect of Catholicizing the space of the South Transept. For while burials continued in the rest of the Abbey (including the North Transept) during the reign of Elizabeth, no one would be buried in the South Transept until Edmund Spenser was entombed in 1599. Clearly something had changed. It's possible that the body of the decidedly Protestant Spenser made the space safe for further burials. Yet it was not until 1616 that anyone else would be buried there. And it would not be until 1620 that Spenser's burial place would receive a marker (although it seems to have been promised earlier).[18] But early in the seventeenth century, anxieties about "Catholic" interpretations of the efficacy of the body were perhaps attenuated. And Protestant rulers, who may have had a healthy suspicion of monuments, also understood that their own power was based, in some sense, on monuments that ensured a memory of the past. In fact, political leaders in sixteenth-century England were forced to legislate against such destruction of monuments, perhaps because, as Russ

Castronovo has pointed out, "without a 'monumental history,' national consciousness remains inert."[19]

Poetry's Anti-Monumental Discourse

But if rulers believed that such monuments were crucial to the maintenance of national consciousness, poets were less comfortable with the privileging of a monumental discourse. One of their attempts to rationalize this need for monumentality was to alter the very idea of "monumentality" itself. Poets in particular returned to the Horatian notion that the monument that lasted was not stone or brass (that could wear away), but poetry itself because poetry could last forever in the memory.[20] Ben Jonson famously located the monumental properties of Shakespeare's poetry in his friend and rival, remarking, "thou art a monument without a tomb."[21] The seeming dissonance between immortal poetic monumentality and impermanent monuments to poets seems to unearth an embarrassment at the heart of Poets' Corner. For what is the use of monuments if not to memorialize those who would be forgotten? And so, if there are material monuments, then poets, like everyone else, are subject to the kind of forgetting brought on by death. The great eighteenth-century memorializer of the Abbey, John Dart, speaks especially well about the mortality that levels not only young and old, captives and slaves but also kings and especially poets:

> Poets themselves like common Mortals die,
> Such are the Laws of hard Necessity;
> Not the sweet Musick of the pleasing Tongue,
> The heav'nly Numbers nor harmonious Song,
> Can plead suspension to the fleeting Breath,
> Or Charm th'inexorable Ears of Death,
> Who interrupts him even while he Sings,
> And with rude Fingers breaks the sounding Strings.[22]

Dart understands the contradiction at the heart of his claim. Later he attempts to say that poets' "lays" are "deathless." And he adds that where the poet "rests, he consecrates the Ground; / Can from rude Hands the sculptur'd Marble save, / And spread a sacred Influence round the Grave."[23] Dart opposes the "rude fingers" of death with the ability of the poet's body to resist other "rude hands" that might erase the material monument. Thus he reinforces the permanence of the memorial with an appeal to a kind of mystical post-mortem poetical influence. But it becomes clear in the next line that it is the poet's tomb itself that grants immortality largely because we can experience it visually: "Thus *Virgil's* Tomb attracts the Trav'ler's Eyes, / While none can tell where great *Augustus* lies."[24]

This invocation of the poet's tomb as the lasting experience of the poet is, of course, crucial to the idea of Poets' Corner, yet it seems to contradict the idea that poetry alone can be the deathless monument. Without the visible medium of the tombs, Poets' Corner would only be an exalted charnel pit. The range of the visitor's emotional response would be restricted to a morbid reflection on the vanity of human wishes. The true power of the site, as we will see, is its ability to elicit a series of emotions that transcend the banal sameness of the *memento mori*. In this way I argue that Poets' Corner mimics the experience of reading itself—laying claim to the power of literature in order to memorialize literature.

If the monuments and memorials are in some sense like the author's texts themselves—things to be read that re-create the bond between absent author and present audience, one might wonder why there is such resistance by poets to these memorial markers. On a very basic level, the ambivalence of writers about these memorials seems perfectly understandable. Poets understood all too well that true immortality cannot depend on material monuments. Monuments, like bodies, are subject to the "rude hand" of impermanence while verse can be seen as immortal because it is incorporeal. The genre of poetry that calls attention to the impermanence of the material monument (perhaps first given voice by Horace's Ode 3.3) is, then, not just the attempt by the poet to displace the monument made of marble or brass with the poetic monument, but is simultaneously the monument that poets rely upon to ensure their own lasting reputations. At the heart of this kind of poetry is an attempt to abstract poetry from the medium upon which it is inscribed. One could certainly see why poets would wish to conceive of poetry as transcending the means by which it was circulated. Too much attention to stone, brass, vellum, or paper draws attention to ways in which poetry lasts only as long as the substance upon which it was written.

Behind this discourse that criticized material monumentality (while exalting writing that seemed dependent on materiality) seems to have been an anxiety about *how* the poet would be remembered. Poets understood all too well that once they were gone, others might be responsible for the way they were remembered. And, in terms of Poets' Corner, it was often true that the poet was not the author of his or her own monument, so who was memorializing the memorializers? The answer can be found in the names of those who were responsible for the erection of the cenotaphs and tombstones in the South Transept. It is perhaps unsurprising that the list includes noblemen and noblewomen, merchants, religious men and women, politicians, critics, and poets. The incredibly varied nature of these sponsors reflects a series of differing agendas: a desire to embody in England's poets a sense of nationhood, a desire to find in art a transcendence that religion has lost, or even, simply, a desire to link one's own name with that of a famous poet. But what all of these desires share is an attempt to elicit an affective response from the visitor to the Abbey—love of country, joy in faith, pride in reflected glory. In other words, those who erected poetic memorials attempted to subordinate Poets' Corner to specific affective ideologies. In varying degrees the sponsors might be said to be successful. The cultural heritage of England undoubtedly supported *some* of the political aims of the state. Art *was* seen by some as a replacement for religion. And the patrons of poets *did* gain a limited amount of fame. But because the space was not subordinated to any one overarching ideology, the differing aims of the various sponsors inevitably configured themselves in unexpected ways.

Of course, the unforeseen configurations of Poets' Corner have as much to do with who was buried there as how they were commemorated. The tangled burial history of the Corner demonstrates that the space we see is a kind of trace of the "real" Poets' Corner. It appears as finished and complete, but its true nature, if we can speak of such a thing, can only be appreciated if we understand that the Corner is haunted by unrealized versions of itself. For instance, Shakespeare's absence from Poets' Corner led to moves to translate his body from Holy Trinity in Stratford-upon-Avon to the Abbey. Failing that, a statue was then erected to make good the absence. Yet the latter history of the Corner makes clear that the bodily absence of the Bard continued to make itself felt well into the late twentieth century. So, too, at least forty of the seventy plus memorials to poets celebrate writers who are buried elsewhere. The absence that these cenotaphs mark, in conjunction with the presence of the sepulchral monuments, gives rise to a vitalizing anxiety that affords Poets' Corner a kind of autonomy within Westminster Abbey. For the mortuary relationship of external sign (a memorial with writing on it) to absent body (the body of the poet) at once signals loss and reenacts the readers' experience with the work—marking the presence of the author's voice even as she or he is absent.

The Beautiful Disorder of Poets' Corner

But if the visitor's encounter with the monument is to be seen as a kind of reenactment of the reading process, one has to admit that the larger space of Poets' Corner cannot be said to be an aesthetically elevating experience. More than a few critics suggest that the real problem with Poets' Corner is that its artistic merit is incommensurate with the artistic value that the place is meant to commemorate. One writer in the nineteenth century was particularly forthright: "The truth is, that Poets' Corner is an eyesore. The monuments in it, few of them of any artistic merit, many of them very ludicrous, and all out of place and character, are mere disfigurements of the south transept. . . . Of these busts and statues, while not one of them is placed in compliance with architectural requisition, many are so ill and confusedly arranged, that any merit they may chance to possess is rendered altogether ineffective."[25] This kind of monumental crowding ultimately led William Morris to launch a full-scale aesthetic attack on the entire fabric of the Abbey, claiming that "the Church is crowded to absurdity with specimens of the gravestone-cutter's art."[26] Even the great nineteenth-century defender and historian of the Abbey, Arthur Penrhyn Stanley, seemed to agree that the lack of regularity rendered suspect the Abbey's ability to commemorate: "We have seen, again how extremely unequal and uncertain is the commemoration of our celebrated men. It is this which renders the interment or notice within our walls a dubious honour, and makes the Abbey, after all, but an imperfect and irregular monument of greatness."[27] Stanley's position as dean of the Abbey and the outsized role that he played in the preservation and advocacy of the Abbey's treasures in the nineteenth century suggests that even true believers of commemoration within the Abbey harbored doubts about the worth of these memorials.

It is in some sense understandable, of course, that a visitor might wish the physical space that celebrates aesthetics to be beautiful. George Santayana once described beauty as "pleasure objectified," and one might believe that the object of visiting Poets' Corner is to feel the pleasure of orderly progress from the medieval period to the Renaissance to modernity—from "Father Chaucer" to his spiritual heirs Edmund Spenser, John Dryden, and T. S. Eliot.

The desire for the beautiful here is a desire for an orderly narrative of literary history. Just such a space has been theorized in T. S. Eliot's famous essay on the relationship between the individual author and his tradition. Though he never explicitly names Poets' Corner, he describes the way that an ideal and completely representative Poets' Corner might work:

> I mean this as a principle of æsthetic, not merely historical, criticism. The necessity that he shall conform, cohere, is not one-sided; what happens when a new work of art is created is something that happens simultaneously to all works of art which preceded it. The existing monuments form an ideal order among themselves, which is modified by the introduction of the new (the really new) work of art among them. The existing order is complete before the new work arrives; for order to persist after the supervention of novelty, the whole existing order must be, if ever so slightly altered; and so the relations, proportions, values of each work of art towards the whole are readjusted; and this is conformity between the old and the new.[28]

In his description of the development of the canon, Eliot slips easily in the first two sentences from talking about the author to talking about the work. And as the quotation moves on, he moves from the work of literature to the monument. Yet, unlike Poets' Corner, Eliot's imaginative space is immaterial and epistemic—a bloodless allegory of how a coherent literary tradition is formed.

In his study of eighteenth-century literary monuments, Philip Connell has argued that to appreciate the importance of Poets' Corner we need to abandon the idea of the "Abbey's poetical quarter as a kind of sepulchral curiosity: an unrepresentative, inchoate record of literary fame that has little significance within the modern institutions of literature, popular or academic."[29] I would extend this idea, asserting that it is within its inchoate, seemingly unrepresentative and curious nature that we might find the importance of the Corner. Dean Stanley said as much one hundred and fifty years ago, admitting to the imperfections of the Abbey, arguing "but it is this also which gives to it that perfectly natural character of which any artificial collection is entirely destitute."[30] Recently, one of the Westminster canons echoed Stanley's words: "It is a very odd, informal and, in some ways, puzzling commemoration of our art. People have suggested that it might be rationalised, set in order, but anyone who will go to Santa Croce in Florence where this has been done, will see what a failure it really is."[31] It is precisely the rational illegibility of Poets' Corner, the lack of form, that signals what kind of place Poets' Corner really is—a place in which felt emotions exceed our own ability to explain why we feel what we feel.

Westminster's poetical monuments will always betray the historical and material traces that go into the attempt to make up the commemorative space because those responsible for the construction of this space were so often intent (albeit sometimes unconsciously) on disordering or at least reordering the "ideal poetical canon." Hence Poets' Corner is a kind of material index of the conflicts that went into the construction of a national canon. As an index of conflict and attempted resolution, it offers a less than perfect, or less than transcendent, space that maps out how literary culture affected and was affected by the shifting cultures of the nation. Poets' Corner is, finally, an irrational, disordered space that (because it is not aesthetically pleasing) can claim that art's power lies precisely in its ability *not* to please.

Of course, even to speak of Poets' Corner as an aesthetical place is a bit misleading. As Irving suggests in the epigraph to this book, it is not really the aesthetic value of the sculptures that brings one to Poets' Corner—rather it is to commune with *manes* or spirits of those literary types that we have lost. Poets' Corner, then, acts by a bit of misdirection. For though it celebrates aesthetics, it is itself not aesthetical in the sense that it is beautifully whole, complete, and regular. What then is the experience that one has in Poets' Corner? It is a strange experience that mimics the reading experience but is also dependent on the presence of the poet's body rather than the poet's work. And if it is not aesthetical, it is affective. In fact, one might well claim that the affective relationship conjured by the work of art is meant to be conjured here in the absence of art. In effect, the poet's body here takes the place of the work of art. This equivalence between body and book extends back at least as far as late medieval stories about how, when Ovid's tomb was opened, they found not his corpse but an ivory casket that contained a perfectly intact book.[32] One reading of the story would suggest the extent to which the author *was* the work of art that he created. As Ovid himself suggests at the end of the *Metamorphoses*, the poet would live through this work. In other words, the story about Ovid supports the extent to which the monument was the work that the author created.

What do we make of the fact that Poets' Corner replaces the immortal text with the body? The effect is clear—the author is idolized to the extent that he or she occludes his or her own work. The space, then, might seem to elevate the status of the author. The work is important because of its connection to its creator. But this idolization of the author has its flip side. For idolization, like fetishization, is "a desperate attempt to render presence"—an attempt to fix and control the author in the here and now.[33] The result is that authors are subject to being used to fulfill the agendas of those who would idolize them. Paradoxically, the power of the poetical corpses lies in their ability to call forth unexpected emotions and thus often escape the control of those who would "use" them.

If, as Walter Benjamin claims, affective connection is ultimately located in the materiality of the thing we feel about, then the special status of Poets' Corner becomes clear.[34] For the "fondness," "friendship," and "companionship" that both Irving and Hawthorne feel for the dead authors suggest the extent to which the so-called idolization of the dead in Poets' Corner does not leave them inert, embodied in "mute stones" as John Frecerro argues. The affective connection tying us to those authors, as Jonathan Flatley argues, dissolves the boundary between reader and author and allows us to "inhabit" the space of Poets' Corner in a way that we are unable to inhabit other parts of the Abbey because we can commune with the dead.[35]

In Chapter 1, I argue that to understand the power of Poets' Corner, we must first understand its plot within the larger space of Westminster Abbey. Like Poets' Corner, this space became a place because of its relationship to the bodies buried beneath it. But what differentiated the earlier space of the Abbey from what would become Poets' Corner was its relative failure to elicit a powerful affective reaction from its medieval visitors. Specifically, I examine how the tears supposedly wept over the "founding corpse" of the Abbey— Edward the Confessor—failed to move either the monks responsible for his cult or members of the larger national community. Paradoxically, this lack of affect led to a kind of anatomization of the Abbey that reflected the English body politic. The importance of this connection between kingly corpse and body politic became apparent as the body was removed and replaced in a new shrine during the brief reign of the Catholic Queen Mary (to replace the one despoiled during her brother's reign). As Abbot Feckenham put it in 1557, "The body of that most holy King, St. Edward remaineth there among us, which body, the favour of Almighty God so preserved during the time of our late schism, that though the heretics had power on that wherein the body was enclosed, yet on that sacred body had they no power."[36] The Abbey, in this formulation, became (and remained throughout the Protestant ascendancy) the inviolable body that linked religion and politics, Church and Commonwealth.

From the corporeal foundation of the Abbey, I move to examine how the medieval idea of "chartered sanctuary" (connected to the inviolable body of the Abbey) was linked to the affective power of Poets' Corner. I argue that, in fact, it was the anger and outrage generated by the violation of a space within the Abbey that led to the sanctification of the Corner. In 1378 an English squire, Robert Hauley, was murdered before the High Altar. This violation of the Sanctuary (a national drama that included John of Gaunt, John Wyclif, and Richard II) not only led to the closure of the Abbey for four months and the suspension of Parliament (which then met in the Refectory), but mapped out a separate space for England's cultural productions. Hauley's corpse, which was reverently buried in what would eventually be Poets' Corner (the South Transept), became a sign of the inviolability and extralegal status of the Abbey. Connected with, and yet separate from, more traditional notions of the saintly body, Hauley's dead body at once redoubles the function of Edward's kingly body (though for the South Transept) and produces a kind of secular reverence that makes possible the corporeal aesthetics of Poets' Corner. Chapter 1 uncovers the ways in which Poets' Corner itself becomes not just a burial site, but a kind of sacred space that insists on its own boundaries. At the same time, it becomes clear that these boundaries limit the power of Poets' Corner by closing it off from the "profane" space of the outer world.

In Chapter 2, I deal with the genesis of Poets' Corner itself, beginning with the move against monumental history during the Reformation and the loss and mourning that followed. I argue that this Protestant attempt to construct what might be called a kind of sublime monumentality drew attention away from the physical monumentality that ultimately makes up the commemorative space in the Abbey. While acknowledging that the trope of the inadequate monument has a classical origin (based in later years on a particularly Horatian formulation), the English Reformation also constructed its own idea of history—one that was at once enabled and frustrated by the attempt to make a fundamental break with the Catholic medieval past. This attempt to break with the past, though ultimately problematized by even ardent reformers, would have an effect on the space of the South Transept throughout its years as Poets' Corner. For it was in the conflict between commemorative monumental materialism and transcendent spiritual spatiality that Poets' Corner was able to locate a constructive melancholia in the corpse of Edmund

Spenser. Spenser could embody Protestant poetics precisely because he dealt with the ruin, loss, and recovery of the poetical and historical past.

The first person to realize the metaphoric potential of the space was Ben Jonson, who alternated between Protestantism and Catholicism. But instead of embracing the analogy linking poetical power with sacred power, he insisted that to commemorate poets in the space of Poets' Corner was to misunderstand the true power of poetry. Specifically, he resisted suggestions that the translation of Shakespeare from Stratford to Westminster would complete the sanctification of the space. Instead he claimed that to create a monument to Shakespeare would be to diminish the true monument—Shakespeare's poetry. Paradoxically, Jonson's resistance to the idea of Poets' Corner actually enabled the sacredness of the place itself. And Jonson's later involvement in the construction of Poets' Corner reflected his contradictory interest both in maintaining a kind of transcendent status of poetry and in realizing that the material aspects of poetry, commemoration and laureateship, were what set these poetic bodies apart from their medieval predecessors.

In Chapter 3, I examine the position of poetry in society during the eighteenth century, and how it was at a moment of anxiety that the space in the South Transept mobilized "public love" in the service of its sacral commemorative status. I argue that when a kind of materialist poetics seemed to emerge to challenge more transcendent notions of art, the material commemoration of art became most important. In one instance—the funeral of John Dryden—the commemorative function of the funeral and by extension the celebration of transcendent poetics were transformed into a cruel burlesque in which the corpse of Dryden became the center of a raucous demonstration in the Abbey. At the same time, Dryden's burial—in the plot that once had contained Chaucer—cemented the Abbey's reputation as *the* burial place for poets. Yet even as the spectacle of commemoration seemed to bring poetry into closer contact with its public, poetry was increasingly seen as vulnerable to concerns that were considered "common." The satirist Tom Brown uses the funeral as an occasion to connect Dryden's literary audience with those who attended his burial—"a crowd so nauseous, so profoundly lewd, / With all the Vices of the Times endu'd."[37]

It is perhaps no accident that during this period the space first known as the "Poets' Quarter" became known as Poets' Corner. Curiously, it was the expansion of the space from a "corner" to the larger space of the South Transept that seemed to have triggered the currency of the new name. It is as if the idea of a corner conjured up an earlier iteration of the space free from the extraliterary influences of commerce and politics. This nostalgic idea of a space devoted solely to aesthetic concerns was given form by the eighteenth-century poet Alexander Pope, who, though he famously rejected burial in the Corner for himself, nonetheless enabled a number of his friends to be buried in the South Transept and was largely responsible for the statue of William Shakespeare as a kind of stand-in for the body of the Bard. Pope here seems to have operated a bit like Jonson; he argued that the space could never truly commemorate poetry (being as it was a material commemoration of that which was necessarily immaterial) even as he acted to ensure that material commemorations of poets played a part in what was increasingly seen as a national space.

In Chapter 4, I discuss how nineteenth-century omissions of poets such as Byron and novelists such as George Eliot (based inevitably on morality or gender) paradoxically energized the space for a time, but ultimately seemed to drain Poets' Corner of relevance. The attempts to make amends for these absences by belatedly raising plaques or inserting medallions in the windows only drew attention to the seemingly regressive nature of literary history. These virtual attempts to compensate for the past have their origin, I argue, in previous failures to create alternative commemorative spaces to supplement the Corner. For instance, the ambitious but failed attempt to create an enormous hall of monuments that would dwarf Big Ben suggests the inadequacy of Poets' Corner. The space, then, would seem almost entirely static—a place that elicits poetic nostalgia rather than any forward-looking projection of the possibilities of literature.

In Chapter 5, I argue that a rash of literary exhumations in the nineteenth century revealed not only anxiety about the corporeal origin of genius (a fundamental belief at the time), but a deeper disquiet about the broader place of literary culture. In England, the site of Poets' Corner seemed to offer a bulwark against this anxiety. But the full effect of this dislocation was only felt in the twentieth century when the second poetical body buried in Poets' Corner—Edmund Spenser—came back, in a sense, to haunt modernity. On the evening of 2 November 1938, there was, as the *Evening Telegraph* put it, "Secret Digging at Poet's Grave." This digging, as it turned out, was an attempt to exhume Spenser's body, buried since 1599. The circumstances surrounding this purported exhumation are, to say the least, remarkable—for the exhumation was undertaken at the behest of the Baconian Society, a group of middle-class men and women whose stated aim was to prove that the author of Shakespeare's works was Francis Bacon. Opposed by Abbey authorities, members of the aristocracy, and academics, this group of advertising men and journalists argued that Shakespeare had thrown a poem into Spenser's grave. Were they able to recover the poem, they reasoned, they could compare the handwriting to Bacon's and, as one member put it, "If manuscripts are found and Shakespeare's signature is on one of them and this is identified as Bacon's handwriting—or anyone elses [sic] for that matter—we shall know that after all 'William Shakespeare' was a pen-name." The conflict surrounding the exhumation reveals how the nineteenth-century attempt to employ literature as a model for civil society ultimately failed, leading to an unexpected middle-class sense of entitlement that frustrated political "uses" of the space.

In the coda, I examine the latest and most ambitious construction of a Poets' Corner—the American Poets' Corner in St. John the Divine. This Corner attempts to escape the premodern Catholic "superstition" of Westminster regarding the sanctity of the body by restricting the commemoration of the poets to smooth-rubbed slate plaques without any burials. But a controversy involving the commemoration of Ezra Pound revealed the extent to which any attempt to conjure up a "new, sublime [poetical] body . . . delivered from the corruption of history" is ultimately a failure.[38] This nonmaterial sublime body offers the promise of a perpetually transcendent American poetics, but Pound's exclusion suggests how the American memorial project is enabled by its own bit of corporeal "superstition" (even if it is an immaterial, "pure" poetical body).

This turn to the "boneless American counterpart to Westminster Abbey" not only signals how a former colony of the homeland might go about constructing its own national Valhalla, but may signal what lies ahead for the original Poets' Corner.[39] As the pleasingly regular plaques in St. John the Divine attempt to aestheticize, one might say smooth out, poetical history, the bodies which are part and parcel of this poetical history disrupt a quiescence which signals death. So too, in the originary place of literature, the discussion about who should be celebrated and how they should be commemorated can continue to evoke the corporeal even in the absence of poetical bodies. For though there are no bodies under these plaques, these memorials point elsewhere. They extract poetry from the isolated realm of aesthetics and figure forth not the circumscription of poetry by ethics, commerce, or politics, but the ability of literature to move from the sanctuary to the larger world.

CHAPTER I

Westminster Abbey and the Incorporation of Poets' Corner

Sometime in the latter half of the seventeenth century, the notorious satirist Tom Brown narrated a kind of tour of London and Westminster that he supposedly conducted for an "Indian friend." After visiting a number of different places (including a tavern and a bawdy house) they finally arrive at Westminster Abbey, where he observes

> *Edward the Confessor's* tomb is the chief piece of antiquity, who was the first royal empirick for scabs and scrophulous humours. He was a whimsical sort of a gentleman, that not being willing or capable to lye with his wife, was yet so jealous of her, that he caus'd her to pass the fiery trial of the *Ordeal*, which she did to the satisfaction of the beholders, but not of the king, who could never be brought to give her his royal benevolence, for which the monks make him a saint, and the nation was exposed to invasion and ruin, in *William* the bastard of Normandy, whom the monks call'd in a barbarous Latin, *Conquestor* or *Conqueror*.[1]

What stands out in this description is Brown's denigration of the character of Edward and the bitter denunciation of the means by which "saints" were "made" in the Middle Ages. Such denunciations might be expected in a seventeenth-century England that has a vexed relationship with its Catholic past. Yet Brown's satire reveals the extent to which the regal and the religious were popularly seen to coalesce in Edward's body.

My argument in this chapter is that the uncorrupted wholeness of the Confessor's body and, paradoxically enough, the failure of his cult originally produced the peculiarly timeless space of the Abbey.[2] Four centuries later, it was the violation of this space and the murder and burial of a fourteenth-century knight by the name of Robert Hauley in the South Transept that led to the sanctification of a space within that space, locating the South Transept in time and shaping a prehistory of Poets' Corner that led to the inclusion of its first poetical corpse, that of Geoffrey Chaucer. I use the term prehistory here advisedly. For much of what was written about the Abbey and the South Transept before 1400 has more the feel of legend than what we would call history. Even the space itself was different. Westminster Abbey in the fourteenth century not only lacked the distinctive towers designed by Nicholas Hawksmoor, but was still connected to part of the original (much lower) Norman nave. At its most basic level, then, the idea of understanding this space might seem at best speculative and at worst a well-meaning fantasy.

One could take an archaeological approach to the space. Like the psychoanalytical attempt to retrace original memories, it would seem to be possible to reconstruct or re-member space though traces of the original buildings. But as Freud suggested, and is now apparent, this analogy has its own problems, for

> just as the archaeologist builds up the walls of a building from the
> foundations that have remained standing, determines the number
> and position of the columns from depressions in the floor and
> reconstructs the mural decorations and paintings from the remains
> found in the debris, so does the analyst proceed when he draws
> his inferences from the fragments of memories, from the associations
> and from the behaviour of the subject of the analysis. Both of them
> have an undisputed right to reconstruct by means of supplementing
> and combining the surviving remains. Both of them, moreover,
> are subject to many of the same difficulties and sources of error.[3]

Freud, of course, believed that such difficulties could be mitigated if not completely overcome. I believe that the archaeological reconstruction to which Freud refers is certainly possible and that even the so-called errors which proceed from it can lead us in a wandering sort of way to "truth."[4] And so I would claim that to get at and inhabit a space one needs to get at its aetiology (or at least its rationalized aetiology). This is not to say that nothing can be learned from entering space *in medias res* merely that to do so is to miss the beginning of what I have called the plot of such a space.

As I argued in the Preface, emplotment of space is not only the report of a succession of events through time, nor is it merely the notion of space conveyed by the meaning of the early modern variant of plot. It is also the plan, one might say the intent or scheme of the work. Poets' Corner certainly can be read for the plot in the classical sense. There was often a plan (or plat) underlying the disposition of bodies, graves, and statues. And it is important to keep this public sense of Poets' Corner in mind if we are to, in some sense, imaginatively inhabit it. But Poets' Corner, being made of scores of monuments constructed at different times to public and private purposes, is also something of a romance. As Lorna Hutson has argued, Romance, with its errant knights, seems to suggest a lack of planning, or plot. But it is, in fact, in the errancy of the construction of Poets' Corner, indeed of the Abbey itself, that the plot can be discerned. The intent, or ground plot of the Abbey, is most often perceived in the ways in which intent is turned on its head. As I suggest above, this is the great strength and the great weakness of the commemorative space of the Abbey. The order that should define the aesthetic object is often missing in the space of the South Transept precisely because plans are often never fulfilled, or if they are fulfilled, they result in unexpected outcomes. Yet the commemorative space often works precisely because ordered planning is frustrated. This organic idea of the South Transept gives a vitality to Poets' Corner that is missing in other, more homogenous poetical commemorations. What I suggest here then is that the space of Poets' Corner often has its own *telos* or end that is often unrecognized until it comes into being. Spaces, especially those that have both public and private uses, have their own logic. To truly inhabit a space is to be there at the beginning so that one can understand what it was projected to be and see how the practice of space transformed it into place.

The Project of Westminster Abbey

The narrative of the space formally known as the Collegiate Church of St. Peter and informally known as Westminster Abbey began with a corpse. If there is any doubt about the power of the corpse to "sanctify" a sense of place, we need only remember how the burial of the *Hero Ktistes*, or founding hero, often gave Greek colonial cities a "centre."[5] As the French philosopher Michel de

Certeau has written, "An inert body always seems, in the West, to found a place and give it the appearance of a tomb."[6] When dealing with a national mausoleum like Westminster Abbey, or, more particularly, Poets' Corner, such an assertion about the power of the dead to give meaning to place might seem self-evident. The sacred nature of the corpse in Christianity—evidenced by the veneration of relics and the theology of the resurrection of the body—has, of course, marked the medieval period as particularly redolent with what Robert Pogue Harrison has termed the "thereness" of places associated with dead bodies.[7] A number of medievalists have detailed the establishment of saints' cults throughout medieval Europe, and what has become apparent is that modern notions of production and advertising are not out of place in discussions of these cults. Patrick Geary, for instance, narrates the establishment of the cult of Saint Helen of Athyra at Troyes in the thirteenth century, demonstrating that the promotion of a cult of this hitherto obscure saint was clearly the product of a need to repair the twin destructions of the cathedral in 1188 and 1228.[8] The hope was that the promotion of her cult would lead to an increase of pilgrims to Troyes and an increase of offerings that could offset the enormous cost of rebuilding. Thus a *vita* was written to order (complete with spurious attribution to John Chrysostom), and "Helen's publicists" promoted the portrait of a thaumaturgic Helen (as opposed to an excessively spiritual Helen) whose wonderworking would appeal to the general population.[9] Like the cult of Helen, these cults almost always relied upon the existence of a previously acknowledged holy person (however unknown) and then used this raw material to invest a place with a specialness that would elicit alms as well as devotions.

The somewhat analogous attempt to make the Abbey of Westminster a special space that could at once produce reverence and money was a bit different from the larger medieval production of sacred space. For the cult that was associated with the Abbey in the High Middle Ages was not that of a local saint or of its patron, St. Peter (though the Abbey did rely on the apostle in its charters). Instead, the Abbey developed a cult that depended on its founder, Edward the Confessor. As we will see, Edward was far from the most popular saint in England; that title would have to go to Thomas Becket, who was given the title of martyr, while Edward was left with the term "confessor"—a kind of second-class martyr who had led a pious life and had been persecuted but had not been killed. Yet, save one small shrine in Dorset, it is Edward's shrine alone that survived the dissolution of the monasteries in 1538, and it is his body that became the focus for what Dean Stanley called in 1868, "the centre of our national energies, the hearth of our national religion."[10] What was it, then, that made Edward different from other English saints? Certainly his status as king distinguished him. One could well argue that it is difficult to have the status of a temporal ruler while at the same time carrying out a life of such complete sanctity that one is canonized, but there are, of course, other examples of kingly saints. Edgar the Peaceful, Edmund of East Anglia, and Edwin of Northumbria were all popularly thought to be saints. Yet the case of Edward is, I argue, somewhat different—his canonization was stage-managed to a larger degree than other British kings. I would, in fact, argue that it was the implicit failure of Edward's cult, along with the unpopularity of his feast day in the Middle Ages, that enabled him, or at least enabled his corpse, to provide the basis for what I have termed elsewhere a necronationalism.

Edward the Confessor, the last Saxon king of England, died in 1066. Before he died, however, he had his own mausoleum built. Finished in 1065, Westminster Abbey only awaited the signed charter from the king to complete its foundation. Unfortunately for Edward, the king's signature preceded his burial before the High Altar by only nine days. Within a year, his tomb became an important political site. On Christmas Day 1066, William the Conqueror, standing on the Confessor's gravestone, laid claim to the throne of England—not by victory but (as the Charter of Battle Abbey put it) by right of "his predecessor King Edward."[11] After William's success in linking the place of Edward's burial with his own claims to the throne, the rite of coronation was inalienably attached to the Abbey at Westminster. Not only the place of Edward's death, but the actual regalia of Edward would supposedly invest the kings and queens who took the oath with the legitimacy of Edward's mantle for almost five hundred years.

It is at this point that the story of Edward takes a strange turn. For, shortly after his burial, stories began circulating about miracles occurring at his tomb, and a life, commissioned by Edward's widow, mentioned the miracles. This, in and of itself, is not abnormal. Miracles supposedly occurred at Thomas Becket's tomb almost from the moment of his burial. Such miracles, in fact, usually set the stage for canonization. What is peculiar about Edward's tomb is that, despite these miracles, there seems to have been no move to proclaim Edward a saint. In fact, the editor of the first life of the Confessor (which was probably written somewhere between 1066 and 1075) detects a certain amount of conscious ignorance, if not outright hostility, on the part of the Westminster monks to the cult of Edward.[12]

There are indications that this hostility was the result of a split between the courtly keepers of the cult and the monks of the Abbey, whose patron remained St. Peter (the "founder" of the Church), rather than Edward. And, in fact, one of the earliest "histories" of the church at Westminster omits any of the miracles associated with Edward. Instead, it focuses on what the eleventh-century monk Sulcard characterizes as the seventh-century foundation narrative of Abbey. In this narrative, St. Peter himself undertakes the consecration of the church in place of the first bishop of London, Mellitus.[13] This hostility or uncertainty about Edward seems to have remained, for in 1102 the Confessor's tomb was opened out of a combination of faith and skepticism concerning the dead king's sanctity. A purported witness for this exhumation (related in the second life of Edward composed by Osbert of Clare) reports that "six and thirty years had Edward lain in the tomb, and many thought that like other men he had fallen to ashes after our common mortal lot. But some there were whose loving thoughts gave them a holy presentiment of somewhat divine attending one whose limbs had never known the loss of virgin purity, and whose body they could not doubt remained in a kind of resurrection glory."[14] The discovery of the incorrupt body of a venerated person or wonder at that incorruption is something of a topos or commonplace in saints' lives; what is unusual here is that Osbert gives voice to those who apparently doubted Edward's sanctity, or at the very least doubted that his sanctity would lead to the existence of his body as whole and unaged some thirty-six years after his death.

But this is not the most peculiar thing about Osbert's *Life*, for, after the lid of the sarcophagus was taken off and Edward's body was indeed found whole and (as Osbert stresses) flexible, Bishop Gundulf reaches down to draw out Edward's long white beard, then, as Osbert tells us:

> when he felt it firm set in the flesh, was this great man astonished at the strange miracle. But yet he essayed to draw gently forth a single hair, if perchance it might yield to his touch, that so of the relics of the holy king he might thus be allowed an abundant enrichment.
>
> But as the lord abbot Gilbert stood and watched, "What is this," he cried, "good bishop, that you do? In the land of the living he hath attained an eternal inheritance with the saints of God: wherefore then dost thou seek to diminish his share of temporal glory? Cease, honored sir, so to presume: vex not the king in his

royal bed." Then was Gundulf wholly resolved in tears, and said, "Venerable abbott, thou has spoken aright. Yet know that not any bold presumption sped me to this deed. The flame of holy devotion, wherewith I burned for love of the glorious king, urged me to take but one hair of that snowy beard, to keep it with solemn reverence in his memory as a treasure more precious than gold. But since my hope is gone, and my wish could not be granted, let him keep his own by his own right in peace. Let him rest in his palace, virgin and incorrupt, till with triumphant joy he shall meet the advent of the Judge, and receive in this his flesh the abiding glory of a blessed immortality."[15]

This bit about the beard—which is repeated in all corresponding versions of the life of Edward (whether in Anglo-Norman or Middle English)—is quite unusual in a saint's life. In fact, it was understood that a bishop who was presiding at such an event would usually get to take a bit of the saint's body to enrich his house's store of relics. Archbishop Langton, for instance, took St. Wulfstan's arm in 1218, and Robert Kilwardby took St. Richard of Chichester's in 1276.[16] This oddity is magnified when one remembers that at the translation of Edward to his shrine in 1163, Thomas Becket was presiding and by all rights should have been able to take the right arm of Edward. Instead, he decided to take the top of the sarcophagus (that had its own peculiar history).[17]

This anecdote, I think, speaks to a number of different cultural formations at once. On the one hand, it certainly focuses on the idea of the virgin body of Edward. The expectation seems to be that virginity, incorruption, and wholeness all go together and, thus, to make the body less than whole would harm the wholeness/virginity of the body. It also suggests a sense that the king's fleshly body, like its metonymic analogue—the body politic—should be allowed to remain unanatomized. For the purposes of my argument, though, I would like to stress the extent to which Gundulph's desire to take one hair that, as he puts it, is "a treasure more precious than gold," seems an attempt to determine how much more precious the entire body?[18] What we seem to have then on the part of Osbert is an effort to imbue the body with value as a prelude to the canonization of Edward. It should be noted here that there was otherwise little to recommend the Abbey as a particularly special place. As the modern editor of Edward's *Life* puts it, "St. Peter could hardly be appropriated to the exclusive service of Westminster. But the Abbey had nothing else. Its collection of relics was not very distinguished, and it had no special right to any English saint."[19]

Osbert was one to cover all of his bases and so, unlike earlier lives of Edward that omitted the story about St. Peter, he made Edward's decision to found the Abbey contingent on the fact that Edward had heard (and believed) the original story about St. Peter's appearance in the seventh century. But if his attempt to suture together the two stories was meant to create a larger and more well-disposed audience for the canonization, it was a failure. Despite the fact that Osbert himself took the petition for canonization to the Curia, the petition was deferred, almost certainly because of a lack of enthusiasm on the part of some in the Abbey, but specifically because (as Innocent II put it) "a genuine cult needed to be supported by the whole realm."[20] However, in 1159 the papal schism gave the canonization of Edward a boost. Henry II had backed Alexander III as pope, and, presumably as partial payment (Henry had sent a letter in support of the canonization), Alexander agreed to the canonization of Edward on 7 February 1161—even waiving the need for a general council. Edward was (after the body was secretly inspected to ensure that it was "whole") translated to his magnificent new tomb, and a new life largely based on Osbert's was drawn up by Aelred, the abbot of Rievaulx. But it is clear that the canonization was not the result of any popular agitation, nor was his festival ever popular. Of eighteen calendars printed by Francis Wormald, only seven contain the January festivals of Edward. The canonization and translation of Edward was thus more the result an attempt to produce sanctity and not incidentally enhance the prestige of the kingship—something in which Henry II was clearly interested—rather than a result of the prestige of Westminster or the popularity of the cult.

After the canonization and translation of Edward, one would think that the cult would become more popular. But Edward is only mentioned in seven (10 percent) of the benefactions to the abbey, and, of these, five benefactors were men of some official status and thus had a special interest in promoting the cult. The laity, then, apparently did not respond to the royal associations of the Abbey.[21] Even when, in 1236, Pope Gregory IX recommended the observance of the feast of St. Edward to the English Church, the feast day did not become popular.[22] The offerings in the Abbey Church first recorded in 1317–18 (as Barbara Harvey has demonstrated) were paltry, and though they would wax and wane, they were never what they should have been for a church with such associations.[23] This failure, I argue, led to the formation (perhaps even consciously) of a kind of secular sanctity that at once derived part of its power from its religious affiliations and maintained its distinctive nature by fore-grounding its connections to secular power.

The moment aspirations for the cult began to change was in 1173 when Thomas Becket was canonized.[24] Though to some degree stage-managed, Becket's canonization was largely the result of popular and clerical pressure despite official resistance. Within four months, miracles were reported at Becket's burial site. The civil authorities, fearing the waxing reputation of Becket, threatened to seize the body, at which point the monks hid it in the crypt. Even then there were stories about the people "finding" the body miracu-lously.[25] In 1174 Henry felt compelled to do penance in front of the tomb of Becket, receiving strokes from each of the bishops, abbots and the eighty monks. Even a fire in 1174 failed to stop the progress of the cult, and on 7 July 1220 the translation of Becket to his shrine was an enormous event that made Becket's body *the* destination for pilgrims within England in the later Middle Ages.[26]

In the wake of the popularity of Becket's cult, the nature of Edward's cult had to change. His became less a popular cult and more a site to mark the placement of royal sepulchers. Part of this alteration in the form of Edward's cult certainly had to do with the inability of Edward's narrative to compete with the martyrological aspects of Becket's narrative. Furthermore, Becket's opposition to Henry offered a site for popular resistance to the idea of monar-chial authority. Henry's penance before Becket's tomb can, then, be seen as a victory of transcendent popular and religious power over the king. In con-trast, Edward's identity as a king trumped his identity as saint. Indeed as the last Anglo-Saxon king he was in some ways a constant point of origin from which a number of English kings derived their legitimacy.[27]

The moment when this alteration in the cult of Edward becomes materi-ally clear is in the third translation of Edward to the shrine in which (with one interruption) he still presumably rests. On 13 October 1269, in a ceremony that, as one writer asserts, was actually suggested by the translation of Becket (a ceremony in which Henry III had assisted as a boy), Henry realized his am-bition of making Westminster an English version of St.-Denis, the French burial place of kings.[28] In fact, he not only planned to be buried in Westmin-ster but was himself translated to a tomb near the Confessor in 1281 by his son Edward I.[29] It was at this point that the Abbey became the site of not only English coronations—the beginning of the reigns of the English kings and queens—but also the end of a reign. Hence the heart of prince Henry was brought home and placed near the Confessor in 1271. Henry III's half-brother

(William de Valence) was buried close by the Confessor in the Chapel of St. Edmund. Edward I buried his queen there, and Edward himself was buried between his father and his brother. The increasing number of sovereign bodies sanctified (in a secular sense at least) the place to the extent that when Henry IV did not bury Richard II in the Abbey, he was forced to translate the king to his proper (and indeed already prepared) resting place some thirteen years after Richard's death.[30]

If, as Augustine claimed, saints' bodies were the limbs and organs of the Holy Spirit, the bodies of the English kings became the limbs and organs of the figure of a national *dignitas*—that fictional person of the king in whom the state was invested—a figure that never died. Ernst Kantorowicz has famously claimed that when the natural body of the sovereign died, there was a separation of the two bodies of the king. The demise of the king thus led to the investment of the new king with qualities of *dignitas* that guaranteed the continuation of the body politic. Yet though the body of the sovereign who had died may not have retained supernatural force, there remained the belief that the natural body of the sovereign, though deceased, continued to house some vital spiritual force. Meditating on the origins and continuation of sovereign power, Giorgio Agamben has suggested that we alter the way that we look at Kantorowicz's formulation. He suggests that it is as if the king "had in himself not two bodies but rather two lives inside one single body: a natural life and a sacred life."[31] After the natural death, the sacred life remains and presumably is passed on to the sovereign's successor. The machinery that ensures this succession is the coronation ceremony. And the regalia involved in the coronation is the outward manifestation of what is supposed to be seen as an inner transformation. In terms of the English ceremony, the crown and ring of Edward indicate a connection with the last Anglo-Saxon monarch *and* ensure that the sovereign will be seen as a worthy heir of the sacred life of the king. But while much of this regalia has been lost or destroyed, one thing has remained constant—the locus of the coronation. The church at Westminster was known as "the head, crown, and diadem of the kingdom" because it is the place of coronation but also because it contains the bodies of those who had been the head of the state.[32] It seems that a certain aura is retained in the sovereign body—enough to require the new sovereign to accept the mantle in the presence of the deceased sovereign.

As Claude Lefort has asserted, what we are really dealing with in the idea of the king's two bodies is "the already politicized theological and the already theologized political."[33] In other words, this way of thinking about the aura

of the king's body is not simply an offshoot of religious belief, rather this belief was already integrated into the idea of the political from its inception. Yet
even if the political and theological were indisputably linked "logically and
historically as a primary datum," medieval subjects often acted as if they were
not linked.[34] In fact, it could be argued that the Abbey in some sense culti-
vated the split between secular and sacred, making Westminster a sanctified
secular site certainly not divorced from—but somehow separated from—the
religious. There is some evidence for this disjunction in Henry IV's own decision to be buried at Canterbury rather than Westminster. He cited his sin-
fulness in this decision, but it is possible that he believed he really didn't
belong in the "resting place of kings" because of his culpability in the death
of Richard.[35]

The kings and queens who lie in shrines, in tombs, and under the masonry at Westminster did not transform the Abbey into a New Jerusalem, a
Compostela, or even a Canterbury. Instead, the coalescence of their corpses
created a kind of sanctified secular, even pre-national, space. Initially this space
provided a counterpoint to the sacred space of Canterbury. But ultimately, with
the Reformation, it was to become the locus of a national church and state.
Edward the Confessor, at the head of all of these bodies, was the crucial and
symbolically irreplaceable beginning point that led to the generation of other
groups of bodies with their own national sanctity. If his religious cult was ultimately a failure, one might argue that it was a fortunate failure because it
enabled the larger space of the Abbey to become more than a place of religious pilgrimage—something that, along with Becket's tomb, would have been
dismantled and abjured after the break with Rome in 1532. Instead, it was able
to repress its Catholic past and be transformed into a space in which the nation could celebrate its own beginnings. The corporeal reality of Edward became, not a celebration of what Dean Stanley in the nineteenth century called
a "disgusting roman ritual," but instead a monumental, national concern that
was putatively freed of the contamination of the body. We see this attitude in
Stanley's own affirmation of the secular memorializing function of the Abbey:
"What a poet, already quoted, said of a private loss is still more true of the
losses of the nation—'A monument in so frequented a place as Westminster
Abbey, restoring them to a kind of second life among the living, will be in
some measure not to have lost them.' The race of our distinguished men will
still continue."[36] The transformation of private loss into public commemoration and of corporeal death into monumental celebration effaces the body
even as it depends on the presence of the bodies of these "distinguished men"

in order to engender "the race." The slippage from nation to race here is enabled by the move from body to monument. It is this move that will ultimately ensure the formation of the space that we call Poets' Corner.

Yet if this slippage is necessary to the formation of the Corner, ultimately, it is not sufficient. It is, in fact, the burial of a nonliterary and nonroyal English corpse that will transform the South Transept into a place of literary commemoration. I suggest that the burial of what is commonly called the founding corpse of the Corner, Geoffrey Chaucer, followed naturally from this prior burial because the two were linked by their connection to the issue of sanctuary—an issue of vital importance for the Abbey and the Church in the fourteenth through the sixteenth centuries. Further this idea of sanctuary became analogically extended to the current notion of Poets' Corner as an enclosed space of refuge for the body of English poetry.

National Trauma and the Production of the Literary

This notion of Poets' Corner as a space of literary sanctuary is echoed in common references to the Corner as a poetical "pantheon," a place of "peculiar glory" and even as the repository of the "sacred reliques of the tuneful train," confirming a metamorphosis from sacred to nationalistic literary space.[37] The reasons behind these characterizations would seem evident enough. As one nineteenth-century writer put it, when a visitor enters Poets' Corner, he "reflect[s] that he is about to tread upon the ashes of genius,—to hold converse with the manes of the illustrious dead."[38] The source of these reflections is a more localized expression of the effects that Edward's body had on the fabric of the entire Abbey. As we saw above, the "thereness" of a saint's body could provide proof that a particular monastic or civic institution had special status.[39] This would explain why the first conceptualization of the space inside the South Transept as especially important to poets refers to it as a "sacred sepulcher."[40] And the poem that first mentions the name "Poets' Corner" (Thomas Fitzgerald's "Upon the POETS CORNER in WESTMINSTER ABBEY") invokes the notion of the "sacred relic."[41] Clearly what is at work here is a kind of literary canonization. Yet for all the similarities between the bodies of poets and the bodies of saints, we will see that these poetical corpses produce a different kind of morbid logic. For where we saw that the bodies and the relics of a saint were acquired in order to localize a cult—to make a particular place important for worship—the bodies in Poets' Corner were gathered together in order to produce a national, secular idea of literature.

But why were they gathered together in this particular "corner" of the Abbey? Geoffrey Chaucer was the first poetical corpse buried in the South Transept, so (unless his burial was a fortuitous accident), any explanation would have to precede his burial in 1400. In fact, some twenty years before Chaucer's death there is a burial in the South Transept that, while now obscure, was at the time the final act of one of the most serious crises in the Abbey's history. It was this crisis, I suggest, that generated the need for a kind of separate space within the larger space of the Abbey.

This crisis (which involved the breaking of sanctuary and murder) had its origins in 1367 at the battle of Nájera in Castile, where Edward the Black Prince successfully restored Pedro the Cruel to the throne (the one whom Chaucer in the *Monk's Tale* calls "O noble, O worthy Petro, glorie of Spayne"). In the battle, two squires, Robert Hauley and Richard Chamberlain, captured the count of Denia and held him for ransom.[42] Some ten years later Hauley and a certain John Shakel (who had bought his share of the hostage from Chamberlain) were still holding the count's oldest son, Alphonso (who stood as pledge for his father).[43] Finally, in August 1377, the count sent an agent to England with a partial ransom and instructions for Alphonso's release. At this time, however, Alphonso had become politically important to the English Crown, and, in October 1377 the Marshal's Court issued a writ demanding that Hauley and Shakel produce the hostage before the king and council in Parliament.[44] When Hauley and Shakel refused to comply, they were, apparently, brought before Parliament and ordered to produce Alphonso. When they refused again, they were taken and imprisoned in the Tower for contumacy and for turning their home into a prison.[45]

In August 1378 Hauley and Shakel broke out of the Tower and fled to Westminster Abbey, taking up sanctuary there. Apparently fearing that the two squires would attempt to flee the country with their hostage, the court ordered the constable of the Tower (Sir Alan de Buxhall) to capture them. He did well enough with Shakel by tricking him into leaving the Abbey precincts, but he was not as successful with Hauley. The result was that Buxhall was forced to break into the Abbey Sanctuary on August 11 during High Mass. Just as the deacon reached the words "If the Goodman of the house had known what watch the thief would appear—" (Matthew 24:43), Buxhall and his men burst in upon the service.[46] With the aid of fifty soldiers, he initially managed to seize Hauley, apparently in the South Transept, but Hauley escaped, and, after fleeing twice around the Choir, he was finally brought down and killed in front of the Prior's Stall at the north side of the entrance to the Choir.[47] The soldiers then took his body by the legs and, as Thomas Walsingham reports, "horribly dragging it through the most sacred part of the choir and the church, bespattering everything with his blood and brains" threw it into the street.[48] This violation of sanctuary led to the closure of the Abbey for four months. And Parliament (which then met in the Chapter House) was suspended, so that the assembly would not be polluted by the desecrated precincts.

Despite the fact that John of Gaunt was away during this desecration, the chroniclers claim that blame for the outrage was assigned to the duke.[49] And though one of the denunciations of those who had violated the Sanctuary specifically exempted the duke of Lancaster, Richard II, and his mother, it is likely that their pointed exclusion would suggest, in fact, that they had something to do with the affair.[50] Thus, though Gaunt probably had little to do with the outrage, he was placed in the position of having to defend the violation of Westminster's Sanctuary. This was especially true since one of the great critics of Gaunt, Bishop Courteny, had refused to appear before the royal council at Windsor to which he had been summoned—an action that Gaunt had reportedly responded to by saying that "if the king so directed, he was willing to hasten to London and bring back that obstinate bishop to the council by force in spite of the ribald knaves of London."[51]

As London was the site of so much unrest, Parliament was summoned to appear on 20 October at St. Peter's in Gloucester. Almost immediately, rumors began to circulate that Parliament had removed to Gloucester in order put forth John of Gaunt's plan to begin the confiscation of church property.[52] In other words, the violation of the Sanctuary had erupted into a full-scale conflict between church and state that at once echoed the murder of Thomas Becket and foreshadowed Henry VIII's break with Rome. Accordingly, after some initial parliamentary business, Archbishop Sudbury formally protested the violation of sanctuary at Westminster. At this time, we are told, "there came into parliament doctors of theology and civil law, and other clerks on behalf of the king, who in the presence of the lords and all the commons made arguments and proof against the prelates on the matter aforesaid by many colourable and strong reasons."[53] Though none of the clerks is named in Walsingham, other sources identify the reformer John Wyclif as one of the clerks pressing the case.[54]

The government took the position that the case of Hauley and Shakel was actually one of debt, as they owed the government their hostage and, by extension, the government's share of the ransom. Further, Wyclif argued that sanctuary did not extend to debtors because neither God nor the pope could grant a local exemption from actions for debt.[55] In addition, the government claimed that Hauley had been the first to pollute the Abbey because he had been the first to draw his sword. The Abbey responded with legendary claims and legal charters that supported the right of sanctuary at Westminster. The Abbey cited an old story about how St. Peter himself had purportedly dedicated the Church in the reign of King Sebert with the help of angels to ensure the sanctity of the principle of sanctuary.[56] The defenders of the Abbey also produced charters from King Edgar and Edward the Confessor that attested to the longstanding nature both of sanctuary and its extension to debtors.[57] Given the intransigence of the prelates, no verdict was returned in this particular case, though the Parliament of 1379 ruled (as had the court in 1355) that sanctuary could protect debtors from imprisonment or seizure, but could not protect the debtor's property outside sanctuary. Thus, in a peculiar fashion, the violation of sanctuary led to a reaffirmation of the idea of sanctuary.

The effect of this violation/sanctification of the boundaries of the Abbey on later thinking about the ecclesiastical space is telling. There are two leading narrators of the violation of Westminster Abbey, Thomas Walsingham and the Anglo-Norman author of the York *Anonimalle Chronicle*. The two accounts are factually quite similar, but Walsingham structures his narrative so that the form of the story in some ways mirrors the transgression that took place in the Abbey. He begins by noting how the story he has to relate is itself a departure: "I who would always have preferred to write comedy, am about to describe something more than tragic (*plus quam tragicam*)."[58] At least two other places in his account he tells us that he is writing in the tragic mode (most notably when he talks about the Rising of 1381), but here he means to communicate something different—that the genre of tragedy cannot contain the enormity of the transgression, or, as he calls it, the crime or sin (*scelus*). The unnameability of the genre seems best communicated by the word he uses three times in the first paragraph, "pollution." In an ecclesiastical sense, the crime at once is categorized as uncleanness and its uncleanness is what makes it a crime. Like the "fro[th]ande fyl[th]e" in the poem *Cleanness*, the threat engendered by sin (that it will overspill its bounds) becomes the sin itself.[59] As A. C. Spearing puts it, "On the one hand, then, we have the ideal of the seamless and perfect enclosure; on the other, we have the nauseatingly uncontrollable expansion of a substance that resists and attacks enclosures, overwhelms and obscures boundaries."[60] Only a tale that itself threatens neat generic boundaries can represent the crime that is made up of threatening these boundaries.

Walsingham goes on to describe, in broad terms, what the crime actually is: "A crime has been committed by men of our world, and moreover, perpetrated alas in our times. Satan's minions, assailing God's temple, have perpetrated a vile form of crime, the pollution of God's house, consecrated by the chief of the apostles, which up to the present day had been unpolluted even by unbelievers and enemies who were without faith."[61] What stands out immediately is the hellish forcefulness of Walsingham's rhetoric. These men are "Satan's minions," later "worse than heathens," and a few lines later "followers of the Antichrist." He tells us that the grief brought about by the transgression is so enormous that it compels him to silence. Yet the scale of the transgression is so great he "shall at least bring to the notice of posterity to those things which, because of their enormity, ought not to remain silent."[62] This topos of unspeakability matches the inability of the genre of tragedy to "contain" the great violation. At the same time, it becomes clear that if language cannot inscribe the emotion occasioned by the violation, to insist that the violation—always overspilling its bounds—cannot be represented is to perpetuate the pollution because language cannot contain it. Walsingham's ability to reinscribe the boundaries of Westminster is thus inherent in the very form of the narrative that he weaves.

Admittedly, Walsingham's task is tricky. He cannot downplay the magnitude of the violation, and yet he must also affirm that the space can be reconsecrated and made holy again. Initially he focuses on the exceptional quality of the transgression. Part of what is important is that "up to the present day" the house of God has remained undefiled. And later, when he narrates the "crime," he portrays one of the monks as "admonishing them not to defile that holy temple wonderfully dedicated to the chief of the apostles and so far undefiled."[63] Yet the curious thing is that Walsingham omits any discussion of reconsecration and instead proceeds to describe the Parliament that had been moved to Gloucester.[64]

One of the reasons that Walsingham does not include the reconsecration of the Abbey in his narrative may be that the very notion of reconsecration was itself politically fraught. The *Continuatio Eulogii* reports that the king "sent many times by his writs to the Abbot of Westminster to appear before him, and to cease his denunciations, and that he should reconsecrate his church and serve God after the foundation thereof, and all the matter should be brought to a good end. But the Abbot would not appear nor would he remain quiet, for he said that the Church of Westminster was consecrated by Saint Peter by miracle, and therefore it did not need to be consecrated by any other man, displaying the chronicle of consecration as follows."[65] What follows this remarkable report is a version of the foundation legend originally penned by Sulcard in which St. Peter arrives at the monastery ahead of Mellitus, the bishop of London, and consecrates the Abbey Church. After the dedication (replete with lights and singing), he tells a fisherman (appropriately enough) that he should go to the bishop and tell him that "I, Peter, have anticipated [*praeveni*] the Bishop and have already along with the citizens of heaven blessed it with the authority of my holy power . . . tell him therefore to leave off his dedication" (*supersedeat igitur dedicationi*).[66] Bishop Mellitus, arriving and seeing the signs of heavenly consecration, agrees.

The more general force of this narrative is, of course, to suggest that things which are already intrinsically holy need not be hallowed by human hands. But one has to confess that as a principle this begs the question of whether, once human hands have sullied a holy thing, it needs to be reconsecrated. Ecclesiastical authorities, at any rate, were pretty clear that "a church must be reconciled on account of any homicide whether with or without the shedding of blood: and also, besides homicide, for any injurious shedding of blood."[67] The abbot of Westminster (Nicholas de Litlyngton) would, then, seem to be mistaken in his assertion that the church did not need to be reconciled. He seems to have in mind the principal that "the holiness of the place itself doth do away with the infamy . . . for reconciliation is performed for an example and a warning, that all behold the church, which in no way sinned, washed and purified for the delict [crime] of another, may reflect how they themselves must work out the expiation of their own sins."[68] The space itself thus cannot be held responsible for its defilement because clearly the men who invaded the space and killed Hauley are the sinners—if the space is reconciled, it is only as an example to those who *need* to be purified.

What Abbot Litlyngton also seems to have in mind is the analogy between the body of the believer and ecclesiastical space. Hugh of St. Victor gives voice to this idea when he claims that "for the faithful soul is the true temple of God by the covenant of virtues which is built, as it were, by a kind of structure of spiritual stones, where faith makes the foundation, hope raises the building, charity imposes the finish. But the Church herself also, brought together as one from the multitude of the faithful, is the house of God constructed of living stones, where Christ has been placed as the cornerstone, joining the two walls of the Jews and the gentiles in one faith."[69] If this particular explanation of the church seems somewhat abstract, gesturing to the Corpus Mysticum rather than the actual building of the church, Dawn Marie Hayes points us towards even more literal explanations of the material ecclesiastical structures—citing Rudolph, the eleventh-century abbot of St. Trond who envisions the Church in anatomical terms—the chancel and sanctuary being the head and neck, the choir stalls symbolizing the breasts, the nave symbolizing the womb, and so on.

What becomes clear in this particular articulation of the temple=body trope is the feminine nature of the church. This becomes particularly evident in the equation of the material church with the bride of Christ in Durandus' *Rationale*: "And it should be observed that consecration . . . appropriates the material church to God . . . in consecration it is endowed and becomes the proper spouse of Christ, which it is a sacrilege to violate adulterously for it ceases to be a place of demons."[70] It also echoes what Walsingham suggests in his initial description of the violation of the Abbey's Sanctuary, "it is very different with Christians in these modern times, for false to their faith, and worse than heathens, not only do they not allow the house of God, the gate of heaven, the door of Paradise, the court of the high priest, indeed the Bride of Jesus Christ, to be free and safe, but they are not afraid to use their polluted hands, their deadly swords, and their vile purposes to enslave or even to defile it with human blood."[71] The pollution of the temple is the violation of the bride of Christ, and this is perhaps one of the reasons that the abbot is so resistant to the idea that the church must be reconciled. Reconciliation should act simply as an example to the sinful, but, in suggesting that the church needs to cleanse itself, it can imply that the church is somehow responsible for its own violation. Ultimately the politics of reconciliation in this case gave way to ecclesiastical necessity, and the church was reconsecrated on 8 December 1378—the feast of the Conception of the Blessed Virgin.[72]

Hauley's murder and the sensational event that followed it might seem distant from the space of Chaucer's tomb in the South Transept. After all, the murder took place in the Choir. Yet it was in the South Transept that the monks decided to bury Hauley. A clue as to why the monks had chosen this particular place might be found in the inscription that the chapter put on the stone where Hauley had been murdered. The stone no longer exists, perhaps being replaced when the Abbey decided to raze the medieval choir stalls in the eighteenth century, but a transcription of the inscription can be found

in John Flete's *History of Westminster Abbey*, which was probably written in
the mid-fifteenth century:

> M domini C ter septuaginta his diebus [dabis sic] octo,
> > Taurini celebrem plebe colente diem
> hic duodena prius in corpore vulnera gestans
> > ense petente caput, Hawle Robertus obit.
> cujus in interitu libertas, cultus, honestas
> > planxit militiae immunis ecclesiae.[73]

> In these days of the Lord, one thousand three hundred and seventy
> > eight,
> As the people celebrated the feast day of Taurinus,
> He was already sporting twelve wounds on each side of his body
> > at this point,
> When a sword came at his head and Robert Hauley died.
> At his death, the freedom, reverence, and integrity of a Church
> > unsullied by a deployment of soldiers lamented aloud.

This inscription would seem to be a kind of elegy for Hauley, but its emphasis
is clearly less on Hauley than on the loss that Hauley's death occasioned.
Beginning, as the inscription does, with the narrative of how the people were
celebrating a holy day—the focus is on the space of the Abbey as a sacred
place that has been sullied. Hauley's death is encapsulated, one might say,
within the poem, surrounded by the *plebs* and the *ecclesia*. We move, then,
through the poem as a kind of narrative—from celebration to violation to
lamentation. What is especially interesting here is the way that the poem
laments, not so much the death of Hauley, as the loss of the church's own
freedom, reverence, and integrity—a kind of lost former self that can never
be restored.

But if Robert Hauley was indeed, as Dean Stanley asserted in 1868, a kind
of "martyr to the injured rights of the Abbey," his burial before the Chapel of
St. Benedict in the South Transept, might be seen as puzzling (fig. 1).[74] After
all, others had been buried in the Choir. One reason might be that, while
Hauley was actually murdered in the Choir, the outrage to the sanctity of the
Abbey began elsewhere. And this, in fact, is what the sixteenth-century antiquarian William Camden seems to suggest in his *Reges, Reginae, Nobiles et
alij* when he says that Hauley "was buried in the place where he was first

assaulted."[75] It is quite possible, then, that Hauley was first approached by Buxhill and his men in the South Transept.

But it is also true that this particular part of the Abbey was already somewhat special, as it was directly in front of the Chapel of St. Benedict—the founder of the monks' order.[76] The Chapel was also purportedly the final resting place of the head of Benedict, which had been brought by Edward III to the Abbey from Fleury. Anyone who journeyed to the relic would receive an indulgence of forty days. The specialness of the place would only be aided by the presence of the body of Hauley, who was a martyr to the cause of the sanctity of the Abbey Church. This is certainly suggested by the epitaph (or what remained of the epitaph) on his grave:

Me dolus, ira, furor multorum, militis atque

————————————

In hoc gladiis celebri pietatis asylo,
Dum Levita Dei sermones legit ad aram:
Proh Dolor ipse meo Monachorum sanguine vultus
Aspersi moriens, chorus est mihi testis in aevum.
Et me nunc retinet sacer [h]is locus, Haule Robertum,
Hic quia pestiferos malè sensi primitùs enses.[77]

I [am overcome by?] the deceit, anger, rage of a soldier and his
    multitude and . . .
    . . . [meet my violent end?] in this sanctuary of piety now full
    of swords,
While the Deacon read his speeches at the altar of the Lord.
Ah the indignation! In dying I myself bespattered the monks' faces
with my blood; the choir is my witness for eternity:
And now their holy place keeps me, Robert Hauley,
Because I in my misfortune experienced the swords bringing evil
    here for the first time.

As might be expected, the epitaph on Hauley's grave has a much more personal feel than the inscription on the stone where he was murdered. Yet Hauley speaks to us from beyond the grave not so much to lament his own murder as to lament the way in which it occurred. The corpse feels the indignation of staining the monks' faces with his blood. And at the end of the poem, his misfortune (his death) takes second place to the bringing of evil (*malum*) to this

Figure 1. The indent from Robert Hauley's grave. The legend was added in the late nineteenth century. Copyright: Dean and Chapter of Westminster.

place (*locus*). Certainly the word *hic* in the final line could mean the sanctuary in a broad sense, but in holding Hauley it specifies the particular place (the South Transept) in which he is buried.

There is, however, an interesting difference between the violation in the Choir (the actual location of Hauley's death) and his burial spot. The corpse says in the epitaph that it is kept (*retinet*) in the holy place (*sacer locus*), which,

of course, is not the Choir but the South Transept where Hauley was supposedly first assaulted suggesting that it was, in fact, the drawing of the sword in
a holy place that constituted the first violation of sanctuary. The first to pollute the Sanctuary, as Wyclif notes, is the first to draw his sword, so it might
well be that the focus for the violation is not so much the murder, however
horrific it might have been, but the actual drawing of weapons in the Sanctuary.[78] It would be here in the South Transept, then, that the pollution first
occurred, and here that the memorial to the violated right of sanctuary
(Hauley's tomb) was placed.

    Punning on the word *chorus*, the corpse points to the stone in the Choir
that narrates Hauley's death and also identifies the choir as the singers of his
death—those who represent him now that he is gone. At the same time, *he*
speaks from the grave to name those who would represent him. Relevant here
are Diana Fuss's twin insights about "corpse poems"—"Death thus animates
the living," and "the speaking corpse operates as a figure for poetry itself."[79]
This drama is enacted each time individuals walk from his grave to the crossing of the Abbey, quite literally taking a spatial tour of the cross—an insight
that would not have escaped a group of men who have dedicated their lives
to the worship of Christ. We might well see that this place was not only
polluted by Hauley's blood, but also has in some sense been consecrated by
it. The very outrage that was Hauley's murder, in other words, led to the
reaffirmation of the sacred space of the Abbey and right of sanctuary—a
reaffirmation memorialized in verses "spoken" by the dead and left for the
visitor to read.

The Debt of the Father

Twenty years after Hauley's death, Chaucer was buried in the South Transept. Speculations about why he was buried in the Abbey have centered on the
idea that because he lived within the precincts of the Abbey, it was natural for
him to be buried there.[80] However, it remains unclear why he was buried in
the South Transept as opposed to some other part of the church. Unlike
other poets who are buried in the South Transept, there are no documents
that show that he had any desire to be buried in the Abbey, much less "near
St. Benedict's Chapel."[81] The Abbey was, at this time, already the "resting place
of kings" (as one source puts it), and kings sometimes honored those who

served them by burying them close to where their own tombs would be, but these tombs are all around the Ambulatory.[82]

So why is Chaucer buried at Hauley's feet? Chaucer certainly would have known about the incident involving Hauley and Shakel. He had recently returned from Calais, and, ten days before Hauley was killed, Chaucer had been sitting on a commission of inquiry in Dartford (Kent). Yet, on the violation of Westminster Abbey, as on so much else, Chaucer is silent.[83] There were events surrounding the murder, however, that might offer circumstantial reasons for Chaucer's burial in the South Transept. Some ten years later, Chaucer began to experience financial difficulties. On 16 April 1388, John Churchman (possibly a moneylender) had initiated an exchequer action against Chaucer for the recovery of a debt of three pounds, six shillings, eight pence. In May, perhaps for political reasons, Chaucer resigned both of his exchequer annuities to John Scalby.[84] The following year he was summoned to court no fewer than five times to answer an action of debt brought against him by Henry Atwood.[85] In the years 1388–1399 there were at least five suits brought against Chaucer for debt, culminating in a warrant that demanded Chaucer's presence in court by June 1399, or he would be declared outlaw. By this time, however, Chaucer had obtained royal protection against creditors until 4 May 1400. It was also around this time (24 December 1399) that he purchased the tenement house within the precincts of Westminster Abbey.

Westminster Abbey, of course, was a chartered sanctuary, and though the events of 1378 had curtailed some of the rights of debtors to claim sanctuary, the reality was that the protection for debtors remained. It is true that a number of critics (and I include myself in their number) have expressed doubt that Chaucer sought sanctuary from his creditors within the Abbey.[86] But I would like to suggest that Chaucer sought to prepare against the possibility that he could not extricate himself from financial difficulties when his letter of royal protection expired. In his lease, he had to agree that "it will not be permitted the aforementioned Geoffrey to receive and give hospitality to anyone seeking the privileges and liberties and immunities of sanctuary of the aforementioned Westminster" without permission, but there is nothing preventing the poet himself from claiming those rights. In fact, one might well see the lease as confirming Chaucer's rights to sanctuary.[87] If Chaucer did avail himself of sanctuary, it would certainly explain why he was buried in such close proximity to Hauley, a martyr to the rights of sanctuary (particularly the rights of debtors) in the Abbey. To return to my earlier trope of emplotment, it is of

course quite possible that I engage in my own sense of errantcy. To resurrect
the idea of Chaucer as old, weary, and financially underappreciated is to an-
ticipate what will become a common theme of poetics in Poets' Corner—
engaging in a romance of the poet's life that is pleasing from a narrative point
of view (and, indeed, has often been repeated in Chaucer criticism) but is more
trope than truth. Yet part of my point in this book is precisely that plotlines
about poets, whether "true" or "false," ultimately become true and condition
how we think about poetics.

In this case there is some evidence that later conceptions of Chaucer as
financially embarrassed actually may have romanced the poet as himself a
debtor. Some ten years after Chaucer was translated from the floor of the
Abbey to the Purbeck marble tomb in which he now apparently rests, there
were a series of payments of debts that ran from 1566 through 1596. The for-
mulae are somewhat different in each of the orders, but they all essentially say
that money has been "tendered vpon [or tendered at] Chawsers tomb within
the Cathedrall church of S. Peter in Westminster" at a certain time (sometimes
very specific) in fulfillment of an earlier decree that said debt be paid.[88] It is
clear, I think, why a debtor might wish to meet to repay his or her loan in the
Abbey. Although the rights of sanctuary had been somewhat eroded with the
dissolution of the monastery in 1559 (one could no longer take sanctuary for
capital crimes, for instance), the Collegiate Church had been refounded as a
royal peculiar (directly under the jurisdiction of the monarch) in 1560. Along
with this special status went the rights of debtors to find sanctuary from their
creditors. Thus debtors were legally safe while they presumably fulfilled their
fiscal obligations. Further, in 1566 (the first recorded year of payments at the
tomb), the Abbey succeeded in defeating a bill that would have done away
with sanctuary, and it may be the strengthening of the right of sanctuary that
led to the suggestion that these particular debts be paid in the Collegiate
Church. Nothing would seem more appropriate than that these monies would
be paid at the tomb of a famous debtor, one who, perhaps enjoyed the protection of sanctuary.

It is possible, of course, that Chaucer's tomb was simply a kind of tourist
attraction that stood out in the South Transept as it was relatively new and
so afforded people a convenient spot to meet. But it is suggestive that, after
1599, there are no more records of payments either at Chaucer's tomb or in the
broader area of the Sanctuary, for in 1604, James would abolish completely the
right of sanctuary at Westminster.[89] What this tells us, I think, is that the space
of the South Transept, beginning with the murder of Hauley on 11 August

1378, was transformed into a symbolic manifestation of the rights of the Church on earth. Whether Chaucer's burial in the South Transept was a part of this symbolism, or accidental, or for some reason that has yet to be discovered, his tomb eventually became an extension of the special status that the church claimed—a status that in its invisibility and sanctity is not so far from the status that those literary corpses would claim in the years that saw the construction of Poets' Corner.

The endplot of the poet's life is thus transformed into the beginnings of the outlines of Poets' Corner. If this is, as I have suggested, a rationalized etiology, it has the advantage of offering a narrative—a plotline—that explains how the space in Westminster Abbey came to be considered not only a holy place, but how a particular part of that space became aestheticized. Behind this creation of literary space, of course, lies not only the body of poet, or the martyr to sanctuary, but the corpse of the founding king. It is, peculiarly enough, the tripartite progression from politics to religion to art that enables a particular kind of place to be made. We inhabit this space by imaginatively re-creating its beginnings and endings. Unlike the quiescent bodies that already dwell here, however, we tell a tale so that the dead may speak to us.

CHAPTER 2

Melancholia, Monumental Resistance, and the Invention of Poets' Corner

One has to know . . . *who* and *where*, to know whose body it really is and what place it occupies—for it must stay in its place. In a safe place . . . nothing could be worse, for the work of mourning, than confusion or doubt: one *has to know* who is buried where—and it *is necessary* (to know—to make certain) that, in what remains of him, *he remain there*. Let him stay there and move no more.

—Jacques Derrida

If Geoffrey Chaucer is said to be the founding corpse of Poets' Corner, one must admit that it was not until the burial of Edmund Spenser in 1599 that anything like a space specifically reserved for poets gained currency, and it was not until Shakespeare's death and burial in 1616 that the space began to be institutionalized (despite the fact that Shakespeare was not buried in the Abbey). Why the delay? The most obvious, but least satisfying, answer is that only in hindsight was Poets' Corner belated. Chaucer was probably buried in the larger space of Westminster Abbey because he lived within its precincts.[1] And, as I argue in Chapter 1, he may have been buried in the more localized space of the South Transept because it was considered an appropriate place for one who had sought sanctuary within the Abbey walls. Thus the idea of the South Transept as a place for poets may begin with Chaucer, but it was not self-consciously realized until almost two centuries after his death. A better question might be why it took so long once he was reburied (1556) for the South Transept to become the burial place for poets.

The answer, I think, lies in the melancholic relationship of Spenser to the medieval past, a relationship that, in turn, transforms Spenser at his death into one of the "moniments" of the past whose loss he laments. Spenser's presence in the South Transept actually signals a double loss—the loss of the medieval past symbolized by Chaucer (near whom he was buried) and the loss of the poet (Spenser) who attempted to make good that loss. Yet far from reinforcing the absoluteness of loss, I argue that this double loss paradoxically leads to a gain. For in troping Spenser as a monument that has been lost, the visitor to the tomb rehearses Spenser's own melancholic relationship to the past. As Spenser melancholically dwelt upon and recreated the past, so the visitor to the tomb recreates the absent presence of Spenser in the space of the South Transept. The South Transept becomes a space that (like any cemetery) is driven by loss, but it is also a space that is different insofar as it necromantically repairs this loss with poetic phantasy. Early in the South Transept's history, then, melancholic affect is key to establishing an almost magical link with the poetical dead.

Yet to suggest that there was monolithic support for the creation of Poets' Corner would be to homogenize the varied reactions to creating a space for the poetic dead. Indeed, shortly after Shakespeare's death, Ben Jonson famously opposed the creation of such a space by invoking the Horatian commonplace that identified poetry (and thus the poet) as a sublime monument that could not be lost because it was not located in any single space. Yet even as Jonson seemed to suggest that a physical space could in no way "contain" poetry, the power of the place seemed to grow, suggesting an increasing need to find a physical site to embody poetry in the seventeenth century.

*   *   *

As W. R. Lethaby and, more recently, Derek Pearsall have argued, Chaucer's reburial during Queen Mary's reign was probably a response to attempts to reform Chaucer into a proto-Protestant.[2] The reburial of the medieval poet in a tomb that recalled earlier Marian forms of devotion was an attempt to appropriate Chaucer to a Catholic "counter-reformation."[3] After Queen Mary died in 1558 and was succeeded by her Protestant sister, Elizabeth, there was an understandable reluctance to acknowledge and celebrate the new burial place of a medieval Catholic poet who had been reburied in commemoration of the old religion.[4] But it is also true that the monumentalization of a poet's grave may have troubled Protestants, for the function of great and extravagant tombs as tools of remembrance was a vexed question. The Calvinist poet

Fulke Greville had designed just such a tomb for himself and his fellow poet Philip Sidney, but had also included an epitaph that condemned such "vaine" attempts "by stones to seek aeternite againe."[5] John Calvin, in contrast, had been buried in an unmarked grave that one late sixteenth-century writer had characterized as surpassing the "marble toumbs" and "sepulchers" of kings.[6] Such English suspicions of monumental remembrance ultimately led to the iconoclasm of the middle part of the sixteenth century when reformers undertook to destroy all funerary monuments that seemed to encourage "idolatrous" (i.e., Catholic) worship of the dead.

Yet the radical solution to this problem (the destruction of tombs) led to the erasure of what a 1560 proclamation called the "honourable and good memory of sundry virtuous and noble persons deceased."[7] In other words, the history conjured up by these tombs and memorials was crucial to the social order upon which political power rested. To destroy such markers of individual history was to threaten the monumental national history. Attempting to discourage the continuing erasure of these material markers of social lineage, the proclamation of 1560 made a distinction between the "monuments of idolatry and false feigned images" and monuments "set up for . . . memory . . . in common churches and not for any religious honor."[8] Despite this attempted distinction between idolatry and memory, the distrust of church monuments continued. For as Sir John Coke suggested in a letter to Fulke Greville, it was "that superstition which taught to worshipp the reliques of the dead [that] brought their tombs into churches."[9] Whatever the present use of monuments, there was no doubt that the impetus to have such monuments in churches was originally Catholic. And as the function of these memorials was to ask people to remember, it was difficult to claim that they should forget the memorials' original religious function.

Behind this critique of funereal monuments was not only a fear that the dead would be worshipped, but an anxiety that such "speaking stones" might elevate the reputation of one who had not lived well. Interestingly, critiques of funereal furniture often did not explicitly encompass this fear. Instead, critics like George Wither asked, "Doost thou suppose, by a few carved stones, / . . . / To be *immortall*? If thou long to live / After thy death; let noble *Vertue* give / And adde that living glory to thy name."[10] It was, in other words, the memory of a life well lived that would give "living glory" and thus a name. At the same time, of course, "vertue" would assure the immortality that only God could grant.[11] This focus on the inadequacy of monuments would seem banal if it did not also suggest the extent to which the residual power of monuments persisted. We also see the Protestant concern about this sepulchral power in the suggestion that such images (or funeral monuments) would lead to idolatrous dealings with the dead. In other words, sixteenth- and early seventeenth-century Protestants were concerned both with the kind of relationship that the living had with the dead *and* with the kind of dead who would have monuments raised to them. At the same time, the history of England, and thus the historical justification for political and aristocratic rule, was in some sense written in the monuments of her dead. Even if some monuments were seen as misleading or "feigned images," it was politically dangerous to claim that all monuments were to be distrusted. The result of this impasse was a kind of Solomonic solution in which monuments were often reared to memorialize their occupants while calling attention to their own inadequacy at memorializing the dead. Against this backdrop I would like to suggest that it was, in fact, this monumental resistance that led to the power of Poets' Corner. By at once drawing attention to loss via the physical monuments and insisting on the monuments' own inability to compensate for loss, the space elicited a kind of productive melancholia.

Generally, of course, melancholia is seen as a pathology that interferes with the healthy mourning process.[12] Perhaps the most famous melancholic was Queen Victoria, who for forty years after her husband's death, had his clothes laid out every evening and the water replaced in his basin every morning. For her, the past was still alive. Hence the loss was not experienced as a loss because of her close memorial tie to Prince Albert. The dangers of this idolatry of the past have been well rehearsed. In psychological terms, the phantom of the past threatens to fill up and control the world of the living. In larger cultural terms, phantasmatic history creates a mirror that offers up a past fantasy of politics and gender that is often deeply nostalgic and can be put in the service of genealogies of ideology.[13] For Renaissance English reformers, such melancholia threatened to lead believers away from the "true" religion by enabling them to dwell in the phantastical Catholic past.[14]

As a Protestant poet, Spenser was sensitive to the seductions of the Catholic past, embodying the Church of Rome in characters like the ultimate seductress Duessa in the *Faerie Queene*. But, like the violent reformer John Bale, he had, as James Simpson puts it, "a deeply divided consciousness" in that "he applaud[ed] the destruction of the [monastic] buildings but deplor[ed] the attendant loss of books."[15] What Bale bewailed above all is the loss of what he calls the "the lyvely memoryalles of our nation." Thus he sought to bring forth "bookes out of the deadly darknesse to lyvele light."[16] Like those reformers who wished to preserve church monuments, he saw learning as an ability to resurrect and preserve not just the classical but the medieval past because to fail to do so would risk losing the national monuments that in large part created English identity.[17] Spenser took a somewhat different tack, generating medievalistic historicisms that recreated and rewrote the legendary Catholic prehistory of Protestant England and simultaneously transformed Spenser himself into a melancholic "ruin" that would itself provide an early modern origin for Poets' Corner.[18]

Spenser's Poetics and the Melancholic Origin of Poets' Corner

From early in his career, Spenser had identified Chaucer, the first poet buried in the South Transept, as the exemplary medieval poet and his own poetical model, saying in the *Shepheardes Calender* that "the God of shepheards Tityrus [identified as Chaucer by E. K.] . . . taught me how to make."[19] And indeed, perhaps the first appearance of the "queene of Fayerye" in English literature is in Chaucer's unfinished *Tale of Sir Thopas*, lending credence to the belief that Spenser's *Faerie Queene* is on some level an attempt to complete Chaucer's tale by substituting Arthur for Thopas. Yet if Spenser asserts a kind of neo-medieval chivalric aesthetic in his works, and if he locates his own inspiration in a medieval poet, he is also all too aware of the lack of continuity between the medieval past and the early modern present. It is this gap that Spenser attempts to bridge with his poetry—an attempt that has profound implications for the early modern reformation of the space that would become Poets' Corner.

  Central to the understanding of how Spenser views poetic history can be found in Spenser's "lamentation," *The Ruines of Time*. In it the narrator encounters Verlame—the embodiment of the late antique/early medieval past. He is, by chance, "beside the shore" of the Thames, near the place where Verulamium "stood of yore," when he sees a "sorrowfullie wailing" woman on the other side. Yet, as he tells us in the first few lines, there remained no memory or monument of the city. Nor (as Spenser's audience would have known) did the Thames any longer flow near the site of the city. The figurative meanings of the river and the weeping woman secure the poem within a tradition of lamenting allegorical figures that includes the Genius of Rome by the Tiber and the Psalmist weeping by the rivers of Babylon for the lost Jerusalem. In this convention, it is lack of presence that leads to lamentation—a state of affairs to which the poem returns after the lamentation ends. For when Ver-lame has "ended all her piteous plaint, / With dolefull shrikes shee vanished away" (252–253).[20] She is, in the end, ultimately a phantasm, a marker for the pathological sense of loss that enables Spenser's own historical project. It is to this pathology of loss that I would like to turn. For key to this historical project is the melancholic affect of the subject in the poem.

The reaction of the poet's persona, once Verlame has vanished, tells us much about Spenser's own melancholic relationship to the past. The "I" of the poem says that he

> . . . sate long time in senceless sad affright,
> Looking still, if I might of her have sight.
>
> Which when I missed, having looked long,
> My thought returned greeved home againe,
> Renewing her complaint with passion strong,
> For ruth of that same womans piteous paine;
> Whose wordes recording in my troubled braine,
> I felt such anguish wound my feeble heart,
> That frosen horror ran through everie part. (475–483)

Spenser here gives an almost clinical description of melancholy. As Hugh of St. Victor put it, melancholy "renders men now somnolent, now vigilant, that is, now grave with anguish, now intent on celestial desires."[21] The speaker's melancholy leads him to turn inward—re-creating the object within to replace the absence of the object without.

This link between melancholia and poetic production is an ancient one. As the pseudo-Aristotelian *Problems* asks, why is it "that all men who are out-standing in philosophy, poetry or the arts are melancholic, and some to such an extent that they are infected by the disease arising from black bile?"[22] As I have shown elsewhere, the short answer to this question seems to be that melancholia produced a near madness—a divine frenzy that was the sign of inspiration—the kind of frenzy that Spenser's poetic persona seems to have experienced when he had access to the vision of Verlame.[23] The psychological process by which this melancholia informs art, however, offers a more instru-mental solution to the connection: the sickness occasioned by melancholia led the victim to conjure up "imaginationes malae" (wicked phantasms), or as Al-bertus Magnus tells us, melancholics "multa phantasmata inveniunt" (make up

many phantasms).[24] The reason why this ability to create phantasms is so help-
ful to artists is because, as the sixteenth-century writer Romano Alberti put it:

> Wishing to imitate, they [artists] must retain the phantasms fixed
> in the intellect, so that afterward they can express them in the way
> they first saw them when present; and, being their work, this
> occurs not only once, but continually. They keep their minds so
> much abstracted and separated from nature that consequently
> melancholy derives from it. Aristotle says, however, that this
> signifies genius and prudence, because almost all the ingenious
> and prudent have been melancholics.[25]

Melancholia, then, deals with loss insofar as it enables the recovery of the
past. There is, of course, a paradox to all of this, one that begins with the notion of melancholy itself. For, as Freud suggests, "In melancholia not only is
it unclear what object has been lost, it is uncertain that one can speak of a
loss at all."[26] This is because the object upon which the melancholic fixates is
not the real lost object, but a phantasmatic creation that appears only once
the object has vanished. In this case, Verlame is the phantasmatic creation that
replaces the lost city of Verlamium—the place that links England to both a
medieval and classical past. The past, as Augustine tells us, has no being and
does not exist in the here and now. Thus, in the attempted melancholic recollection of the past, "the object," as Giorgio Agamben puts it, "is neither appropriated nor lost, but both possessed and lost at the same time."[27]

Reformers in the sixteenth century well understood the seductions of
phantastic productions and were quick to connect poetic imagery with het-
erodox ecclesiastical imagery. John Jewel, in his *A Reply to Harding's Answer*,
writes that "For painters and poets, for liberty of lying, have of a long time
been coupled both together. . . . And therefore, like as Plato commanded all
poets for their lying to be banished out of his commonwealth; so likewise Almighty God, for like liberty, banished all painters out of Israel."[28] Jewel lumps
all painters and poets together because they produce images or idols which
dishonestly *seem* to re-present that which really is. In much the same way,
Thomas Nashe adapts a passage from Roger Ascham's *The Scholemaster* to
attack contemporary writers because they wish

> to restore to the worlde that forgotten Legendary license of lying,
> to imitate a fresh the fantasticall dreames of those exiled Abbie-

lubbers, from whose idle pens proceeded those worne out impressions of the feyned no where acts, of Arthur of litle Brittaine, sir Tristram. . . . It is not of my yeeres nor studie to censure these mens foolerie more theologicallie, but to shew how they to no Common-wealth commoditie, tosse ouer their troubled imaginations to haue the praise of learning which they lack.[29]

"Abbie-lubbers" (Catholics) continue to affirm the medieval "fantasticall dreames" of Arthurian romance that threaten the current age because these romances present fantastic and seductive idols of the Catholic medieval past, idols that threaten to corrupt the Protestant commonwealth. Nashe here makes explicit what remains implicit in Jewel, that the real danger lies in mistaking poets for historians. Underlying this critique, then, is an attempt to escape the problem of the Middle Ages—what Nashe's source (Ascham) terms "Papistrie," which "as a standyng poole, couered and ouerflowed all England . . . in our forefather's tyme."[30] Such imaginings had been forgotten but now must be resuppressed by an English form of history that increasingly defines itself in negative terms: it is not medieval, nor fabulous, nor Catholic.

Yet if Protestant reformers would seem to distinguish between Catholicism, imagination, and error on the one hand and Protestantism, learning, and truth on the other, this series of oppositions is frustrated by poets like Philip Sidney who, despite his Calvinist leanings, avers that historiographers often lay claim to "veritie" even as they borrow from poets.[31] So too, Sidney would frustrate the idea that poets are necessarily beguilers, arguing that fiction need not beguile if writers use "narration but as an imaginative ground plot of a profitable invention."[32] In this way, then, phantastical creation proceeds from absence and ultimately leads not to a false presence but a "true-seeming" presence that is activated by absence.[33]

Monumental Melancholia

The vehicle for this presence of absence was the binary meaning of the word "monument." For even as physical monuments in some sense conjure up presence, they point to absence. Monuments to poets posed a further problem because poets had long made the claim that they, and not physical monuments, were the makers of reputation and fame. As early as Horace, the argument was that without the poet, fame would simply vanish.

Exegi monumentum aere perennius
regalique situ pyramidum altius,
quod non imber edax, non Aquilo impotens
posit diruere aut innumerabilis
annorum series et fuga temporum.[34]

I have finished a monument more lasting than bronze, more lofty
that the regal structure of the pyramids, one which neither the
corroding rain nor the ungovernable North Wind can ever destroy,
nor can the countless series of years, nor the flight of time.[35]

Horace's poem, of course, is about the timelessness of poetry and the ability
of the poet to defeat time, a topos that Simonides, Ovid, and Shakespeare,
among others, would rework to advance the immortality of the poet. Most
notable is the suggestion that an immaterial or abstract "monument" could
outlast the material stone or plaque, even if only in the memories of the living.
The advantage of poetry was that it gave form to the reputation of the dead
even while eschewing materiality. It became, in other words, a vessel for history that could participate in all the various senses of the word "monument"
without being subject to the depredations of time.

Like his fellow poets, Spenser believed in the monumental power of
poetry precisely because of its insubstantial nature and its seeming resistance to
the vagaries of history. Enduring monuments, for him, were his own poems.
He makes this particularly clear at the end of his *Epithalamion* where he claims
that the "song made in lieu of many ornaments" is "an endless moniment."[36]
So too, in the final stanza of *The Ruines of Time*, Spenser's praise of Sidney
acknowledges that the dead poet's art has made him "heavens ornament" (a
counterpoint to the unlasting earthly ornaments of *Epithalamion*). His own
poetry guarantees Sidney's immortality as a "moniment of his last praise."[37]

Yet if Spenser exalted Sidney as a sublime ornament, Spenser paradoxically enough became the ruin that he wrote about in the *The Ruines of Time*.
The antiquary John Weever, who wrote the first full-length treatment of
English church monuments, characterized him as a figure who is at least
structurally similar to Verlame and the other figures of loss in the poem.

Spencer is ruin'd of our latter time
The fairest ruine, Faeries foulest want:
When his *Time ruines* did our ruine show,

Which by his ruine we vntimely know:
Spenser therefore thy *Ruines* were cal'd in,
Too soone to sorrow least we should begin.[38]

These obituary verses recapitulate the melancholic poetics that characterize Spenser's attempt to recuperate the past. As Weever repeatedly returns to the ruins of the past, he compulsively reenacts Spenser's own return to the premodern past. Of course, the figure recuperated here is not Verlame or some figure from Spenser's poetry, but Spenser himself who then stands as a figure for that past.[39]

If Spenser himself becomes a ruin, a figure for that which is lost, his commemoration in Poets' Corner might seem to offer the possibility of monumental presence. Yet even his monument seems to dwell on loss. William Camden prefaces his report of the epitaph that originally appeared on Spenser's grave with the expected iteration of Spenser's fame, but he also notes the manner of his death.

Edmundus Spencer Londinensis Anglicorum poetarum, nostri saeculi facile Princeps, quod ejus poemata faventibus musis & victuro genio conscripta comprobat. Obiit immatura morte, anno salutis 1598. & prope Galfredum Chaucerum conditur, qui felicissime Poesin Anglicis literis primus illustravit.

EDMUND SPENCER, born in *London*, and chief Poet of our Age; which his Works, written with a happy spirit, and masterly Genius testify. He died by a too early Death in the Year 1598, and lies buried near *Chaucer*, who was the first that successfully wrote Poetry in the *English* Language.[40]

In suggesting that Spenser "died by a too early death," Camden may simply be engaging in a well-worn topos, but it is true that stories began to circulate that Spenser's death was somehow noteworthy. As Camden put it (some sixteen years after Spenser's death [1615]), he "had scarcely secured the means of retirement and leisure to write when he was ejected [from Ireland] by the rebels, spoiled of his goods and returned to England in poverty, where he died immediately afterwards and was interred at Westminster near to Chaucer."[41] The cause of Spenser's death remains in some doubt, but if we are to believe the poet John Lane and Ben Jonson, who wrote some twenty years after

Spenser's death, Spenser died of want, famously declaring (in Lane's words) that when the earl of Essex sent him a "crown of good store," "the medicine comes too late to the patient."[42] In his report, Ben Jonson avoids the medicinal metaphor, claiming that Spenser "refused 20 pieces sent to him by my Lord of Essex, and said that he was sorry he had no time to spend them."[43] In both reports, however, Spenser is coded not only as someone already dead, but someone who knows it. He is a kind of walking corpse that has no future.

The belatedness of Essex's "patronage" has an analogue in a much later story that purports to narrate an interchange between Spenser and the ultimate patron, Queen Elizabeth. As the English churchman and historian Thomas Fuller tells the tale in his *Worthies of England:*

> There passeth a story commonly told and believed, that Spencer presenting his poems to queen Elizabeth, she, highly affected therewith, commanded the lord Cecil, her treasurer, to give him an hundred pound; and when the treasurer (a good steward of the queen's money) alledged that the sum was too much; "Then give him," quoth the queen, "What is reason;" to which the lord consented, but was so busied, belike, about matters of higher concernment, that Spencer received no reward, whereupon he presented this petition in a small piece of paper to the queen in her progress:—
>
>> I was promis'd on a time,
>> To have reason for my rhyme;
>> From that time unto this season,
>> I receiv'd nor rhyme nor reason.
>
> Hereupon the queen gave strict order (not without some check to her treasurer), for the present payment of the hundred pounds she first intended unto him.[44]

Ostensibly, the story seems to address aesthetic and economic concerns. Elizabeth is deeply moved by Spenser's work, but Cecil balances her aesthetic response with his own pecuniary concern. Elizabeth then turns to rationality to make her case for the need to recompense the poet. Cecil agrees, but "higher concernment," presumably with matters of state (though what is highlighted here is his concern about money) then leads him to overlook the reward. Having received a promise for reasonable recompense for his "highly affecting" poetry, Spenser (unlike Chaucer) does not offer more poetry, but turns to doggerel in order to secure what he has already been promised. The suggestion seems to be that without support for poetry, there can be no truly "affecting verse," only poor poetry. Far from identifying poetry as immortal and divorced from the material concerns of the world, the story (which is repeated several times in the seventeenth century) seems to demonstrate the extent to which poetry depends on patronage.

Yet later versions of the same tale focus less on Cecil's thrifty resistance to Spenser's reward and more on how economic concerns not only mask political partisanship, but lead to the death not only of art, but of the artist. In a version of the story that was put down on paper some thirteen years after Fuller's account, Elizabeth's act of reading is suppressed and the hostility between Spenser and Cecil is highlighted. In his *Theatrum Poetarum*, Edward Phillips (John Milton's nephew) narrates how Spenser "return'd into England, and having lost his great friend Sir Philip, fell into poverty, yet made his last refuge to the Queen's bounty, and had 500_l. ordered him for his support, which nevertheless was abridged to 100_l. by Cecil, who, hearing of it, and owing him a grudge for some reflections in Mother Hubbard's Tale, cry'd out to the queen, What! all this for a song? This he is said to have taken so much to heart, that he contracted a deep melancholy, which soon after brought his life to a period."[45] The anecdote seems to tell the story of how politics once again trumps art. Spenser had been of Leicester's party and had indeed taken the time to savage Cecil in *Mother Hubbard's Tale*—a move that even Spenser's friend Gabriel Harvey went out of his way to distance himself from, saying "I must needs say, Mother-Hubbard in heat of choler, forgetting the pure sanguine of her sweete Faery Queen, willfully over-shott her malcontented selfe."[46] This choleric attack on Cecil leads, in this story, to a further imbalance of humors the result of which is the deep melancholy that leads irrevocably to death.[47]

These narratives that focus on the connection of poetic production to patronage and politics are directly linked to the erection of Spenser's monument. The earliest visual record we have of any kind of marker is the monument that the effigy maker Nicholas Stone erected in 1620. As he put it in his notebook, "I allso made a monement for Mr Spenser the pouett and set it up at Westminster for which the contes of Dorsett payed me 40 pounds."[48] Yet many seventeenth-century versions of Spenser's death state that Essex paid not only for Spenser's funeral but for his tombstone. Perhaps echoing the epitaph contained on the monument (fig. 2),[49] one of the earliest representations of the monument, the 1679 folio of Spenser contains a little addendum below an engraving of the stone:

> Such is the Tombe, the Noble Essex gave
> Great SPENSER's learned Reliques; such his grave
> How 'ere ill-treated in His Life he were
> His sacred Bones Rest Honourably Here.

Two things stand out about this quatrain. First, even as late as 1679, we find a kind of apologia for Spenser's treatment by his contemporaries. The effect is that the four lines posit the tomb as a kind of replacement for the lack of recognition that Spenser received in his own day. Spenser's "learned reliques . . . Rest Hourably Here," a status that anxiously repeats what the epitaph on the stone has already made clear that here "*Here* Lyes . . . the body of Edmond Spencer" (my emphasis). Second, the poem gives Essex the credit for raising the "tomb."[50] Yet despite the assurance that a monument was raised to the poet at his death, Spenser had to wait twenty years to receive his commemoration.

There was apparently an epitaph that existed over his tomb, but it was probably a temporary plaque. A year after Spenser's death Camden tells us that the epitaph read

> Hic prope *Chaucerum* situs est *Spenserius* illi
> Proximus ingenio, proximus & tumulo.
> Hic prope *Chaucerum Spensere* poeta poetam,
> Conderis & versu quam tumolo proprior,
> Anglica te viv, vixit plausitque poesis,
> Nunc moritura timet te moriente mori.

> Here plac'd near *Chaucer, Spencer* claims a Room,
> As next to him in Merit, next his tomb.
> To place near *Chaucer, Spencer* lays a claim;
> Near his Tomb, but nearer far his Fame.
> With thee our English Verse was rais'd on high;
> But now declin'd, it fears with you to die.[51]

This epigraph suggests that Spenser's body lay quite close to where Chaucer's body was supposed to reside, probably somewhere near the entrance to St. Benedict's Chapel.[52] The topography of the South Transept recapitulates

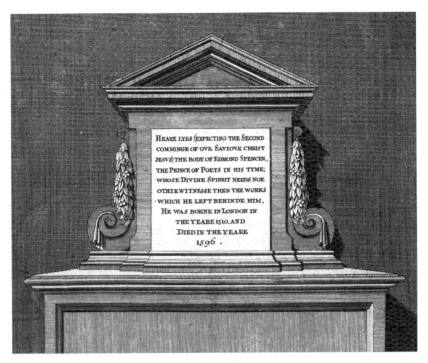

HEARE LYES (EXPECTING THE SECOND
COMMINGE OF OVR SAVIOVR CHRIST
JESVS) THE BODY OF EDMOND SPENCER,
THE PRINCE OF POETS IN HIS TYME;
WHOSE DIVINE SPIRRIT NEEDS NOE
OTHER WITNESSE THEN THE WORKS
WHICH HE LEFT BEHINDE HIM,
HE WAS BORNE IN LONDON IN
THE YEARE 1510, AND
DIED IN THE YEARE
1596 .

Figure 2. An early engraving of Spenser's monument from John Dart's *West-monasterium*. At its restoration in 1778, the birth date and death date were revised. Copyright Dean and Chapter of Westminster.

in symbolic form what most readers would already understand—that the physical space recapitulates the symbolic nearness of the two poets.[53] Yet if Camden implies that Spenser was buried "near to Chaucer" because he was symbolically his neighbor, then William Warner only seven years after Spenser's death concurs, but asserts that Spenser was *"Per Accidens,* only interr'd / Nigh Venerable Chaucer."[54] If we are to believe Warner, the beginning of Poets' Corner, then, seems to proceed from an "accident." It is only after the erection of Spenser's monument in 1620 that the logic of the burial next to Chaucer is too strong to be denied, and in what might be a kind of mortuary back-formation Sir James Ware (the editor of Spenser's *A View of the Present State of Ireland*) asserts in 1633 that Spenser "was buried according to his own desire in the collegiat church there, neere unto Chaucer whom he worthily imitated," a statement that is repeated in later accounts until it becomes "fact."[55]

The story of the oft-delayed monument tells us much about the idea of how poetry fit into the workings of the polis. As William Browne (one of the so-called Spenserians—imitators of the poet) tells us in 1616, Elizabeth apparently designated funds for the stone, but they were embezzled. Browne's story is suspiciously close to Fuller's story about how Cecil diverted funds from Spenser, and though Fuller's story is considerably later than Browne's poem, the story is rehearsed in a much earlier (1602) version in the diary of John Manningham.[56] Browne's poem, however, not only seems to recycle the story about Elizabeth, albeit with monumental concerns, but also invokes the topos of the enduring monument even as it undermines it.

> When mighty Nereus Queene
> (In memory of what was heard and seene)
> Imploy'd a Factor, (fitted well with store)
> Of richest Iemmes, (refined Indian Ore)
> To raise, in honour of his worthy name
> A Piramis, whose head (like winged Fame)
> Should pierce the clouds, yea seeme the stars to kisse,
> And Mausolus great toombe might shrowd in his.
> Her will had beene performance, had not Fate
> (that neuer knew how to commiserate)
> Suborn'd curs'd Auarice to lye in waite
> For that rich prey: (Gold is a taking baite)
> Who closely lurking like a subtile Snake
> Vnder the couert of a thorny brake,
> Seiz'd on the Factor by faire Thetis sent,
> And rob'd our Colin of his Monument.[57]

By invoking "Mausolus" and his tomb, Browne's poem is in dialogue with Spenser's own *Ruines of Time*. Spenser's poem, as suggested above, calls attention to the ways in which physical monuments, in particular the pyramids of princes and the tomb of Mausolus, fail to ensure fame. Spenser claims,

> In vaine doo earthly Princes then, in vaine,
> Seeke with Pyramids, to heaven aspired . . .
> To make their memories for ever live:
> For how can mortall immortalitie give?

Such one *Mausolus* made, the worlds great wonder,
But now no remnant doth therof remain. (407–408, 412–415)

Browne invokes this poem in order to certify that Spenser deserves a monument that would "shroud" the others. At the same time, as Browne is narrating the failure to raise a monument to Spenser, he suggests the deeper problem with monumentality—such commemorations are undependable. By default, then, Browne seems to confirm the Horatian idea that poetry is the only enduring monument. Yet one cannot help feeling that it is the loss, the lack to which Browne's poem points, that in fact makes Browne's poem possible. To return to the notion of poetic melancholia, it is the conjuring up of the phantasm of the tomb that enables Browne to construct his poem. And it is, finally, the lack of monumentalization that affirms the poetic commemoration of the poet in material terms. The "loss" of the tomb in some ways reenacts the original loss of Spenser himself—and peculiarly, then, it is absence that leads to the conjuration of a presence.

The Absence of Shakespeare and the Making of a Place

The same year as the publication of Browne's poem (1616), the third poetical corpse (Francis Beaumont) was laid to rest in Poets' Corner. But it was less his presence than the absence of another poet that actuated what might be called a mortuary imaginary. William Shakespeare, of course, was not buried in the Abbey; instead he was buried in Holy Trinity Church in Stratford-upon-Avon where he had been church warden. As in the Middle Ages, it was not unusual for poets to be buried in churches with which they had a connection. While Beaumont was buried in the Abbey, his partner John Fletcher was buried in the cathedral at Southwark because it was his parish. John Donne was buried in Old St. Paul's probably because he had been dean there. Yet some six years after Shakespeare's death in 1616, the poet William Basse imagined the space in the South Transept of the Abbey as appropriate for the dramatist:

Renowned *Spenser* lie a thought more nigh
To learned *Chauser*, and rare *Beaumont* lie
A little nearer *Spenser,* to make roome,
For *Shakespeare* in your three-fold, four-fold Tombe;

To lodge all foure in one bed make a shift,
Vntill Doomes-day, for hardly will a fift
Betwixt this day and that by Fate be slaine,
For whom your Curtaines need be drawne againe.
But if precedencie in death doth barre,
A fourth place in your sacred Sepulchre.
Vnder this carved Marble of thine owne,
Sleepe rare Tragedian *Shakespeare*, sleepe alone;
Thy unmolested peace, unshared Cave,
Possesse as Lord not Tennant of thy Grave,
That unto us, or others it may be,
Honour hereafter to be laid by thee.[58]

Not only did these verses circulate widely in the seventeenth century (they existed in over a dozen manuscript copies), but they were printed five times, the first time in the 1633 edition of Donne's poems.[59] While we cannot claim, as Dean Stanley did, that after Beaumont's burial there immediately came "the cry and counter-cry over the ashes of another who died within the next year," it is true that Basse's lines seem to be the first recorded evidence that the space in the South Transept was conceived of as a kind of generalized space for poets.[60] Basse, of course, has a highly conservative notion of what that space should be—a single bed (that sleeps four) rather than a space for many tombs. Yet, if he seems to express the view that the golden age of poetry has departed, he nonetheless gives voice to the idea of an eternal canon of like-minded poets who will live, or at least sleep together until doomsday— even if Shakespeare is missing.

In this claim Basse's imaginative reshaping of the South Transept might be seen as fundamentally different from other contemporary imaginings of the space that was Westminster Abbey. Francis Beaumont, in fact, had written a poem "On the Tombs in Westminster Abbey" that perhaps expresses a more widespread view of what the Abbey was at this time—a royal sepulcher:

MORTALITY, behold and fear!
What a change of flesh is here!
Think how many royal bones
Sleep within this heap of stones:
Here they lie had realms and lands,
Who now want strength to stir their hands:

Where from their pulpits seal'd with dust
They preach, "In greatness is no trust."
Here's an acre sown indeed
With the richest, royall'st seed
That the earth did e'er suck in
Since the first man died for sin:
Here the bones of birth have cried—
"Though gods they were, as men they died."
Here are sands, ignoble things,
Dropt from the ruin'd sides of kings;
Here's a world of pomp and state,
    Buried in dust, once dead by fate.[61]

Beaumont's poem might be seen as a fairly conventional example of *memento mori*. Kings once ruled their realms. Now death rules them. They were great. Now they are dust. They had power. Now they are powerless. Yet by invoking the idea of "an acre sown . . . / With the richest, royall'st seed," the poet also employs an agricultural metaphor that highlights the specialness of the place. Beaumont seems to suggest that out of death can come a life that transcends death. In fact, the entire poem is a kind of defeat of death. It celebrates the Abbey as a place which recalls the "world of pomp and state" that was "once dead by fate," but now has been enlivened by the recollection which itself gave birth to the poem.

At the same time, by celebrating the graveyard of kings, Beaumont points to the fundamental flaw inherent in the idea of a royal graveyard—that in such places one might remember not the enduring nature of power, but its evanescence. In writing a poem on the Abbey graveyard, Beaumont recalls Cicero's assertion about the need for poetry in an impermanent world: "How many historians of his exploits is Alexander the Great said to have had with him; and he, when standing on Cape Sigeum at the grave of Achilles, said, 'O happy youth, to find Homer as the panegyrist of your glory!' And he said the truth; for, if the Iliad had not existed, the same tomb which covered his body would have also buried his renown."[62] Present in Cicero's assertion, and implicit in Beaumont's poem, is a kind of anti-monumental aesthetics. For Cicero, the tomb ensures immortality only through the agency of poetry. Beaumont, on the other hand, uses poetry not only to draw attention to the inadequacy of sepulchral commemoration, but also to show the extent to which monuments themselves call attention to their own inadequacy. Thus both the ancient writer and the early modern poet render monuments and tombs as signs that immortalize only to the extent that poetry gives them meaning.

Basse's poem suggesting that Shakespeare should be buried in Poets' Corner more overtly celebrates the defeat of death because it is dealing with poets instead of kings. As we have seen, Basse's task is made easier because of the Horatian tradition that links a poet's works to an immortality that transcends temporal power. In fact, his poem may be the first call to close off that space as he claims that the bed should only be fit for four because "hardly will a fift / Betwixt this day and that fate be slain / For whom your curtains may be drawn again." His imaginative reshaping of that space is, as he acknowledges, improbable. For it is unlikely that the three poets' "sacred sepulcher" will be reopened for Shakespeare. And so he turns his gaze to Holy Trinity in Stratford, which he hallows by claiming that Shakespeare's body alone makes it an "Honor hereafter to be laid by thee."

Yet if Basse's exhumation and reburial of Shakespeare's corpse was a fantasy, Ben Jonson, at least, took it seriously enough to respond in his famous elegy from Shakespeare's First Folio (1623).

> My Shakespeare, rise: I will not lodge thee by
> Chaucer, or Spenser, or bid Beaumont lye
> A little further, to make thee roome:
> Thou art a Moniment without a tombe,
> And art alive still, while thy Booke doth live,
> And we have wits to read, and praise to give.
> That I not mix thee so, my brain excuses;
> I meane with great, but disproportion'd Muses.[63]

Unlike Basse, who lumps all four writers together and suggests that a fourfold tomb may be all that "should" exist in the South Transept (hence attempting to put an end to "Poets' Corner" before it has had its proper beginning), Jonson's elegy works on at least two levels. First, much as Spenser suggested the sublimation of Sidney, Jonson suggests that Shakespeare's "moniment" has nothing to do with his grave. In this he temporarily abandons Basse's invocation of a hallowed sepulchral space. The reasons for this seem to have to do with the relationship between the poets' graveyard and Shakespeare's reputation. For a grave suggests death, when Shakespeare is, according to Jonson, "alive still," and will be as long as his "Booke doth live." In other words, as long as the folio that the reader is holding in his or her hands exists, Shakespeare will survive. In fact, I would go so far as to suggest that here, at least, Jonson wishes to distance the idea of Shakespeare from any corporeal connection to the "sepulcher." His poetics here is not a poetics of the charnel house, but of the spirit. As Jonson defines him, the playwright is the "Soule of the Age!" He is emblematic of an early modern *Geistgeschichte*, an exemplification of the early modern spirit that enables his "recovery" via this folio. To monumentalize him in the Abbey would be to bury him as the kings in Beaumont's poem were buried—to bring his existence and influence to an untimely end.

This attempt to draw attention away from the body is understandable. The body is the repository of all that is contingent, earthly and mortal. Jonson's mission in this poem is to establish a Shakespeare that (as he says later in the elegy) is "not of an age, but for all time." To this end he suggests that to "mix . . . [Shakespeare] . . . with great, but disproportion'd Muses" is a mistake. Instead, Jonson says that we might "commit [Shakespeare] . . . surely with . . . his [dramatic] peeres" like Thomas Kyd, Christopher Marlowe, and John Lyly (a physical impossibility since they predeceased Shakespeare and were all buried in different locations).[64] Jonson's reference to "muses" here seems to use the word as a kind of synecdoche for the writers who are buried in the Abbey. And notions of mixing recall that Basse wanted to "mix" the bodies of the four poets in one bed. Jonson at once uses the materiality of corporeal mixing and the spirituality of the muses as a kind of jarring contrast suggesting by implication that to try to bring them together is absurd.

Jonson continues with this metaphoric notion of miscibility by saying that he would *not* mix Shakespeare with Chaucer, Spenser, and Beaumont because they are "disproportion'd." What he has in mind hinges on the meanings of "disproportioned" in this line. First, he certainly seems to suggest that these three writers do not bear comparison with Shakespeare because Shakespeare is somehow greater. But I also think that he is acknowledging that the writers already buried in the Abbey are not comparable to Shakespeare because they did not all work in the genre at which Shakespeare excelled. Jonson's solution to this problem of comparison is resolved when he conjures up the name of three contemporary playwrights in the next few lines (Kyd, Marlowe, and Lyly). They are, of course, weighed and found wanting. Jonson avers that "from thence to honour thee, I would not seeke / for names but call forth" the ancient dramatists, Aeschulys, Euripides, Sophocles, and the somewhat less well-known Roman tragedians, Pacuvius and Accius. Jonson obsessively keeps his eyes on judging Shakespeare not as a great writer, but as a great playwright.

Part of the reason for this focus on drama, as Richard Helgerson has pointed out, is that Jonson was interested in creating himself as a laureate dramatist—something that even in 1623 was not completely recognized.[65] His goal was to address the prejudice against drama by writers such as Philip Sidney (who famously observed that English drama caused "her mother Poesy's honesty to be called in question").[66] What Jonson wished to establish was a recognition that drama could lead to the "poetic dignity toward which he aspired."[67] To this end, he uses the publication of Shakespeare's works in order to raise the general reputation of drama, just as he used the publication of his own works seven years earlier to advance his own reputation. This obsessive attempt not only to avoid "mixing" of corporeal forms but also to avoid mixing formal genres at once highlights Shakespeare's reputation as a playwright, serves as a kind of advertisement for the First Folio, and highlights the extent to which drama is now identified as a project fit for laureates.

Jonson's response to Basse's poem about Shakespeare seems to have three major implications for the space that would become Poets' Corner. First, Jonson takes issue with the "four-fold" tomb because, if the poets did not share a genre, they should not share a bed. In some ways, just as Jonson does not wish to mix genres, so he does not wish to mix the reputations of poets who work in different genres. The idea of a "Poets' Corner" would seem to create a jumble of genres that heaps different kinds of writings and reputations together. Second, the very materiality of the poets' corpses would seem to militate against the idea of a place of commemoration. It too readily recalls their deaths and interferes with the popular humanistic trope that it is not monuments of stone that will bring immortality but the immortal nature of the poet's literary work. Finally, Jonson seems to disable a specifically English canon of writers. For, if we compare Shakespeare with his English dramatic contemporaries, Shakespeare, according to Jonson, still continues to "outshine" them. In fact, he asserts that these names are not nearly august enough to rank with Shakespeare, and he invokes the great ancient playwrights as those who might be compared with "the swan of Avon." This move from Father Chaucer to contemporary playwrights, then to the great playwrights of the ancient world denatures the idea of a national Valhalla that is material and focuses on a more spiritual notion of the canon. Thus even while Jonson insists "Triumph, my Britaine, thou hast one to showe. / To whom all scenes of Europe homage owe," it is (in this poem at any rate) a canon of one. Hence, while Shakespeare is of the England of "Eliza and our James," he is also outside of a temporal setting and creates a metaphoric space that ultimately resolved itself only when, at the end of the elegy, he becomes a constellation in the heavens. He has at this point surpassed the merely English or even worldly to "shine" his literary light from the "Hemisphere."

We are, here, a long way from the idea of a graveyard of poets. Indeed, one might say that one of Jonson's aims in this poem is to demolish the whole idea of a poetic graveyard because it infects sublime and immortal poetry with the disease of mortality. Yet, if the idea of laureateship seems to be impeded by thoughts of the grave here, the epitaph written for the poet Michael Drayton (for many years attributed to Jonson), seems to take issue with this line of thinking.

> Michael Drayton Esquier a memorable Poet of this age exchanged
>   his Laurel
> for a Crowne of Glory
> Doe pious Marble! Let thy Readers knowe
> What they, and what their Children owe
> To DRAYTON's name, whose sacred dust
> We recommend unto thy Trust.
> Protecte his Mem'ry and preserve his storie,
> Remaine a lasting monument of his Glorye.
> And When thy Ruines shall disclame
> To be the Treas'rer of his Name,
> His Name, that cannot fade, shall bee
> An everlasting Monument to thee.[68]

The epitaph, perhaps written by Francis Quarles, inflects the monument with the ability to "protecte his [Drayton's] Mem'ry and preserve his storie." In a further reversal, it claims that when the monument falls to "ruines," then the name itself will do the work of monumentalizing the "monument." A cynical reading of this epitaph might suggest that the author was uncertain that Drayton's "storie"—both his history as a poet and the work for which he was best known, the topographical poem *Poly-olbion*—would stand the test of time. If, for a moment, we indulge in this cynical reading, then Drayton's epitaph would seem prophetic. For readers separated by only a hundred years were surprised to find Drayton in the Abbey. Indeed, as early as 1762, Oliver Goldsmith portrayed his Chinese philosopher Lien Chi Altangi visiting the Abbey and remarking, "Drayton! I never heard of him before."[69] And the eighteenth-century satirist Tom Brown, obviously playing on the suggestion that Drayton's name would outlive the monument, reported that "Drayton with half a nose [his bust had been disfigured], was next, whose works are forgotten before his monument is worn out."[70]

But there is good evidence that at his death in 1631, Drayton was actually seen as a worthy addition to the same bed in which Chaucer, Spenser, and Beaumont lay.[71] He was friends with Jonson and Shakespeare (in fact one report has it that Shakespeare died shortly after drinking with them).[72] A collected edition of Drayton's poems came out in 1606 (which was rare for the time). A deluxe edition (with frontispiece) was produced in 1619 and his *Poly-olbion* was much admired. In addition, Drayton was only the second Renaissance writer to receive a monument in the Abbey (joining Spenser). In fact, one could argue that when Lady Anne Clifford, countess of Dorset, decided to erect a monument to Drayton, she made herself the godmother of the modern notion of Poets' Corner. For if Basse was the first to give expression to the idea of the South Transept as a kind of sacred poetical space, the countess of Dorset's monument to Spenser in 1620 and her monument to Drayton in 1631 gave rise to a monumental notion of Poets' Corner.[73]

The notion that monumentalism began to make itself felt in the construction of the space of the South Transept would seem to be confirmed by a disagreement about whether Drayton's body was indeed under the monument raised to him. In his discussion of the burial place of Chaucer, Thomas Fuller asserted in 1655 that "Hie lies buried in the South-Isle of *St Peters, Westminster*, and since hath got the company of *Spencer* and *Drayton* (a pair-royal of Poets) enough (almost) to make passengers feet to move metrically, who go over the place where so much *Poetical dust* is interred."[74] What we see here is the establishment of a space that is made special by the presence of "poetical dust"—as if the mere presence of the bodies of poets would be enough (almost) to make metrical the otherwise quotidian passings of "passengers" through the Abbey—to transform tourists into poets. Some four years later, however, Peter Heylyn, prebendary of Westminster, quoted Fuller's claim and responded:

> Not *Drayton's* company I am sure, whose body was not buryed in
> the South-Isle of that Church, but under the North wall thereof in
> the main body of it, not far from the little dore openeth into one
> of the Prebend's houses. This I can say on certain knowledge, being
> casually invited to his Funeral, when I thought not of it; though

since his *Statue* hath been set up in the other place which our
Author speaks of.[75]

Heylyn's claim that Drayton was buried under the north wall would seem to
be supported by the antiquarian John Aubrey, who in the late seventeenth
century claimed "Sepult. In north + of Westminster Abbey."[76] In addition,
Heylyn's position as prebendary and his assertion that he was at the funeral
would seem unimpeachable evidence that Drayton was buried in the Nave.
Fuller, however, remained unconvinced. In a heated reply to Heylyn he quotes
the epitaph on the monument in the South Transept and then asks, "Have
Stones learnt to *Lye*, and abuse posterity? Must there needs be a *Fiction* in the
Epitaph of a *Poet*? If this be a meer *Cenotaph*, that Marble hath nothing to
doe with *Draitons Dust*: but let us proceed."[77] Given the number of cenotaphs
in Poets' Corner (monuments to writers whose remains are elsewhere), such
concern about "stones lying" seems a bit misplaced. But at the time it is clear
that such stones were *meant* to mark the place where a body was buried.[78] Not
to mark the place was seen as a form of dishonesty that Fuller, interestingly
enough, connects with the fiction that poets seem to concoct. One almost
might read his plea as an indictment of the very task that poets seem to undertake (i.e., abusing posterity with "fictions" or "lies"). In other words, Fuller
seems to connect the epitaph with a certain kind of truthfulness that should
exist in the final words that exist over a body—even if that body is the corpse
of someone who perhaps was not connected with truthfulness in a historical
sense.

   Though one would not want to identify this as a crisis in the construction
of Poets' Corner, I would argue that it gave rise to an anxiety that shaped the
fiction of the space. Monuments are meant to "remind" the passersby of a
cause, an event, or, in this case, the person buried underneath the stone.[79]
As I have argued elsewhere, the stones that mark the burial place have a strange
epistemological function. They do not denote, as so often is true of a sign,
absence, but point to what Robert Pogue Harrison calls the "thereness" of a
space. The stone, then, must needs be more than a "meer cenotaph" in order to
carry the kind of significance that opens up a particular space and makes it
special. We can see the extent to which the stone needs to mark the spot of
the corpse, I think, in Fuller's shoulder-shrugging conditional wording—"If
this be a meer *Cenotaph*." Without the body, the marble is mere stone, and as
Fuller no doubt means to suggest in his final four punning words ("but let us

proceed"), we can pass this particular monument by, for it is an empty memorial that signifies only absence.

The reason for Fuller's anxious denial of Heylyn's seemingly indisputable evidence can be found, I think, in the epigraph from Derrida that began this chapter. Without a marker for the body, we cannot tell where the body is. Not to know where the body is creates problems for the project that begins, in some measure, with the erection of the markers to Spenser and Drayton. Fuller understands all too well that to call into question the epitaph on Drayton's marker is to make a liar of the project of monumentalization before it has even begun. Without a marker that is actually connected with the interment, there can only be epistemological uncertainty.[80] As Derrida suggests, in order to carry out the work of mourning, there should be no question of epistemological doubt. The work of mourning is ultimately engaged in a search for certainty in that it attempts to "ontologize remains, to make them present."[81] This presence, in the psychoanalytical understanding of mourning, is meant to replace the absence that death has brought about. Yet the work of mourning or melancholia, if we can call it that, that these monuments undertake is different from the more personal, intimate mourning that is generally characterized by psychoanalysis. This work engages the visitor not in severing ties with the deceased poet (enabling the mourner to successfully navigate loss), but in recollecting that which had never truly existed for most of the English public—a personal connection with the poet.

*   *   *

It is, of course, well to remember (as Philip Connell has asserted vis-à-vis the eighteenth century) that "if . . . Poets' Corner could be represented as a physical and symbolic locus for the celebration of national literary genius, the creation and consolidation of this public commemorative space remained notoriously dependent, throughout the century, upon the vagaries of private munificence rather than systematic state subsidy."[82] In some instances, as in the case of Alexander Pope, this private intervention is crucial to the understanding of the meaning of individual memorials and the factional politics of Poets' Corner. At the same time, even at this early date, the space seems to have developed a public logic of its own. It is difficult to put one's finger on the precise nature of this logic, but if Chaucer was originally buried in the South Transept because of a kind of fourteenth-century national trauma, his reburial in 1556, we now understand, seems to have been motivated by the larger attempt to reconsecrate the space of the Abbey as Catholic.[83] So too, the erection of Spenser's monument in 1620 followed by Basse's poem in 1622 and Jonson's rejoinder in 1623 suggest that in the early part of the seventeenth century thinking about the space had coalesced into a public consciousness of the space as "poetic." Despite the fact that most of the monuments are erected by private individuals, the work that these monuments make manifest is a kind of national mourning or commemoration that links poetry with the idea of England.[84] In other words, with the construction of Spenser's and (later) Drayton's monuments we begin to see the outline of a canon of writers written in stone. Even Fuller's initial claim about the "poetical dust" of the bodies enabling "passengers feet to move metrically" suggests not so much a mourning as a participation in the larger project of poetry that is enabled by the dead bodies that exist beneath the "passengers' feet."

Jonson's Displacement

Yet as the outlines of what is now known as Poets' Corner take shape in the early seventeenth century, it is possible that there was one final attempt to frustrate the formation of a specialized place of poetry with its speaking stones. As one who had so much to do with the imagining of poetical space, it may, perhaps, not be so surprising that Ben Jonson was buried in Westminster Abbey. Robert Herrick, in fact, composed an epitaph to Jonson that "purport[s] to be the inscription upon Jonson's tomb" and speaks to his presence among the other poetical bodies:[85]

> Here lies Jonson with the rest
> Of the Poets; but the best.
> Reader, would'st thou more have known?
> Ask his story, not this stone;
> That will speak what this can't tell,
> Of his glory. So farewell![86]

Part of the classical tradition of epigrammatic epitaph, Herrick's epitaph suggests the inadequacy of the genre of which it is a part, but also suggests that the monument is ultimately mute. As Joshua Scodel argues, the so-called "reader" or visitor to the imagined monument must seek Jonson's "story" in "Jonson's 'own account of the events of his life' in his self-portraying poems."[87]

The "epitaph" then reiterates what Jonson had said of Shakespeare—that his poetry was ultimately his lasting monument, not the stone that is over his grave. Given that the actual epitaph only reads "O Rare Ben Johnson" [*sic*], we might read Herrick's poem as a satire on the muteness of stones. In fact, if Aubrey is to be believed, there was originally to be no inscription at all, until a certain Jack Young (later knighted) "was walking there when the grave was covering [and] gave the fellow eighteen pence to cutt it."[88]

But this casual attitude toward inscription is not the strangest thing about Jonson's tomb. What is most peculiar is that Jonson was not really buried with the "rest of the poets." Instead he was placed under an eighteen-inch-square stone in the North Aisle of the Nave in front of what is now the Parson's Window.[89] Like Chaucer, he spent his final days as a resident of the Abbey precincts, so it is likely that this is why he was buried in the Abbey.[90] Abbey tradition also has it that he picked his own burial spot close to what may be his friend's (Drayton's) grave in the north crossing of the Abbey. The only eye-witness account of the funeral suggests that "he was accompanied to his grave with all or the greatest part of the nobility and gentrie then in the towne," so he may have been granted the honor of choosing his own burial place.[91] If so, it is telling that he did not choose the South Transept for his grave. As we saw earlier, at least in 1623, he seems opposed to the idea of a space in the Abbey that was particularly designed for writers perhaps because he felt that different kinds of writerly reputations should not be lumped together. But he seems also to have paid no attention to conceiving a monument (or even a gravestone) for himself. He received a monument in Poets' Corner.[92] But unlike Spenser and Beaumont, this monument was erected quite late—possibly because its installation was delayed by the Civil War.[93] What this suggests is that Jonson, who certainly paid attention to his status as laureate poet and was deeply interested in the idea of a poetic reputation, felt (even as late as the 1630s) that a recognizable tomb or monument was not something that a laureate poet should need, or something to which he should aspire. Like Spenser, Jonson seems ready to embrace the rejection of such monuments in favor of lasting poetry. But, unlike Spenser, Jonson's afterlife did not lead to a monumental aesthetics, perhaps because he was buried outside the poetic space of the South Transept (the monument in Poets' Corner was not erected until 1728). And, in fact, if we look back at his epitaph for Drayton, we can see a suggestion that these monuments must necessarily fail as they themselves must rely on the "storie" or reputation of the poet.

Lest we think, however, that Jonson's influence on the South Transept died with his death, we need only turn to the man who followed him in the laureateship—William Davenant. According to Jodocus Crull, at Davenant's death in 1668, "this Gentleman, out of a peculiar Affectation, order'd Ben's Epitaph (but how justly, I leave to the publick Voice) to be put upon his Grave-stone. O RARE SIR WILLIAM DAVENANT" (fig. 3).[94] This appropriation of Jonson's epitaph not only seems (as Crull's comment would seem to suggest) a bit cheeky, but also speaks to how much Davenant saw himself in a kind of di-rect line from Jonson—not only as laureate or dramatist, but also as another celebrated poetic corpse in the Abbey. In addition, his appropriation of Shake-speare's title for Jonson ("Rare Ben") might indicate his attempt to solidify his spiritual connection (at least) with the Bard himself, a connection he ap-peared to relish during his lifetime.[95] His burial in the South Transept might seem a conscious expansion of the poetical graveyard that would become Poets' Corner, but only retrospectively. The space was originally occupied by Thomas May who "stood Candidate for the Laurell after Ben Johnson; but Sir William Davenant carried it: manet alta mente repostum [it remained deeply embedded in his mind]."[96] May was a parliamentarian and was buried in the South Transept in 1650 but was disinterred in 1661 at the Restoration, and his place lay empty until Davenant, a royalist, occupied his grave. This exhumation and burial certainly speaks to the extent that political consider-ations governed burial in the Abbey. After all, Oliver Cromwell had been bur-ied in the Abbey in 1658 and was disinterred in 1661.[97] It will not be surprising to learn that political considerations like these (though perhaps less heated) continue to haunt the burial place of poets. But for the moment it is enough to observe how the space itself became a habitary place for poets and writers to the extent that improper poetic burials were effectively erased by newer ones and lines of connection with earlier poetic traditions were highlighted in or-der to determine who should and who should not be buried in the South Tran-sept and, by extension, who should and who should not be admitted in the English canon of poets.

The burial that first celebrated the space as a place of poets was most likely Abraham Cowley's in 1667. Though little read now, he was at the time a highly considered poet whose patron was the duke of Buckingham (in fact, he erected the monument). He was also a close friend of the dean of the Abbey at the time, Thomas Sprat. His epitaph proclaims him "the English Pindar, Horace, Virgil: the delight, glory and desire of his age." Sprat tells us that "his Body

Figure 3. Davenant's broken stone (replaced in 1866) which, if an accurate reproduction of the original, differs from early reports in that it emphasizes that he was (unlike Jonson) knighted. Copyright Dean and Chapter of Westminster.

was attended to Westminster Abby by a great number of Persons of the most eminent quality, and follow'd with the praises of all good and Learned Men. It lies near the Ashes of Chaucer and Spencer, the two most Famous English Poets of former times."[98] If we are to believe Dean Stanley, Cowley received "the greatest obsequies that Poets' Corner ever witnessed."[99] And the elegies at his death recall and enact many of the conventions that will be observed in future poets' burials in the corner.

For instance, Cowley's epitaph and translated amplification (a rhetorical repetition and variation of the epitaph perhaps written by his friend Dr. Scarborough) state that the place Cowely lies in is sacred (*Sit sacer iste locus*) or, in terms that recall the epitaph of Robert Hauley, "a sanctuary."[100] They add that the nine muses are perpetually to keep watch over "the grave thy corps to keep." In terms that represent the body more as relic than corpse, the epitaph and amplification warn that no one is to disturb the stone with unhallowed touch nor "with his breath profane this sacred tomb."[101] The English politician and diplomat Thomas Higgons elegized Cowley by recalling the opposition between the fame of rulers and of poets, writing that "His memory Fame from Death shall save; / His Bayes shall flourish, and be ever green, / When those of Conquerors are not to be seen."[102] Roger Boyle, earl of Orrery, both reiterates the connection to Horace's ode and, in his invocation of the pyramids, seems to recall Spenser's *Ruines of Time* when he writes "His works shall live, when Pyramids of Pride / Shrink to such ashes as they long did hide."[103] This sanctity of the place, the presence of the muses, the opposition between the secular glory of rulers and the more rarified fame of poets, and the invocation of Horace's Ode 3.3 all will be used to characterize future burials in the Corner and can be seen as formulaic even at this early date.

What is a bit unusual in Boyle's otherwise conventional elegy is an almost religious suggestion that the bodies in the Abbey actually have some kind of supernatural efficacy in the world. Immediately following his invocation of Horace's ode (and apparent recollection of Spenser's *Ruines of Time*), Boyle suddenly turns topical and suggests the presence of so many sanctified bodies may have enabled Westminster Abbey to avoid (as old St. Paul's did not), the Great Fire of 1666:

> That sacrilegious fire (which did last year
> Level those Piles which Piety did rear)
> Dreaded neer that majestick Church to flye
> Where English Kings and English Poets lye:
> It at an awful distance did expire,
> Such pow'r had sacred Ashes over fire;
> Such as it durst not neer that Structure come
> Which Fate had order'd to be Cowley's Tomb;
> And 'twill be still preserv'd, by being so,
> From what the rage of future Flames can do.
> Material Fire dares not that place infest
> Where he who had immortal flame does rest.
> There let his Urn remain, for it was fit

Amongst our Kings to lay the King of wit:
By which the Structure more renown'd will prove
For that part bury'd than for all above.[104]

Perhaps because Boyle was titled and a poet, he locates a power to resist destruction in the remains of *both* rulers' and makers' bodies. Indeed he makes
Cowley a king among kings and insists that the separation of "material fire"
from "immortal flame" will prevent the "rage of future flames." Oddly enough,
then, the inferiority of the material to the immaterial world is employed here
in order to guarantee the preservation of the material monument. And the
bodies themselves, far from being empty shells, are considered sacred, a kind
of subterranean monument that guarantees that which lies above. It is the ability of this place in the South Transept to make the invisible (that which is
below and peculiarly enough above) visible and to give the place its name.

CHAPTER 3

Love, Literary Publicity, and the Naming of Poets' Corner

With equal foot, Rich friend, impartial Fate
Knocks at the Cottage, and the Palace Gate:
Life's span forbids Thee to extend thy Cares,
And stretch thy hopes beyond thy Years:
Night soon will seize, and You may quickly go
To story'd Ghosts, and *Pluto's* house below.
                            —Addison, quoting Creech's translation of Horace

When was the name Poets' Corner first applied to the South
Transept of Westminster Abbey?
                            —*Notes and Queries* (1851)

Until the early eighteenth century the South Transept existed as a kind of private space in which one might acknowledge the resting place of poets. Such journeys to this particular part of Westminster Abbey seem to have been governed by the solitary relationship that one might have with a writer. It is this seeming solitude that, as we have seen in the previous chapter, gave the space its melancholic air. Around 1723 this attitude changed. Part of this change had to do with an alteration of the space that would become Poets' Corner, but the space also reflected a fundamental change in the relationship of poetry to what might be called the public sphere. In many ways it was at this moment that the South Transept became Poets' Corner—no longer a private graveyard of poets for poets, but a space that began to have national implications.

In becoming a public or even national space, Poets' Corner participated in the transformation of the larger space of the Abbey into what can only be called a tourist destination. As Matthew Craske has argued, the decades following 1720 saw the Abbey become something of a place of public resort or even a site of promenade.[1] The sculptures created for this space competed "for attention in the public sphere."[2] And, in fact, the monuments in the Abbey were the first to inspire a "widely read critical literature."[3] The Abbey became at once a "shop window" for the sculptors John Michael Rysbrack, Peter Scheemakers, and Louis-François Roubiliac and a site of competition—a competition that ultimately culminated in the spectacular production of monuments outside of the Corner such as that to Lady Elizabeth Nightingale. This tomb, with its full-length skeleton emerging from the vaults of the Abbey and the vain attempt by the husband (Joseph Gascoigne Nightingale) to ward off death's blow, was created to terrify but also to elicit sorrow. As one commentator put it,

> At this sad tomb shall many a pair attend,
> While varying passions their fond bosoms rend;
> See pleased the strokes of art with nature vie,
> While rising sorrows swell the tearful eye.[4]

Craske sees in these increasingly theatrical productions a move towards the "celebration of feeling."[5] But this theatricality had its critics. Horace Walpole, for instance, saw the Nightingale monument as departing from the more classically oriented Rysbrack, who had "taught the age to depend on statuary for its best ornaments. . . . We seem since to have advanced into scenery. Mr. Nightingale's tomb [sic], though finely thought and well executed, is more theatrical than sepulchral" (fig. 4).[6]

Yet these theatrical sculptural productions that drew attention to their own production of affect lay outside what Addison in 1711 called "the poetical quarter." Familial tombs, with their elaborate sculptures of grieving widows and daughters, are for the most part absent from the space. And the larger tombs with their overt appeals to patriotism tend to be located in the more central space of the Nave. The one seeming exception, the monument to the second duke of Argyll and Greenwich (also a product of Roubiliac, erected 1749; fig. 5), is important insofar as it reminds us that the limits of Poets' Corner were still very much in flux. If one visits Poets' Corner today, it appears that the monument is squarely in the middle of the Corner, and the

Figure 4. The so-called Nightingale tomb (1760). Copyright Dean and Chapter
of Westminster.

monument could certainly be characterized as theatrical. The figure of History stands over the statue of the duke leaving the word Greenwich unfinished to signal that his line dies with him. Helmet-clad Minerva "looks up" to the wisdom of the duke, and Eloquence (who in the original drawings turned inward) turns with hand outstretched to the visitor as if to highlight the need to stop in front of this monument.[7] The effect, as one guide put it, is to "pathetically display . . . the public loss of his death."[8]

But when this monument was erected in the South Transept, it was most likely not seen to be in Poets' Corner proper but west of it (and on the other side of the door to St. Faith's Chapel where there were no poetic monuments). In fact, no poetic monument would cross over the imaginary line that ran from the doorway of St. Faith's to the South Aisle until 1809.[9] The space of the Corner in the middle of the eighteenth century was more circumscribed than the space of the South Transept. And, more importantly, the logic of the Corner was intensely nostalgic—resisting the increasingly homogenous national space of the rest of the Abbey.

The reasons for this attempt to circumscribe the limits of Poets' Corner can be found in one of the more famous meditations on Westminster Abbey, Joseph Addison's *Spectator* 26. In it he narrates a pursuit of melancholy that he describes as "not disagreeable." This "thoughtfulness" is born of his discovery of people's names on "the tombstones and inscriptions that I met with in those several regions of the dead" in the larger space of the Abbey.[10] In fact, the whole of the number is really a meditation on naming. Initially Addison reads "these registers of existence . . . as a kind of satire upon the departed persons." The reason for this, he says, is that "they put me in mind of several persons mentioned in the battles of heroic poems, who have sounding names given them, for no other reason but that they may be killed, and are celebrated for nothing but being knocked on the head."[11] The desire of these people is to be remembered after they have died—to continue in a kind of afterlife in the memories of those who view their memorials. But, as they have left "no other memorial," they are remembered only for dying.

As he continued walking in the Abbey, Addison mediates on how beneath the Abbey floor "multitudes of people lay confused together." Even if they have epitaphs, their bodies lay "undistinguished in the same promiscuous heap of matter."[12] If they have distinguished themselves in the past, they can no longer be physically distinguished, for they have moldered together in the earth with other bodies. And the epigraph from Horace would seem to

Figure 5. The Duke of Argyll's monument (1749). Copyright Dean and Chapter of Westminster.

confirm the status of *Spectator* 26 as a kind of familiar reiteration of the dictum that death is the great leveler. His continuing use of words such as "confused . . . blended . . . mass . . . undistinguished . . . heap" when talking about the corpses of the dead suggest that he is not only looking forward to the end of time— "that great day when we shall all of us be contemporaries, and make our appearance together," but is meditating on the notion of human identity. If Ben Jonson objected to the miscible nature of a poetic graveyard, Addison worries that the inability to distinguish one body from another might lead to a "lack of distinction."

What might calm anxieties about the threatening homogeneity of corpses is the distinction of space (like Poets' Corner) within the Abbey. But even here the markers can't be trusted. As he says, "In the poetical quarter, I found there were poets who had no monuments, and monuments who had no poets."[13] This quotation, perhaps the first to name the South Transept as the burial place of poets, indicates a discomfort with the absence of the body that can be traced to a kind of early modern version of the medieval obsession of the relic. As Peter Brown has argued, relics, and indeed entire bodies, had a special significance indicating *hic locus est*. To fail to have the body is to take away the thing that defines the space as a particularly important geographical location. Thomas Fuller's reaction to the suggestion that Drayton's tomb is nothing but an empty monument (discussed in Chapter 2) indicates how important the body was to the space. Indeed, for Addison this particular space is "the poets' quarter," in other words, the place where the poets themselves in some sense "reside." Should their bodies be absent, the name becomes an empty signifier—more remarkable in what it does not signify.

So too, Addison suggests that to have a space that has no marker (though it contains a body) might be even more of a problem for a poet who relies on his "story" in order to retain his place in people's memory. If naming is a product of human identity, then to lose one's name is to lose one's distinction from the heap of bodies that have been buried in the earth. In 1711 the poets who "had no monuments" would have included John and Francis Beaumont, Abraham Cowley's friend John Denham, and lesser lights like Sir Robert Stapleton. But the poet who most clearly lacked a monument and whom Addison undoubtedly has in mind is John Dryden. This absence would have been especially apparent because of Dryden's fame, but also because the national nature of Dryden's funeral, and his belated monument reflected the uneasy relationship between satire and commemoration that had a special significance for the poetical space.[14]

Dryden's Folly

Some years earlier Dryden had been buried with what seems to have been great fanfare. As the newspaper *The Postman* reports it:

> Dryden was buried on May 13, 1700. One of the accounts has it that He was carried in great state to *Westminster Abbey*, from the Colledge of Physicians, whither it was removed some days ago, and was attended by above one hundred Coaches of the Chief of our Nobility and Gentry, who shewed on this occasion what respect they had for this excellent Poet; but before he was removed from the Colledge, Dr. *Garth* made an Eloquent Oration in Latin, in praise of the Deceased, and the Ode of Horace beginning, *Monumentum exegi AEre perennius*, set to mournful muskick, was saung there, with a consort of Trumpets, Hautboys, and other Instruments. There was a world of people, and his Highness the Duke of *Gloucester* was pleased to send one of his Coaches to attend the Funeral, which was performed at the charge of several persons of quality, lovers of Poetry.[15]

Such a funeral had not been seen since Cowley's burial some thirty years before. Not surprisingly, there seems to have been a plan to erect a monument to Dryden. As the *Post Boy* put it optimistically, "I am assured that a Person of great Quality who has a mighty Esteem for the Works of that Ingenious Gentleman, will erect at his own proper Charge, a Noble Monument upon him, and so perpetuate the Name of that great Man."[16] Pepys claimed that the persons who were to erect the tomb were Lord Dorset and Lord Montague.[17] Yet, as Tom Brown observed some years later, "At Chaucer's feet without any name, lies John Dryden his admirer and truly the English Maro."[18]

The singing of Horace's ode which heralds the ability of poetry to provide a "monument more enduring than brass" would therefore *seem* particularly appropriate here precisely because no material monument was erected. Yet if, as we saw, poets like Spenser, Jonson, and Pope all argued for the primacy of poetry as a monument, it seems that the stone monument nonetheless continues to be important even to those poets who seem to abjure such monuments. In an epitaph proposed for Nicholas Rowe's monument, Alexander Pope went so far as to suggest that the real worth of Nicholas Rowe's tomb was that it pointed the way to Dryden's unmarked grave:

> Thy reliques Rowe, to this fair urn we trust,
> And sacred, place by Dryden's awful dust.
> Beneath a rude and nameless stone he lies,
> To which thy tomb shall guide inquiring eyes.[19]

This kind of poetical tourism in which the "relics" of Rowe become important insofar as they lead the way to other bodies indicates two things. First, though it may seem that Rowe's own status is posed as secondary, it is true that Pope talks of Rowe's relics as "sacred." What Rowe's body does, then, is accomplish a kind of double task. For it keeps in memory the place of Rowe's purported burial, and it also serves as a kind of signpost in the absence of a stone upon which Dryden's name might appear. Hence Rowe's body and the tomb that contains it make good what is missing in Dryden's case—a visible, posthumous identity that can be perceived by "inquiring eyes." In some ways, Pope makes virtue of necessity by claiming that the search for Dryden's grave will continue precisely because there must be a search. The second thing that Rowe's tomb does is maintain the *nachleben* or afterlife of Dryden by enabling those eyes to find the tomb. It keeps alive, then, the special status of Dryden's dead body, even as Dryden's grave continues to lack a name. Dryden's afterlife, his "place" in Poets' Corner is maintained by the fact that other corpses remain near him.

This afterlife was aided by the fact that Dryden's final resting placed was, as Samuel Pepys states in his diary, planned for Chaucer's grave. And despite some still incompletely explained confusion about the burial, Dryden was apparently buried in what was considered Chaucer's original resting place in the eighteenth century—not the Purbeck marble tomb to which Chaucer was purportedly translated in 1556, but an area some distance from the tomb in front of St. Benedict's Chapel. Dryden's burial in the grave of the Father of Ancient Poetry signaled not only that Dryden had what he termed a "soul congenial" to the "ancient poet" (and had in fact produced a translation of his works and thus brought him back to life), but that he laid claim to the title of

Father of Modern Poetry and thus should rest with that older father.[20] As Henry Hall put it in verses commissioned to memorialize the poet:

> Nor is thy latest Work, unworthy thee
> New Cloath'd by You, how *Chaucer* we esteem;
> When You've new Polish'd it, how bright the Jem!
> And lo, the Sacred Shade for thee make's room,
> Tho' Souls so alike, should take but up one tomb.[21]

As I suggest elsewhere, Hall celebrates Dryden's translation of Chaucer's works and reiterates Dryden's own assertion that Dryden and Chaucer had "souls congenial."[22] But knowingly or not, Hall also seems to pick up on the rhetoric of Basse's much earlier suggestion that the space in the South Transept is a bit like a bed, in which "Renowned Spenser . . . [might] . . . lie a thought more nigh / To learned Chaucer . . . to make room / For Shakespeare." In other words, the space itself has acquired a certain logic that has made it into the place of Poets' Corner.

I would, in fact, argue that the treatment of Dryden's funeral indicates a kind of institutionalization of the space in the South Transept. For though the funeral service seems to have been fairly decorous, this was not the way it was reported in a number of sources. The most famous of these is Samuel Johnson's *Lives of the Poets* in which he reports that the funeral was to have been a private and relatively modest affair until Lord Jeffries "with some of his rakish companions, coming by, in wine, asked whose funeral? On being told, 'What,' cries he, 'Shall Dryden, the greatest honor and ornament of the nation, be buried after this manner? No gentlemen, let all that loved Mr. Dryden, and honour his memory, alight and join with me in gaining my Lady's consent to let me have the honour of the interment, which shall be after another manner than this; and I will bestow 1000 on a monument in the Abbey for him.'"[23] Though Jeffries does not secure consent, nonetheless he manages to have the body sent off to the undertakers, but then purports to forget all about the corpse, the funeral, and the planned monument. The result is that the funeral turns into a mock service with a rotting corpse. An orator falls into a beer barrel and the rabble become so unruly that the few gentlemen who could enter the Abbey had to cut their way in with swords.

One must read the account with an eye upon the fact that Dryden, as a satirist, opened himself up to satire, and that some ultimately attempted to characterize him as one who prostituted his muse in an attempt to appeal to a larger audience. But the satirical focus on the Abbey itself, the double burial, and the lack of a monument all signify that burial in the South Transept had become institutionalized. And this institutionalized solemnity delighted those like the satirist Tom Brown who in his satire on Dryden's funeral, begins

> Of Kings Renown'd and Mighty Bards I write
> Some slain by Whores, and others kill'd in Fight;
> Some starving liv'd, whilst others were prefer'd;
> But all, when dead, are in one place inter'd.
> A Fabrick stands by Antient Heroes built,
> Design'd for Holy Use t'atone their guilt;
> Here sacred Urns of Majesty they keep,
> Here Kings and Poets most profoundly sleep;
> Here Choristers in Hymns their Voices raise,
> And charm the dreadful Goblins from the Place.
> Tho throng'd with Tombs, no Specter here is found,
> They sing the very Devil off the Ground.[24]

The focus here, as is evident in the phrase "some slain by whores," is on the unworthiness of a few of those who are buried in the Abbey. But Brown seems more restrained when writing about the "Fabric," meaning the "holy" space of the Abbey that was built by "Antient Heroes," to atone for "their guilt." As we might expect from Brown this "Holy use" itself comes in for some ridicule, particularly in the suggestion that the Westminster choristers could "sing the very Devil off the Ground." But Brown's approach here is to acknowledge the uncanniness of the place of the dead even if he constructs a kind of mock supernatural in order to draw off some of that Gothic quality. In other words, he is all too aware that the place itself has a kind of "awfulness" that he must disable in order to proceed with his mockery of Dryden's funeral.

Brown specifically writes about the Corner late in the satire by invoking those poets who had earlier been buried there. These poets—Cowley, Chaucer, and Spenser—are themselves not mocked, but are witnesses to the "crowd of fools [that] attend him [Dryden] to the grave." Brown tells us that "Cowley's Marble wept to see the Throng, / Old Chaucer laugh'd at their unpolish'd Song, / And Spencer thought he once again had seen / The Imps attending on his Fairy Queen."[25] We would expect the invocation of Chaucer, as Dryden was purportedly placed in his grave. But the recollection of Spenser and Cowley, I think, indicates the extent to which Brown wanted to emphasize that this place was to be a burial place of "great" poets in order to contrast the burial of Dryden with the burial of those English poets who had been deemed great. The point of the satire, then, is to contrast Dryden "the poet squab," his audience, "a crowd so nauseous, so profoundly lewd, / With all the Vices of the Times endu'd" with the place in which he is buried and the company that he will henceforth keep. In some ways, though in a different vein, Brown rehearses an argument about the appropriateness of the burial of various poetic bodies together that had started with Basse and Jonson. Whether it was the appropriateness of Beaumont, Spenser, and Chaucer residing with Shakespeare or Dryden being buried with Spenser, Chaucer, and Cowley, the conflation of these bodies in this place bespeaks an imaginative construction of the South Transept as a space that had special significance for the construction of a kind of poetic reputation, the memory of a poetic tradition, the construction of poetic canon, and the meditation on and anxiety about the significance of this tradition.

From Quarter to Corner

If the eighteenth century saw the construction of the South Transept as a locus that served a series of competing agendas, the naming of the South Transept as "Poets' Quarter," or "Poets' Corner" as it has come to be known, completed the transformation of this particular piece of ecclesiastical space into a visible expression of the invisible canon. At the same time, perhaps inevitably, the Corner became an index of anxieties about the function and use of poetry. The earliest use of the name "Poets' Corner" seems to have been in a poem entitled "Upon the POETS CORNER in WESTMINSTER ABBEY." The poem appears in the Reverend Thomas Fitzgerald's 1733 *Poems on Several Occasions*:

> Hail, sacred Reliques of the tuneful Train!
> Here ever honour'd, ever lov'd remain.
> No other Dust of the once Great or Wise,
> As each beneath the hallow'd Pavement lies,
> To this old Dome a juster Rev'rence brings;
> No, though she keeps the Ashes of our Kings.
> Yet you the Herald's idle Art disdain,
> ('Tis yours to give, and not to borrow Fame)

> No Vaunts of far-fetch'd Ancestry are here,
> Nor dusty Trophies waving in the Air;
> No blazon'd Metals spread their tawdry Charms,
> And only *Shadwell* shews a Coat of Arms:
> Though those who foremost of our Nobles stand,
> Peers of the Realm, and Princes of the Land,
> Croud to appear to your high Merits just,
> And rear the Tomb, and place the breathing Bust;
> VILLIERS is read with *Cowley* on the Stone,
> And SHEFFIELD adds to *Dryden's* Name his own.
> And this in future Times shall be their Boast,
> When all Memorials else of Fame are lost;
> When Time shall have devour'd whate'er proclaims
> The Grandeur of their now illustrious Names,
> And levell'd, as successive Ages pass,
> The proud Inscription and the sculptur'd Brass;
> Your Sanction then Eternity shall give,
> In Your immortal Lustre Theirs shall live;
> As still *Mecaenas* our lov'd Theme we make,
> And Honour *Pollio* for his *Virgil's* sake.[26]

Fitzgerald, a sometime poet and usher of Westminster School, was dedicated to the preservation of antiquities.[27] In this piece he rehearses the by now familiar Horatian admonition that inscriptions on brass are not enduring while literary reputation is. Yet here, because he is dealing with the Abbey, there is a slight twist to this literary convention, because Fitzgerald's object is not so much the poets as the other famous corpses that are buried about the Abbey. The "dust of the once Great or Wise" does not bring "a juster Rev'rence . . . to this old Dome." Instead, that honor is reserved for the "sacred relics of the tuneful train." Lineage, which in many cases determines the rationale for burial at the Abbey, is dismissed as inadequate as are "dusty trophies" and blazon'd Metals." In what must be a bit of a critique, Shadwell (the object of Dryden's scorn) is the only poet to display his coat of arms. The implication seems to be that it was by virtue of his lineage rather than his poetic talent that he gained the honor of burial in the Abbey. Fitzgerald thus suggests the inadequacy of Dryden's rival *and* uses that inadequacy to critique those who are honored simply for their bloodlines.

Fitzgerald goes so far as to suggest that "Nobles . . . Peers of the Realm, and Princes of the Land" are put in the position of justifying their own positions by erecting tombs or monuments to poets. Hence George Villiers, second duke of Buckingham, is buried in the Abbey (in a small chapel in the apse of Henry VII's chapel), but his real claim to fame is that his name is "read with Cowley on the Stone." So too, John Sheffield, first duke of Buckingham, is buried in a chapel to the east of Villiers, but his accomplishment is that he "adds to Dryden's name his own." This idea of fame by association is given some form of historical confirmation by mentioning the great Roman statesmen Caius Maecenas and Gaius Asinius Pollio at the end of the poem and claiming that it is their patronage of Horace and Virgil that enables us to remember them at all.[28] Maecenas (as trusted advisor of Augustus) and Pollio (as a successful general, a well-known politician, and consul of Rome) mirror Villiers and Sheffield. These two men were among the most influential of their age. Villiers was privy councillor and intimate of Charles II (just as Maecenas was advisor to Augustus) and later a member of the famous "cabal" that advised Charles II. Sheffield, like Pollio, was a successful general and became Lord Chamberlain under James. Fitzgerald's assertion here is that soldiers and politicians may seem to possess power and notoriety but it is the poets who "give" rather than "borrow fame." It is the patronage of these men rather than their political careers that led to their remembrance, or, as he puts it, it is the "sanction" of the poets that shall allow these men to live "in . . . immortal lustre."

History, which seems to favor those who are intimately involved with the political machinations of the nation, will recognize poets because it is, in Fitzgerald's formulation, the poets who make history. Behind this belief (as behind Basse's initial mapping out of the space in the South Transept) is Cicero's assertion that it is poets who possess the power because it is in their power to memorialize politicians. Yet far from indicating a kind of certainty about the place of poets, I would argue that the insistence on political power actually speaks to an anxiety about the power of poets.

In other words, Fitzgerald takes Horace's injunction that poetry is the most enduring monument and not only applies it to the statesmen (by suggesting that they will only live by having their name associated with the poets), but goes further and claims for poets the task of producing that which is immortal. In a rhetorical move similar to the epilogue of the *Metamorphoses*, in which Ovid claims that his work will exist "beyond Time's hunger," Fitzgerald asserts that, though "time shall have devour'd" and "levell'd" the "Great," poets still retain the ability to defeat time and make immortal those who are associated with them (even if their association extends to the patronage of the poet). The function of poets and poetry, then, becomes clear. Whereas politicians, statesmen, and kings all operate within time, poetry is able to construct a place that is outside of time. What is so curious about Fitzgerald's assertions is that they are all dependent on a physical space, a locus that exists within time. He asserts that "all Memorials else of Fame" will be lost, but then bases the fame of Villiers and Sheffield on the fact that their names are joined with Cowley's and Dryden's on "the tomb." Even as Fitzgerald asserts the transcendent, immaterial being of poetry, he depends on the space that is Poets' Corner to generate that being.

This space, in and of itself, was by no means fixed. There is good evidence to suggest that the "Corner" was originally just that, a small, enclosed or even hidden space. In 1881 Henry Poole, the master mason of the Abbey asserted that, "one would naturally hesitate to accept the word *Corner* as applicable to so large a space in the Abbey as that occupied by the transept . . . in dictionaries of the early and middle part of the last century, the word *corner* is defined to mean an angle, or remote place. It is also applied to an enclosed space, secret or retired."[29] Poole goes on to demonstrate that the large space which we now know as "Poets' Corner" was originally much more hemmed in by the eastern wall of a chapel dedicated to St. Blaize. This chapel was gradually dismantled until any sign of it had disappeared completely. The earliest known representation of Poets' Corner (in an Initial of John Dart's *Westmonasterium* [1723]) shows the older version of the corner (fig. 6). There is no way of telling when the first bits of the chapel were taken down (apparently the western wall), but according to Poole, about 1723 "[James] Gibbs, the architect, and Rysbrack, the sculptor, removed the eastern wall and part of the northern wall with its corner pillar, to erect the monstrous wall between the detached main pillar of the fabric and the corresponding wall half-pillar southward."[30] Matthew Prior's monument designed by Gibbs and executed by Rysbrack was then attached to this pillar and, as Poole puts it, "thus seems to have begun the erection of the enormous walls and corresponding monuments, which continued throughout the eighteenth century, thereby shutting out light, obstructing the grand view of the ancient architecture, and causing damage and destruction to it, to the great detriment of the magnificent beauty of almost all parts of the Abbey" (fig. 7).[31]

The erection of the Prior monument and the large monument to Dryden two years earlier (also designed by Gibbs) initiated the process whereby much

Figure 6. The earliest visual representation of Poets' Corner from John Dart's *Westmonasterium* (1723). Copyright Dean and Chapter of Westminster.

larger monuments made their way into the Corner. Ultimately, as we will see, the addition of so many monuments would require action, but for now it is enough to observe that by 1723 the Corner had gained a certain synergy so that portions of the Abbey were actually removed to make room for it. In addition, it is possible to surmise that the modern term for the poets' graveyard, Poets' Corner, was probably in use even before Thomas Fitzgerald's 1733 poem as it would not really describe the much wider space encompassed by the Corner after 1723. If we can assume that Addison would have used the term had it been in wide circulation, then a workable hypothesis would be to assert that even if the term was not invented between 1711 and 1723, it was not in wide usage until then. One might further surmise that the removal of the east wall

Figure 7. The eastern part of Poets' Corner in 1860. Copyright Dean and
Chapter of Westminster.

of St. Blaize's Chapel, the building of the "monstrous wall between the detached main pillar of the fabric and the corresponding wall half-pillar," rede-
fined the space to such an extent that the notion of this part of the South
Transept was fundamentally altered. In addition, the erection of a bust to
Dryden in 1720 (fig. 8), the erection of a memorial to Samuel Butler in 1721,
the burial of Matthew Prior (at the feet of Spenser at Prior's request) in the
same year, and the placement of Matthew Prior's tomb next to the half-pillar

Figure 8. The monument to Dryden with its enormous marble arch and surround still intact, from John Dart's *Westmonasterium* (1723). It was taken down in 1848 and only the bust remains. Copyright Dean and Chapter of Westminster.

in 1723 might well have been responsible for the new name of what Addison had called "Poets' Quarter." In other words, it is possible that at just the moment that the Corner expanded to become more than a retired space in the Abbey, the name that described that space became firmly established. But even if the enormous amount of activity in the early 1720s was not responsible for the "christening" of Poets' Corner, it is clear that the modern idea of the corner was created at this time.[32]

Perhaps no memorial proclaimed this new reality as much as the monument to Shakespeare that was erected in 1740. As we have already seen, there were early questions about why he had not been buried with his fellow writers. In fact, Beaumont may be seen to have anticipated the larger idea of the Corner by asking if Chaucer and Spenser could make room for Shakespeare just as Jonson resisted the idea that Shakespeare should be buried with the other poets.[33] In 1740, perhaps emboldened by the additional space that the Corner had taken to itself, a public subscription was undertaken which led to the creation of the statue by Scheemakers. As we will see, the erection of this statue was not a merely a disinterested act that in some sense "returned" Shakespeare to the aesthetic place that he belonged. Indeed, the subscription and even the statute itself were the product of what might be called the politics of Poets' Corner. But in terms of external aesthetic logic, the erection of the statue made good a kind of lack in the Corner that had disabled the Corner's status as a material, hence public, version of Parnassus. The presence of this *sine qua non* highlighted the absence of other poetic bodies and monuments as the idea of Poets' Corner took hold in the popular imagination.

Alexander Pope, Patronage, and the Sponsorship of Poets' Corner

Curiously, it was the absence of the man who was in some sense responsible for the monument to Shakespeare that occasioned some of the most trenchant criticism. In his *Citizen of the World* (1762) Oliver Goldsmith, for instance, portrayed his Chinese philosopher, Lien Chi Altangi, wandering through the Abbey being guided by the "Man in Black." At one point he asks, "I have been told of one Pope. Is he here?" To which the guide replies, "It is time enough, these hundred years: he is not long dead: people have not done hating him yet."[34] The Chinese philosopher's question and, along with it, the guide's rationale for Alexander Pope's exclusion at once supports and undermines the purported function of Poets' Corner. Pope, Goldsmith seems to suggest, *should* be buried in the Abbey, but his poetic talent was not enough to trump the enmity that was aroused in those who read him. This disconnection between feelings about the poet and appreciation of his poetry is something that would haunt the Corner for the next three centuries and speaks to a crisis in the understanding of how poetry and ethics should be weighed against one another. Increasingly, the dean and chapter would be put in positions in which the aesthetic appreciation of art and the ethical/religious questions about the individual would come into conflict. In other words, the nature of the Corner changed, becoming not so much an index of the worth of poetry as a measure of whether the poet was worthy.

Of course, occasionally it was the poet himself who decided not whether he was worthy of Poets' Corner, but whether Poets' Corner was worthy of him. Despite Goldsmith's assertion that Pope was denied burial in the Corner, it was actually Pope's request that he be buried near his mother in Twickenham. In fact, he launched a kind of peremptory strike on the Abbey in the epitaph that he wrote for himself. His friend William Warburton had it inscribed on a white marble tablet above the gallery in St. Mary's the Virgin:

> POETA LOQUITUR.
> *For one who would not be buried in Westminster Abbey.*
> Heroes and Kings! your distance keep:
> In peace let one poor Poet sleep;
> Who never flatter'd folks like you:
> Let Horace blush and Virgil too.

One might well see in this quatrain a bit of bluster that was meant to deny those who would deny him an honored burial place. In other words, Pope's protestations to the contrary, he might well have understood that Dean Sprat would not allow him to be buried in Poets' Corner because he was Catholic. But his words also set forth a kind of creed about the kind of work that the poet should carry out.

Pope's words seem to suggest that burial at the Abbey is tantamount to an admission that conflict and politics influence the poet's work in unfortunate ways. The poet believes that he has earned "peace," as opposed to the hurly-burly of war or the internecine strife of politics. Further, far from comparing himself to Virgil or Horace here, he positively distances himself from their seemingly obsequious ways. Behind this lies an idea about poetry that somehow transcends the more mundane qualities of the world. Indeed, even earlier in Thomas Fitzgerald's poem "Upon the Poets Corner in Westminster-Abbey," we see an attempt to elevate the work of the writer over the politician. Fitzgerald, of course, goes so far as to suggest that it is the reflected glory of the poet that will stand the politician in good stead because he will be remembered as a good patron. Pope seems less sanguine about any connection between poetry and politics, or, one might say, between poetry and the state.

In fact, one might well see his epitaph as a kind of riff on the last four lines of the epitaph that he composed for John Gay, who was buried in the Abbey in 1732 and who received his monument (upon which the epitaph was written) in 1737:

> These are thy honours! Not that here thy bust
> Is mix'd with heroes, nor with kings thy dust,
> But that the worthy and the good shall say,
> Striking their pensive bosoms—"Here lies Gay."[35]

Pope expresses a kind of ambivalence about the location of Gay's monument and body in the Abbey precisely because he does not want the visitor to think that the great honor that should be afforded the poet is bought with his association of heroes and kings. Samuel Johnson famously commented that the last line "is so dark that few can explain it, and so hard when it is explained that still fewer can understand it."[36] But I would argue that the line is an affirmation of the poet's resting place *qua* resting place rather than as another burial/monument that gains its honor from the monuments (especially the monuments of rulers and warriors) that give the place its honor. In other words, the honor derives from not from what surrounds Gay's "dust," but the fact that *hic est locus*—this is the space of Gay's grave.

Pope's willingness to write an epitaph for Gay, of course, reveals something of a paradox in his attitude towards the Abbey. Even if he critiques the other burials in Westminster as not of the same importance as those of the poets, nonetheless he participates in the economy of epitaph that maintains or perhaps in some sense creates the idea of Poets' Corner. Indeed, we might well see Pope as the godfather of the Corner, for he was materially involved in the erection of half a dozen monuments and tombs in the South Transept.

His interest in poetic memorials seems to have started with Dryden, for in the notes to the *Epistle to Arbuthnot,* Pope remarks ironically about the earl of Halifax's relationship to Dryden that "still the Great have kindness in reserve, / He helped to bury whom he help'd to starve."[37] Pope here was referring here to the magnificent funeral that the earl of Halifax (and others) provided for Dryden, who of course did not receive such largesse during his lifetime. As we saw earlier, neither did Dryden receive the monument that he was to have had of Halifax, a circumstance that Pope drew attention to in the epitaphs intended for Nicholas Rowe. His complaint is something of a topos that stretches back at least (as we have seen) to Spenser. Yet Pope's critique of the pretensions and hypocrisy of these great men, his constant satire of their attempts to ally themselves with the producers of culture actually seemed to have produced that which he purportedly scorned. For the result of his satire of Halifax was that the duke of Sheffield provided the funds to raise the monument, and Pope apparently took a keen interest in the placement and design of the sculpture as well as the epitaph that appeared on the base.[38]

Further, the particular epitaph that he constructed for Dryden seems, if anything, a model of the harmonious patron-poet relationship. It is true that he rejected Dean Francis Atterbury's suggestion, "This SHEFFIELD rais'd, The Sacred Dust below / Was Dryden Once: The rest who does not know?" in favor of a simple Latin inscription that had Dryden's name first.[39] But the inclusion of Sheffield's name on the monument occasioned a good deal of criticism. An anonymous epigram from some years after the monument was erected (1733) declared that "Great Peers, 'tis known can in Oblivion lie: / But no great Poet has the Pow'r to die. / At cheap Expence behold engrafted Fame; / . . . / S—d shall borrow Life / From Dryden's Grave."[40] This epigram which, curiously enough, appears in the same year as Fitzgerald's "Upon the POETS CORNER in WESTMINSTER-ABBEY" suggests, as does Fitzgerald's poem, that "SHEFFIELD adds to *Dryden's* Name his own" and that "this shall be . . . [his] . . . boast." The epigram goes even further than Fitzgerald, however, in claiming a kind of ghoulish role for Sheffield. He "borrow[s] life / from Dryden's grave," thereby stealing the vitality that should be the poet's and extending his own life by cannibalizing the reputation of the writer. There was no explicit critique of Pope's role in the creation of the epitaph, perhaps because his participation in the raising of the monument was not widely known. But one writer, at least, has gone so far as to claim that Pope may have composed his own epitaph with the controversy over Dryden in mind.[41] By separating himself from the Abbey and claiming his own burial ground, he was able to claim an

independent monumentalization for himself—far from the whims of those
notable men who were so often responsible for the erection of monuments in
the Abbey.

Whether or not Pope had this in mind when he was composing the epitaph "for one that would not be buried in Westminster Abbey," it is true that
his interest in Poets' Corner seems to have been sparked by what he saw as an
inadequate memorialization of those who were responsible for the cultural life
of the nation. The sheer number of projects that he was involved in concerning the Abbey would seem to speak to a desire to create a single place where
English men and women could come to remember the arts. In fact, in the
same year that Pope was engaged in raising a tomb to Dryden, he also became involved with the erection of the monument to Samuel Butler. Just what
Pope's role was remains a bit unclear, but Pope "probably advised Alderman
Barber concerning the monument which Barber in 1721 erected in the Abbey
to the author of *Hudibras*."[42] Pope was certainly involved in the writing of
the epitaph, and, as in so many others, he expresses dissatisfaction with the
way the world honors the poet:

> Samuel Butler Who was born at Strensham, in Worcestershire, 1612
> and died in London, 1680; a man of uncommon wit and probity: as
> admirable for the product of his genius, as unhappy in the rewards
> of them. His satire, exposing the hypocrisy and wickedness of the
> rebels, is such an inimitable piece, that as he was the first, he may
> be said to be the last writer in this peculiar manner. That he, who,
> when living, wanted almost everything, might not, after death, any
> longer want so much as a tomb, JOHN BARBER, citizen of London,
> erected this monument in 1721.[43]

When taken in concert with the way that the Dryden monument came to
be, it is clear that Pope's reaction to the monumentalization of poets was
complex. He felt that these monuments should memorialize the career of the
poet, but he also seems to have felt that these monuments should speak to the
lack of attention to poets while they live. Too often, he seems to suggest (as in
the case of Halifax and Dryden), more attention is paid to the poet after his
death than when he was living. As we have seen, such observations about the
hypocrisy of patrons are relatively conventional and (in the context of Westminster Abbey) had been made as early as Spenser's death and burial. Pope
appears to look with approbation on John Barber (alderman and Lord Mayor

of London) who "erected this monument . . . [so] that he, who when living, wanted almost everything, might not, after death, any longer want so much as a tomb." Yet if he did so, he must have changed his mind. For in the fourth book of the *Dunciad* (1742), in a series of lines with the footnote "the *Tombs of the Poets, Editio Westmonsteriensis*," Pope has the Goddess Dulness refer to Barber (in his role as alderman), "So by each Bard an Alderman shall sit, / A heavy Lord shall hang at ev'ry Wit, / And while on Fame's triumphal Car they ride, / Some Slave of mine be pinion'd to their side."[44] If this dismissal of Barber's role in raising the monument is not clear enough, Pope launches a more generalized attack on what he characterizes as "the practice of tacking the obscure names of Persons not eminent in any branch of learning, to those of the Most distinguished Writers . . . by setting up *Monuments* disgraced with their own vile names and inscriptions."[45] Even for Pope, this inconsistency and hostility seem, at least superficially, puzzling. It is doubtful that he or anyone else had forgotten his own role in the perpetuation of this practice and his relationship with Barber was extremely cordial.[46]

An anecdote about Barber and Pope, however, may give a clue as to why Pope insisted on the strict separation of writer and patron. In an entry dated 1744, Pope's friend, Joseph Spence, claims that

> Mr. Pope never flattered anybody for money in the whole course of his writings. Alderman Barber had a great inclination to have a stroke in his commendation inserted in some part of Mr. Pope's Works. He did not want money, and he wanted fame. He would probably have given four or five thousand pounds to have been gratified in this desire, and gave Mr. Pope to understand as much. Mr. Pope would never comply with such a baseness, and when the Alderman died, he left him a legacy only of a hundred pounds, which might have been some thousands if he had obliged him only with a couplet.[47]

The story belongs to a type that seems to demonstrate Pope's relationship to "pure" art, and given Spence's partiality toward Pope, we might well distrust it. But, having been circulated by Pope, it also suggests that Pope was not above using his friends (especially after they were dead) to ensure that his own reputation would remain unsullied by the more commercial aspects of artistic production.[48] So even if the story is not true, it stands as an example of Pope's desire to advertise his own commitment to the objective and sublime nature of poetry. In other words, he seems not to have thought that monuments in and of themselves were futile, rather he seems to have come to conclusion that how these monuments are erected is at least as important as the fact that they are raised.[49]

To understand Pope's refiguring of the poet/patron relationship it is also important to understand that the cultural climate of England had changed after 1720. Not only did England have a new king, but the South Sea stock crash had revealed the ministry's involvement in manipulating the market to its advantage. Any investigation into the scandal had been blocked by the House of Commons until (so the thinking was) the Court could sell out. The result was that the Hanoverians were so unpopular that it seemed like a restoration of the Stuarts might actually be possible. But far from aiding the Jacobites, the resultant unrest had the opposite effect as Sir Robert Walpole cast the threat from abroad as an excuse to suspend habeas corpus, impose on Catholics a fine of one hundred thousand pounds, and pursue the leader of the opposition Tories, Francis Atterbury, dean of Westminster, for aiding Jacobite plans to invade after the elections of 1722. Atterbury was not completely guiltless, but the trial (which resulted in Atterbury's exile) was a mockery. Further, Pope, whose loyalties were seen as questionable because of his religion, came under suspicion because of involvement in the publication of the writings of the patron that he had so recently praised. Apparently, because the wife of Sir John Sheffield, duke of Buckinghamshire, was the natural daughter of James II, the writings came under scrutiny and were found to be partially seditious. Though Pope was not responsible for obtaining the license for publication of the duke's works, he was nonetheless taken into custody and questioned.[50] Ultimately, the works were published after being "castrated" (as one wag put it) and were in full circulation as they had formerly been by 1726.[51]

These occurrences that were brought on by "great men" of England—the loss of his friend and aid in raising monuments in the Abbey, the calumniation of his dead friend Sheffield, and the proscription of his own religion—might be thought to be enough to sour him on the idea of the "greatness" of politicians. But Pope (and the writers who surrounded him) believed that there was an even greater wrong in which Walpole and his minions were engaged. After Walpole's ascent, the Pope circle felt, and would later express, that the patronage system had become politicized.[52] In order to "earn" a living, writers now had to prostitute their talent to the state. One of this circle, John Gay brings together the concerns expressed by Pope and Fitzgerald in his *Epistle to . . . Paul Methuen*:

Why flourish'd verse in great Augustus' reign?
He and Mecaenas lov'd the Muses strain.
But now that wight in poverty must mourn
Who was (O cruel stars!) a Poet born.
Yet there are ways for authors to be great;
Write ranc'rous libels to reform the State:
Or if you chuse more sure and ready ways,
Spatter a minister with fulsome praise;
Launch out with freedom, flatter him enough;
Fear not, all men are dedication proof.
Be bolder yet, you must go farther still,
Dip deep in gall thy mercenary quill.
He who his pen in party quarrels draws,
Lists an hir'd bravo to support the cause;
He must indulge his Patron's hate and spleen,
And stab the fame of those he ne'er has seen.
Why then should authors mourn their desp'rate case?
Be brave, do this, and then demand a place.
Why art thou poor? exert thy gifts to rise,
And banish tim'rous vertue from thy eyes.[53]

Just as Gay suggests that Mecaenas "lov'd the Muses strain," so too Gay also seems to embrace the thoughts expressed by Thomas Fitzgerald when he suggests, in his apostrophe to poetry, that "In Your immortal Lustre Theirs shall live; / As still *Mecaenas* our lov'd Theme we make." He opposes the ideas of a virtuous patron to the modern poet who needs to "Write ranc'rous libels to reform the State" in order to "indulge his Patron's hate and spleen." The result is that the poet will not be poor, but only at the cost of banishing "tim'rous vertue from thy eyes."

While Gay's nostalgia about the virtues of the patronage system might seem in line with Pope's celebration of Sheffield's patronage of Dryden (and himself), we should also recall that later in his own epitaph Pope would find fault with Virgil (whose patron was Pollio as well as Augustus) and Horace (whose patron was Mecaenas) for engaging in the flattery that often characterized the patron/poet relationship. Pope finds fault, then, even with those who seem to have an ideal relationship with their patron—one that ensured that "art" would adhere to the older idea that secured the place of the poet as "legislator of Parnassus."[54] On the other hand, Pope well understood and attacked the new literary system that he himself had helped to bring about. Though the role of professional writer led to a kind of freedom from literary patronage, it was also clear that substituting the reading public for a single patron had its own dangers. Booksellers like Edmund Curll, a particular target of Pope's, not only were able to lay claim to the rights of authors and bring out works in their names (like the pirated versions of Sheffield's works), but also were responsible for hiring untalented hacks who would turn out ephemera that would be able to compete with other more worthy writings. The "unspeakable Curll," of course, was a special case.[55] But even Pope's close relationship and eventual quarrel with Curll's rival, Bernard Lintot, revealed the precarious position (at least in Pope's mind) of the writer vis à vis the reading public.[56]

Pope himself, in the *Dunciad Variorum,* speaking through the person of the "editor" Scriblerus, said of the author of the poem, "he lived in those days, when (after Providence had permitted the Invention of Printing as a scourge for the Sins of the learned) Paper also became so cheap, and printers so numerous, that a deluge of authors cover'd the land: Whereby not only the peace of the honest unwriting subject was daily molested, but unmerciful demands were made of his applause, yea of his money, by such as would neither earn the one or deserve the other."[57] In Pope's apocalyptic scenario, the great invention of printing becomes a curse. British production of paper, the dearth of which had restricted English printing in the seventeenth century, has cheapened the available literature. Earlier governmental restrictions on printers to a theoretical total of twenty had lapsed and hence a kind of second flood (of authors) has taken place.[58] The result was that the "unwriting subject" (as Pope puts it) is constantly badgered for his or her applause and, more important, money. Pope, I think, is being generous to the public—neither condemning it for having bad taste, nor implicating it in the death of the idea of high art. Yet, at the same time, Pope clearly differentiates between those consumers of texts who write and those cannot write. One thinks here of Dryden's and Pope's patron John Sheffield who, if he was not a great author, nonetheless was enough of a writer (at least in Pope's mind) to understand that Dryden and Pope were great writing talents that should be supported. The problem with having the general public as a patron was that the booksellers like Curll or (according to Pope anyway) Lintot produced writing in much the same that one might produce any other commercial product. They both understood that one could not simply assume a market but had to create one by advertising and making writing (on some level at least) commensurate with money. Those authors who were commercially successful were, thus, seen as the authors who were worth publishing. In other words, for these booksellers, the worthiness of writing was exactly the same as commercial success—and, by the lights of the Pope circle at least, this not only subjected literature to the public, but subordinated public taste to the taste of the booksellers.

Pope was too much of a realist to believe that he could turn back the clock, but it was possible to use the memorials in Poets' Corner as a kind of counterweight to the booksellers. The most salient example of this commemorative strategy is Pope's involvement in the erection of the Shakespeare memorial in 1740. This memorial has received more attention than any other in Poets' Corner not only because was raised to the writer widely regarded as England's greatest, but because it crystallized a number of different anxieties about the role of the poet vis-à-vis his public and the state. Behind the erection of the statue, of course, was the fact that Shakespeare did not have a memorial in the English poetic graveyard. Pope signaled the belatedness of the memorial with an epigram: "After an hundred and thirty years' nap / Enter Shakspear with a loud clap."[59] But why did it take until 1740 to have a monument reared?

Michael Dobson suggests that until the early eighteenth century Shakespeare was not really missed in Poets' Corner. In fact he asserts that the first intimation that Shakespeare's absence from Poets' Corner occasioned any comment comes from an anonymous correspondent in the *Weekly Register* in 1736: "I believe that everyone that visits this sacred Repository of the illustrious Dead, cannot help looking round, like me, for the divine *Milton*, and the immortal *Shakespear*; names which are the Honour of their Country, and yet have receiv'd no Honour from it."[60] As we have seen this is not strictly speaking correct. As early as 1622 William Basse had expressed the thought that the space in the South Transept was absent a body. But it does seem to be true that the early eighteenth century saw a revival of interest in memorializing Shakespeare in the Abbey. The poet's reputation with the public grew both as a kind of cultural patriotism and (on the part of the influential Shakespeare Ladies' Club) a reaction in the 1730s against Italian opera and the scurrilities of Restoration comedy.[61]

Yet until this point, as we have seen, it was usually the contribution of a rich patron that led to the erection of a monument. With Shakespeare it was purportedly to be different. Pope served on a committee with Lord Burlington and Dr. Richard Meade that was formed to raise funds for the monument through public subscription. This was the first monument that Pope had been involved in that was not to be the product of private patronage. And the thinking seems to have been to transform patronage from a remote private affair to a nationalistic public one. As the *London Daily Post and General Advertiser* gravely intoned:

> Britons with virtuous pride your merit know;
> You've done, what kings of old, were fond to do:
> Then, when the poet died, the monarch mourn'd;
> And by command, his ashes were inurn'd.[62]

Clearly, as others have argued, Pope attempted to create the public patronage of Shakespeare as a rejection of the subordination of art to the politics of the Walpole government. But what also seems to be true is that the statue of Shakespeare appears as a kind of effigy of the absent poet—something that, in the words of Joseph Roach, can "evoke an absence, to body something forth, especially something from the distant past."[63] This doubling—marking absence and bodying forth presence precisely replicates both the work of the medieval relic and (especially in the Abbey) the work of the monarchial corpse. As Carlyle would note a hundred years later, in the burial place of kings, the statue of Shakespeare represents the poet as a king, but one who is not subject to the depredations of politics or time.[64] The attempt to embody a sublime Shakespeare in the first full-length statue in Poets' Corner, then, would seem to have been a success.

Yet if the public, out of some sense of national pride, was to take the place of the state, the reality was that the subscription was not as successful as it might have been, and Lord Burlington had to make good the shortfall. When the monument was finished, Pope insisted against objections from Meade that the words "Amor Publicus Posuit" be placed on the memorial to commemorate the fact that it was the public rather than any private patron that led to the construction of the memorial.[65] So too, Pope apparently proposed that on the vacant scroll under Shakespeare's bust be placed a couplet that read, "Thus Britain lov'd me; and preserv'd my Fame, / Clear from a *Barber's* or a Benson's Name" (fig. 9).[66] Pope's simultaneous emphasis on the love of the public and his dismissal of patrons like Barber suggests that Pope's thoughts on fame had altered somewhat. As the first professional writer, we might not be surprised that Pope would move away from the traditional poet-patron relationship. And indeed his idea that the public should be supporters and praisegivers of poets fits in well with the notion of the literary marketplace that the 1710 copyright act enabled.

Figure 9. Pope's satirical suggestion for the Shakespeare statue scroll. Frontispiece to *Poems on Several Occasions. By Shakespeare* (London, [between 1760 and 1780?]). Used by permission of the Folger Shakespeare Library.

But it would be erroneous to believe that Pope abandoned the idea of literary patronage completely. For even as he earned his living through what might be termed the democracy of the marketplace, he never, as far as we know, distanced himself from Sheffield's involvement in the erection of Dryden's monument.[67] This, I would argue, has more to do with the special relationship that Sheffield had with Dryden than with any hypocrisy on Pope's part. Sheffield had collaborated with and been praised by Dryden as a "friend of poets." And Pope had edited Sheffield's works.[68] Indeed, it may be that in Pope's mind the difference between Sheffield's involvement with Dryden's monument and Barber's erection of Butler's memorial can be found in Dryden's own words. For in 1736 Pope reiterates them in his *Epistle to Arbuthnot* "(great *Dryden's* friends before) / With open arms receiv'd one Poet more" (ll. 141–142). It is ultimately "friendship," a personal virtue, that Pope identifies as the singular quality of Sheffield especially as it was applied to him.[69] Friendship, in other words, defined Sheffield as the model patron and the great failing of those who followed him was that they were not like him. Pope's complex reaction to the poet/patron relationship, his simultaneous rejection and embrace of such homosocial bonds reveals, I think, a deep nostalgia for the kind of relationship that Dryden had with Sheffield. Pope, of course, is located on the other side of a kind of a divide that Pope himself created. And what we have from Pope is a series of ambivalent reactions to the past when patron and poet were linked not only by bonds of friendship, but by money. His recollection of Dryden's relationship with Sheffield, however, and his suggestion that he has joined Dryden in his close relationship with Sheffield conjures up a time before Pope essentially created the notion of the professional writer and idealizes these bonds as unpolluted by filthy lucre.

Almost twenty years after Pope's death, the nostalgia lingers. In Goldsmith's fictionalized tour of the Abbey, the writer asks, "But are there not some men of distinguished taste, as in China, who are willing to patronize men of merit, and soften the rancor of malevolent dullness?" His guide, the Man in Black, assures him that "there are many . . . but . . . the book-answerers [those employed by publishers to attack authors] crowd about them, and call themselves the writers of books; and the patron is too indolent to distinguish; thus poets are kept at a distance, while their enemies eat up all their rewards at the mandarine's table."[70] It is interesting here that Goldsmith only puts part of the blame on the patrons. They are "indolent," it is true, but they still have the taste to distinguish if they choose. And the main problem seems to be that the "book-answerers" are so numerous that it quite literally is difficult even to see the men of "genius" valued by Goldsmith. The main problem, then, is that the modes of production have become so widespread that patronage is unable to operate in the way it should. Discernment becomes more difficult when there are so many choices. Like Pope, then, Goldsmith locates the problem mainly in the material realm—cheap paper and cheap printing lead to an erosion of the quality of literature.

Goldsmith goes even a bit further than Pope, however, in suggesting that the real root of the problem is money. When the Chinese traveler asks if every poet has suffered the indignation of the book-answerers, his guide responds that if the poet has money, "he may buy reputation from your book answerers, as well as a monument from the guardians of the temple."[71] Goldsmith conflates and attacks the monumental nature of the Abbey and literary reputation here, for the temple that Goldsmith speaks of is Westminster Abbey, and the guardians are the Dean and Chapter. Yet Goldsmith's attitude toward the Abbey is complicated because he at once claims that money is needed for any monument (because that is the only way that reputation is got) *and* that the poets who lie in the Abbey have been attacked by the book-answerers. He shows, I think, a continued investment in and criticism of the idea of Poets' Corner. Pope has no monument, but there are monuments to "Shakespeare, and Milton, and Prior, and Drayton." Like Pope he seems to understand the importance of a place of commemoration of poetry, but he also almost intuitively understands that its very importance heralds something important for the status of poetry. It is as if the very commemoration of poetry in Poets' Corner also symbolizes a passing of poetry, or at least what the eighteenth-century wits would have considered poetry of genius.

This attempt by Pope to disentangle the poet from the politician anticipates and attempts to combat assertions about the interconnectedness of politics and poetry that seems so obvious in the tombs that line the Abbey. Dean Stanley, for instance, sees the dead poet (as well as other great men of the land) as a kind of prop for the monarchy—something that ensures its stability:

> Let those who are inclined bitterly to contrast the placid dignity of
> our recumbent Kings, with Chatham gesticulating from the
> Northern Transept, or Pitt from the western door, or Shakespeare
> leaning on his column in Poets' Corner, or Wolfe expiring by
> the Chapel of St. John, look upon them as in their different ways
> keeping guard over the shrine of our monarchy and our laws—
> and that which seems at first incongruous will become a symbol
> of the harmonious diversity in unity which pervades our whole
> commonwealth. Had the Abbey of St. Denys admitted within its

walls the poets and warriors and statesmen of France, the kings
might yet have remained inviolate in their graves.[72]

Stanley puts the poet (symbolized, of course, by Shakespeare) in the role of
handmaiden to the monarchy. Along with the other three figures mentioned
here, he guards one of the four directions of the compass ensuring that the
"shrine" of the monarchy will remain inviolate. The result is something that
will be familiar to nineteenth-century aesthetics—a harmonious political diversity that is mirrored in the harmony, or beauty, brought on by the aesthetic
experience. Incongruity thus becomes diversity that in turn becomes harmonious in the experience of the Abbey. The not so subtle suggestion here is that
continuity of the nation depends on the relationship between art and politics
(among other things). The stark contrast of France figures forth the ways in
which the "inviolate" grave of kings (ensured by the inviolate nature of the
other graves) actually extends the inviolate nature of kingship itself. Ultimately
this contrast with France links poetical burial with the kingly corpse not so
much in a poetics/politics of death as in a promise of continuity that can be
extended to the nation. What comes to mind here is the primal corpse of
Edward the Confessor who, as we saw in Chapter 1, provided at once a kind
of material governing body to the Abbey (having been its founder and king)
and a spiritual aspect as well. Continuity thus depends on the ways that poetry and politics are in harmony. This is not, one suspects, a view that would
have been unproblematic to Alexander Pope. The practice of selling commemorative space in the Abbey to whoever had the requisite funds was notorious, but the uneven shift from private to public patronage in both the
Abbey and the literary spheres sometimes seemed to emphasize the less salu-
brious similitude between monumental and literary fame.[73] It may, in other
words, lay the groundwork for what in the nineteenth century would be a
deep interest in how the poetical corpse at once embodies a political continuity and signals the dangers of a poetical death.

CHAPTER 4

Absence and the Public Poetics of Regret

> The first visitor that I remember was Queen Emma of the Sandwich
> Islands (1865, or 6). . . . She showed a most unexpected knowledge
> of the various monuments. Amongst other things she was greatly
> disturbed at not finding a monument to Coleridge, the author of
> "The Ancient Mariner."
>
> —Dean Arthur Penrhyn Stanley

Queen Emma Kalanikaumakaʻamano Kaleleonālani Naʻea Rooke's search for
the monument to Coleridge seems at first blush a kind of quaint story that
exemplified the anecdotally irresistible history of the Abbey. In this particular story the exotic visitor from a far-away land who might not be expected to
know anything of English culture reveals, in fact, not only knowledge of the
people who are monumentalized in the Abbey, but a recognition that the absence of a monument in Poets' Corner was in some sense meaningful. Such
stories certainly play into notions of empire, in which the center of the cultural world is not only England but Westminster Abbey, the site of coronation and the burial place of both kings and poets. Queen Emma's status as
royalty of a land that is by its very nature on the margins of civilization demonstrates the wide-ranging extent of England's influence and marginalizes indig-
enous culture even further.[1] But the story also shows the extent to which the
Abbey had become a kind of virtual ideal in which it was not only who was
buried there, but who should be buried there that mattered. The expectation,
engendered by the ideal, enabled the Abbey to function as a *lieu de mémoire*
that gave the visitor a sense of belonging. As Jeop Leesen has suggested, "Such
monuments proclaim a Burkean sense of national community—'community'

both in a synchronic sense (encompassing all those who share the location and its symbolic charisma) and in a diachronic one (linking present-day users to the past ones)."[2] Queen Emma, of course, was the consort of a king who ruled an independent land far from Westminster, and so it might seem odd to suggest that she felt a sense of "national community" in Poets' Corner. But her conversion to the Church of England, her English foster parents, her friendship with Queen Victoria, and the fact that her mother's father was English also identified her as one who felt close ties with England. Further, as an English speaker, she was able to lay claim to a feeling of belonging within the Anglophone community.

But what about Queen Emma's "great disturbance"? The fact that she searches for something that is ultimately lacking points to her inability to participate in the sense of "national community" that Poets' Corner might otherwise be seen to engender. In this reading, Coleridge's missing monument becomes an impediment to Queen Emma's ability to form a virtual link to a larger sense of English poetical tradition. Her search for that which is not present might, in an allegorical sense, suggest her inability to locate her own place in the Anglophone community. Yet the importance of absence here perhaps has more to do with the nature of the Abbey in the nineteenth century than the queen's anxieties. In fact, I would argue that it is Dean Stanley, the great nineteenth-century chronicler of the Abbey, who is disturbed. Some two or three years after Queen Emma's visit he gives voice to his own anxiety that Poets' Corner had lost its relevance, or, more accurately, its quasi-mystical power: "The remaining glories of Poets' Corner belong to our own time and to the future. It would seem as if, during the opening of the century, the place for once had lost its charm . . . of the three greatest geniuses of that period two (Burns and Walter Scott) sleep at Dumfries and Dryburgh, under their own native hills; the third (Byron) lies at Newstead."[3] It was understandable that Burns and Scott would be buried in Scotland. But as both Samantha Matthews and Nicola Watson have pointed out, more troubling was the defection of the entire generation of Romantic writers.[4] But while absence certainly created problems for the space in the nineteenth century (limiting the extent to which Poets' Corner was able to function as a memorial and commemorative locus of belonging), it also led to what Matthews has characterized as a late Victorian revival of the space.[5]

The Productive Absence of Byron

It was, perhaps unsurprisingly, Stanley himself who took the lead in turning disadvantage to advantage by "creating a powerful mythology" in which corporeal absence actually signaled the power of the Corner's presence.[6] There were, as Stanley suggested, national reasons for the absence of Burns and Scott from the Corner. But Byron was a different matter. When Byron died in 1824, Thomas Babington Macaulay wrote (and Stanley quotes at length), "We cannot even now retrace the close of the brilliant and miserable career of the most celebrated Englishman of the nineteenth century, without feeling something of what was felt by those who saw the hearse with its long train of coaches turn slowly northwards, leaving behind it that cemetery which had been consecrated by the dust of so many great poets, but of which the doors were closed against all that remained of Byron."[7] Stanley claims that "it was understood that an unfavourable answer would be given to any application to inter Byron in the Abbey."[8]

Yet it was precisely to be interred in Westminster Abbey that Byron's supporters brought his body back from Greece. John Cam Hobhouse's sentiment is perhaps exemplary, "to lose no time in doing my duty by preserving all that was left to me of my dear friend—his fame."[9] In terms of receiving a state funeral at Westminster and being buried in Poets' Corner, they were to be disappointed, as the Abbey's dean at the time, Dr. Ireland, suggested that instead the best thing to be done was "to carry away the body, & say as little about it as possible."[10] This attempt to downplay Byron's death ultimately turned out to be impossible. When the undertaker's barge made its way down the Thames on the afternoon of the fifth of July, the shores were lined with spectators. Byron lay on view for a week at 20 Great George Street, and the press was so great that London police sergeants had to be brought in and a wooden frame erected around the coffin. Watching the throngs at Byron's funeral procession, the poet John Clare (later to be commemorated in the Abbey) commented that "the common people felt his merits and his power and the common people of a country are the best feelings of a prophesy of futurity."[11]

Nor did this interest in the commemoration of Byron flag. Four years later, under the name "Sydney," a proponent wrote in to the *Morning Courier* to complain about the exclusion of a statue of Byron from the Abbey:

I am no advocate for the failings of Lord Byron. They may have
been many—where there is Light there will be Shadow.—But
when we talk of *Christianity*, let us, with an accordant spirit,
employ its sacred hand to draw a veil over his frailties. . . . Is no
homage due to genius? Is no allowance to be made for its youthful
aberrations? Is England's greatest Poet, with a mind teeming with
sublime conceptions, and a heart glowing with all the fervour of
heroic charity—is the man who sacrificed his life for virtue—(for
where is the Englishman that shall *dare* to separate *her* cause from
that of Freedom?)—Is such a man, I ask,—the bard—the Soldier—
to be banished, (like the image of Brutus in the procession of
Tiberius) from his rightful place (amid the "laurelled crowd,") only
the more distinctly to disclose the vacancy he leaves, and louder to
proclaim the ingratitude of his unfeeling country?

One would have thought the *Poet's Corner* have received Lord
Byron's statue *without a crime.* But it seems it has been decided
otherwise.—One consolation at least remains, which the author
of this paper offers to his Child, and to the breasts of those who
loved him:—

> *All Greece will be his monument, while that from which he is*
> *now excluded, shall be itself a Ruin and a Tomb!*[12]

The writer attempts to make the case for the inclusion of the bust in terms that
are partially predictable. Byron is a "genius" and thus desires "homage." He is
sublime, so one would have to expect some darkness, for "where there is light,
there will be shadow." He does not excuse the faults of Byron, and (less predict-
ably) transforms the metaphor of light and darkness into a kind of Christian
argument for the inclusion of the statue. For though he does not actually suggest that the "redeeming light" may be able to illumine those dark parts of his
character (in fact, he suggests that Christianity should draw a veil over them),
there are other aspects of his character that were cast "unduly into shade." Thus
the redeeming light is not there to aid Byron, but to ensure that we may look
upon his character with the proper appreciation of its "generosity"—part of
which, of course, was his sacrifice of his life in the cause of Greek "freedom."

The end of his letter is perhaps the most interesting, for it suggests that
in the exclusion of Byron, there will be consequences for the Abbey itself.
Because he will not be able to take his "rightful place . . . amid the laurelled
crowd," he will "disclose the vacancy he leaves." This absence, in turn, will

reflect badly on England itself. For it shall "proclaim the ingratitude of his unfeeling country." It is, thus, not only a lack of recognition that the exclusion speaks to, but a kind of ghostly absent presence that will reveal to visitors a lack of appreciation or poetic feeling on the part of the entire nation. This ingenious attack, based on the ability of the Corner to elicit affect, suggests that Poets' Corner without Byron will signify a lack of national affect. The Abbey, in its refusal to accept the bust, ensures that it will cease to add to the immortality of those who are commemorated there. Instead, it will become a "tomb" in the sense that it will enshrine the dead, but by doing so only reinforce the deathly aspects of such tombs, for it will also become ruined. This bombastic conclusion suggests, in fact, that the bust's exclusion will lead to the ruin of England's poetical heritage—a point he amplifies in a later letter.[13]

"Sydney's" letters, of course, only give the views of one writer. And, as we might expect, Dean Stanley gives a very different account of the Abbey, contending that Byron's supporters never asked for his burial in the Abbey, but also diagnosing the poet's absence as a symptom of the Abbey's "naturalness."

> We have seen, again how extremely unequal and uncertain is the commemoration of our celebrated men. It is this which renders the interment or notice within our walls a dubious honour, and makes the Abbey, after all, but an imperfect and irregular monument of greatness. But it is this also which gives to it that perfectly natural character of which any artificial collection is entirely destitute. In the Valhalla of Bavaria, every niche is carefully portioned out; and if a single bust is wanting from the catalogue of German worthies, its absence becomes the subject of a literary controversy, and the vacant space is at last filled. Not so in the Abbey, there, as in English institutions generally, no fixed rule has been followed. Graves have been opened or closed, monuments erected or not erected, from the most various feelings of the time.[14]

At least initially, Stanley wishes to claim that, as the admission of burials and monuments into the Abbey is not a regularized process, admission into the Abbey is thus "a dubious honour"—something that, he later claims, devolves not so much from greatness, but from "political and ecclesiastical prejudice."[15] At the same time, he cannot resist supplementing the supernatural "charm" of poets' corner by comparing it with the "artificial collection" in the Valhalla of Bavaria.

The Valhalla, or Walhalla, was built over a twelve-year period (1830–1842) in Donaustauf bei Regensberg by King Ludwig I of Bavaria. Modeled on the Parthenon, the building contains busts of the "greats" that were initially chosen by Ludwig, but eventually selected by the Bavarian Academy of Sciences (fig. 10). As Stanley suggests, these busts are placed at regular—one might say geometric intervals. In fact, everything about the Walhalla is entirely regular, and it is this regularity that Stanley apparently feels is artificial. There is, one gets the feeling, a kind of organic quality to Stanley's commentary. For what guides the burial and commemoration of persons in the Abbey are "the most various feelings of the time." The Abbey's history thus becomes a kind of affective history of the nation that in its co-extensiveness is natural, if imperfect. In this way, Stanley also critiques the relatively recent construction of the Walhalla. The Abbey had, of course, been around since 1065 and thus mirrored the complete post-Conquest history of the English nation. The Walhalla had been completed only twenty-six years before Stanley wrote. Further, its geographical reach was somewhat attenuated by the fact that it had been built by the king of one part of a patchwork of small states that had not yet coalesced into one nation. Though Stanley does not press the issue, he clearly sees the Walhalla, with its classical origins, well-ordered statuary, and provincial roots as an attempt to create a feeling of national pride where there was as yet no nation.

If we return for a moment to the connection between harmonious aesthetics and harmonious politics that I discussed briefly in the introduction, we can see why Stanley would need to respond to this German ideal of the well-ordered Walhalla. Unlike the ideal of beauty that rested on the ideas of harmony and orderliness, Stanley seems to be making the case for a kind of beautiful disorder. He locates this beauty in the "naturalness" of the development of the Abbey, taking the position that this aesthetic disorder reflects the disorderly but natural and organic history of the nation-state. Stanley, then, might be seen to be a Romantic at this particular moment, even as he is justifying rejection of one of the great Romantic poets for burial in the Abbey on the basis of a Romantic aesthetic.

Stanley's position illustrates the uncomfortable juxtaposition of two desiderata: first that the dean and chapter should decide who will be buried in the Abbey and second that the Abbey should be considered a national church. The factor that links them is a kind of aesthetics of imperfect perfection. One particularly trenchant example of how this organic functioning of the Abbey

Figure 10. A nineteenth-century view of the Walhalla's interior.

worked imperfectly is an attempt to create by a kind of fiat a space called "Little Poets' Corner." Shortly after John Keble died (1866), Stanley determined to place a tablet to him—not in Poets' Corner, but in St. George's Chapel then known as the Baptistry. As Stanley put it, "Wordsworth, by the sentiment of a kinsman, is seated in the Baptistry—not unsuited to the innocent presence of childhood at the sacred font—not unworthy to make that angle of the Nave the nucleus of a new Poets' Corner of future years. Beside him, like a concord of ideas, will be the tablet of Keble, author of the 'Christian Year,' who himself wrote the reverential epitaph on Wordsworth's monument at Grasmere."[16] Later recollections of the event are less coy about Stanley's intent. As the 1905 guidebook to the Abbey put it, "This chapel was chosen by Dean Stanley to receive the bust of Keble, and since the statue of Wordsworth already consecrated this part of poetry, he re-christened it: 'Little Poets' Corner.'[17] The guide is reverent towards Stanley's accomplishment, suggesting that the statue of Wordsworth had already consecrated the ground and that Stanley merely "re-christened" the area called the Baptistry. In fact, he had done a good deal more than this—placing busts or tablets to Thomas Arnold and Charles Kingsley in the chapel and removing the baptismal font to the chapel of Henry VII (figure 11). This attempt to rechristen the Baptistry was ultimately unsuccessful, as in 1932 it was determined that the chapel would be remodeled and turned into a Warrior's Chapel in order to honor those who fought in World War I. There is evidence that some saw the removal of these monuments as "vandalism," but on the whole, the repositioning of the monuments in Poets' Corner was seen as a positive thing. One reader wrote

> these five acts of "vandalism," [the removal of the five monuments] or of improvement, offer hints of some of the motives which might induce further acts of the same kind. At the bottom lay the desire—or rather the need—to make the Warrior's Chapel practicable and to fit it for its special purpose as a unit in the great place of worship. This motive was supported by the obvious fitness of Poets' Corner as the place for Wordsworth, close to Coleridge and Southey; Keble's right to be there is equally plain; and when Keble had gone, his friend Arnold was due to go also.[18]

The writer of the piece has a two-pronged argument—first, he claims that the transformation of the Baptistry into the Warrior's Chapel, if motivated by "desire," was nonetheless a "need." Presumably, the identity of Westminster Abbey as a national Valhalla required that the Great War and those who died in it be commemorated in some way. The second prong of the writer's argument was that the proper place for the statue of Wordsworth was in Poets' Corner both because he had a right to be there (as did Keble) and because it was somehow seemly for him to be grouped with Southey and Coleridge. The argument, then, is against a kind of doubling of space in the Abbey. Each transept, section, or chapel had its purpose as a "unit in the great place of worship," and the writer goes so far as to characterize the statues as animated by friendship to dwell in the South Transept.

Of course, what made this movement possible was that all of the memorials in the Baptistry were sepulchers rather than tombstones. As I have argued, it is the placement of the body that gives the place of memorialization a "thereness." If the body is absent, the space falls prey to other seemingly more pressing concerns, such as the celebration of those who have sacrificed their bodies for the good of the nation, or even more cogently, aesthetic considerations. And indeed, it seems that Stanley's idea to create a "Little Poet's Corner," whatever its merits, failed at least partially because of the aesthetics of the memorials to Wordsworth, Arnold, Keble, and Kingsley.[19] This is not to say that the monuments in Poets' Corner itself were necessarily considered any more beautiful (in fact, all of the above monuments can now be found there), but because the South Transept was already "made sacred" by the existence of material bodies, it did not need to be hallowed by an aesthetics that located beauty in regularized order.

Aesthetics and the Valhalla-like quality of the Abbey had always been in tension, and in fact there had been, over the years, a number of critiques of all of the memorials that crowded the Abbey and, in the view of some, inhibited the Abbey's aesthetic qualities (fig. 12).[20] In fact one might well claim that these empty memorials had been considered suspect at least as early as Addison's time when he remarked that he found in Poets' Quarter "poets with no memorials and memorials with no poets."[21] Such thoughts found their way into *The Londoner* two centuries later when Oswald Barron, apparently echoing the thoughts of the dean, averred that

> humbly I applaud the Dean when he grumbles against the portrait
> statues and the like memorials of men who have their graves
> elsewhere. Things which have no more business in the abbey
> church than has Lord Nelson's waxen image, set up there by the
> nineteenth-century vergers to gather in six pence which might

Figure 11. Little Poets' Corner circa 1909. Copyright Dean and Chapter of Westminster.

else have been spent in the cathedral church of St. Paul. We know where William Shakespeare lies at Stratford-on-Avon. Why then should Westminster keep an eighteenth-century marble shape of him?[22]

These virtual burials, in other words, had always existed in tension with the "genuine" burials that initially made up the substance of Poets' Corner. The suspicion voiced by the letter writer was that, like the wax funeral effigies stored in the Abbey, the monuments were less in celebration of those whom they were

Figure 12. An interwar view of Poets' Corner that reveals shows how crowded the space had become. The Chaucer windows (above his tomb) would be destroyed in a bomb blast in 1940. Copyright Dean and Chapter of Westminster.

modeled after and more in the way of a tourist attraction that might enable the vergers to extort more money from the unwitting public.[23] There seemed, as Watson suggests, a new distrust of the cenotaph that as early as the nineteenth century led literary tourists to leave London and travel to Grasmere (Wordsworth) and Stratford (Shakespeare) in order to "emphasise a personal sentimental relation between the physical remains of the poet and literary pilgrim."[24] She further argues "by Victorian times there was much more pressure to collect the real thing than there had been in the eighteenth century" and thus this nineteenth-century emphasis on the real thing—the body— "undid the centrality of the Abbey as the site upon which the writers were commemorated."[25]

Yet, as we have seen, the tension between the physical presence (or absence) of the body and the commemorative monuments existed in discussions of the Corner as early as the seventeenth century. It was in the productive tension of presence and absence that the Corner maintained a kind of vitality in

the unfulfilled expectations of the audience of the Abbey. In fact, when these
empty sepulchers or memorials were constructed, they were thought of as a
substantial part of the South Transept.[26] Unlike the military pantheon that
was constructed in St. Paul's (after the erection of Nelson's tomb) and then
dismantled, the poetical monuments tended to stay in one place.[27] The reasons for this are various—St. Paul's was certainly a public space like the
Abbey, but it was also a city church rather than a royal peculiar like the Abbey.
Hence it was subject to the authority of the ecclesiastical hierarchy, which was
concerned about the potential distraction of idolatrous images and statuary.[28]
In addition, St. Paul's was a late arrival to the business of commemoration,
only being open to monuments in 1793, after the Abbey was already full.[29] In
other words, St. Paul's was an incomplete supplement to the Abbey, having
neither the history nor the variety of the Abbey. And one may also advance
the argument that what was most important was the linkage between the
function of the place and literary (as opposed to fleeting military) fame. To
be constantly moving monuments, or worse yet, removing them, is to call
into question the stability of poetic fame. There are, to be sure, a number of
instances in which the fame of the poet did not last, and thus we have reactions like those of Goldsmith's philosopher about Michael Drayton ("Drayton! I have never heard of him"). But the reputation of any poet, like the
reputation of Drayton, may well suffer its vicissitudes and yet be assured that
it will maintain its presence in the Corner. Given the seemingly organic or
naturalistic idea of Poets' Corner, it is strange that Stanley (who had argued
against the artificiality of a space like the Walhalla) engaged in a project very
much like the Walhalla in his attempt to create a "Little Poets' Corner." Both
spaces were consciously created to celebrate the "greats." Both had their origins in a nineteenth-century desire to map out a particular space as a celebration of the nation. And finally, both spaces were absent the bodies that
could lend to the space their materiality and thus make it more than an
empty memorial. In fact, though it is apparent why Ludwig chose the name
"Walhalla" for his temple of fame, the name is in many ways inappropriate
for a hall that is ultimately a national cenotaph. The term "Valhalla," of course,
originates with the Norse idea of the bodily rescue and transportation of the
war dead to the Hall of Odin. In some ways, then, the term might be applied
more aptly to the place of the fallen in the land conquered by the Anglo-
Saxons than to a hall in Bavaria.

It was, in fact, after Stanley's invocation of the Bavarian "Walhalla" that
the term "Valhalla" becomes inextricably intertwined with the history of the

Abbey. In 1893 William Morris pens a critique of the Abbey that locates its aesthetic failings in the probability that it had become a Valhalla: "We fear, therefore, that in following out this curious superstition of the last two centuries, that it is necessary that Westminster Abbey should serve the purpose of a 'National Valhalla,' the public have neglected all other uses to which this building might serve, except that of a place for the decent celebration of the services of the Church of England." Morris's main attack is on the "restoration" effort of such architects as Edward Blore, but the superstition that he refers to here is the desire to create what he calls "a kind of registration office for the names of men whom the present generation considers eminent in various capacities."[30] His attempt is to evacuate any sense of the "charm" of the place (except for its religious function) in order that it may remain what it once was, a thirteenth-century example of the stonecutter's art.

Though Morris had an especial dislike of the monumental function of the Abbey, even those architects and "forward thinkers" who felt no animus toward the idea of the monumental began to feel that the Abbey was being overcrowded with memorials. Hence a number of proposals came forward to construct a national "Campo Santo" or "Valhalla" that might enable the clearance of the monuments from the venerable fabric. As early as 1863 Gilbert Scott, the Surveyor of the Fabric of the Abbey, proposed that all the houses in Abingdon Street be cleared away and that an enormous double-aisled cloister be built to the southeast of the Chapter House at the cost of half a million pounds to accommodate all of the monuments. John Loughborough Pearson (who succeeded Scott as Surveyor of the Fabric of the Abbey) designed a monumental aisle to the north of the Nave for the same purpose, and in 1884 James Fergusson designed a plan for a "New South Transept" where Scott had originally had placed his "Campo Santo."[31] The most ambitious plan however was the Imperial Hall and Tower that would have dwarfed both the Abbey and the Victoria tower, proposed in 1904 (fig. 13). Such buildings certainly spoke to the imperial ambitions of the nineteenth century and in some cases would have provided what the *Guardian* recently called "a stirring Gothic home to British heroes," so it is fair to ask why such buildings were not built.[32] Anthony Hyland suggests that part of the problem was money, but one might well understand that such spaces are ultimately seen as a kind of afterthought—artificially constructed to resolve a problem of overcrowding rather than put together for the celebration of national heroism. If we return for a moment to Stanley's insight about the Abbey, the naturalization of the national Valhalla *as* the Abbey might well preclude the artificial construction of such a palace of heroes.

Figure 13. The Imperial Monumental Hall was only the latest vision of a hall of heroes by John Pollard Seddon (with Edward Beckitt Lamb). RIBA Library Drawings & Archives Collections.

This state of affairs is, of course, different from the Bavarian construction of a hall of heroes in the nineteenth century in at least two important respects. First it is clear that the new hall would be built not only to contain cenotaphs, but to house new burials as well. Second, even if the new English "National Valhalla" had been built, the Abbey would still exist as a kind of primary Valhalla—housing all of the bodies that might be considered founding corpses (e.g., Edward the Confessor and Geoffrey Chaucer). The New Hall would always be a displacement of the Abbey proper—something that belatedly became clear to Scott in his plans for a Campo Santo. Originally his plans did not provide for any connection between the proposed building and the Abbey. Later he added a "winding passageway around the Chapter House to the South Transept" in order to construct a connection between the founding space and the displaced (nearly five hundred feet away) Campo Santo.[33] The attempts by Scott, Fergusson, Pearson, and others indicate a kind of divided consciousness about the space. It clearly had to exist connected to or near the Abbey, yet there also seems to be some understanding that it would always be separate. With the exception of perhaps Fergusson's design, all of these projects extended well beyond the idea of Poets' Corner. Yet their goal (ultimately in every case frustrated) to construct a separate Campo Santo ran into the same kinds of problems that any secondary place of commemoration would—it was necessarily a pale imitation of the "original." In addition, the artificial nature of the space would have severely restricted any sense that its growth was somehow organic, hence "natural." Finally, while some of the proposed spaces had an option to include burials, the lack of the founding "sacred ashes" of the revered dead would severely limit the ability of the place to conjure up something that was often referred to as supernatural. Yet even as it becomes clear that the spatial power of the Abbey in general and Poets' Corner in particular relied on a kind of originary corporeal presence, the desire to supplement the space signals the beginnings of what might be called a national poetics of regret.

In Absentia: Women Writers and Poets' Corner

For late modern visitors to the Abbey, the most notable absence and cause for regret is the marked lack of women writers in the South Transept. Of the twenty women who are buried in the South Transept, almost half have some connection (wife or daughter) to men who were prebendaries or vicars at the Abbey. Most of the others are what might be called "private burials"— burials sponsored by husbands or fathers. Only Mary Eleanor Bowes (countess of Strathmore by her first marriage) could be characterized as a writer. Author of a play (*The Siege of Jerusalem*), which was well received, and *The Confessions of the Countess of Strathmore,* which was a sensation and served as the basis for William Thackeray's *Barry Lyndon,* she was best known for her indiscretions while married to John Lyon-Bowes (tenth earl of Strathmore and Kinghorne) and her subsequent marriage to Andrew Robinson Stoney, an Irish adventurer. In the process of trying to obtain her fortune, Stoney imprisoned her in her own house, apparently beat her, and carried her and her daughter off to Paris. When she finally escaped his custody and sought a divorce, he kidnapped her and threatened her with rape, but was finally caught and, after a lengthy and sensational trial, was imprisoned until his death. The countess lived a quiet life after this and was buried in the Abbey on 10 May 1800 in the magnificent wedding gown from her first marriage.

It is unlikely that the countess was buried in Poets' Corner because of her status as a writer. More probable is that her status and wealth led to her interment there.[34] If this is so, then it is interesting that her moral qualities did not bar her entrance into the Abbey. Since her burial was a private affair, not designated to memorialize her writing, it is possible that it would not be seen to sully the more transcendent world of poetry. If we compare her burial with the interment of Aphra Behn, a woman who was buried in Westminster Abbey (though not in Poets' Corner) on the strength of her writings, we see a kind of double standard at work. Behn was buried in the East Cloister outside the South Transept on 20 April 1689. Dean Stanley positively celebrates the fact that she did not reach Poets' Corner saying, "Aphara Behn [sic], the notorious novelist, happily has not reached beyond the East Cloister" (fig. 14).[35] Strathmore, in contrast, is treated as if she herself were not a writer but a kind of story from an era long past: "Another trace of the strange romances of the North of England is the grave of Mary Eleanor Bowes, Countess of Strathmore, who . . . was buried in the South Transept, in the last year of the past century, after adventures which ought to belong to the Middle Ages."[36] Stanley medievalizes Strathmore, denaturing her adventures as romance—a kind of quaint story that must be judged by the tenets of the fiction of a pre-Anglican past.

But if Stanley attempts to rationalize Strathmore's presence in the South Transept by medievalizing her, there were certainly differences between Behn and Strathmore that might better explain their very different treatments. Countess Strathmore was an aristocrat while Behn was the wife of a merchant. And while Strathmore's notorious private life was made public by gossip and rumor and her attempt to dissociate herself from her second husband, Behn herself ensured that her life was made public and embraced her identity as a courtesan. It is difficult to escape the notion, however, that it was Behn's status as a professional writer—especially a Restoration dramatist—that differentiated her from Strathmore. And lest we think that Stanley's attack on Behn was somehow unusual, we might turn to an eighteenth-century publication that seemingly makes a case against Behn while addressing the appropriateness of commemorating another poet in the Corner—John Milton.

In 1737 a statue of Milton had been placed to the right of Spenser's monument. Because of Milton's role in supporting Cromwell's Commonwealth, his entry into the company of the "spirits of the Bards" at the Abbey

Figure 14. Aphra Behn's stone in the East Cloister—recently recut. Copyright Dean and Chapter Westminster.

had understandably occasioned some discussion. A series of imaginative essays written a year later and attributed to Samuel Johnson (but actually written by the Scottish historian William Guthrie) in the *Gentleman's Magazine* addressed the controversy by transforming it into a dream vision. The author relates that, being locked in the Abbey accidentally one night, he fell asleep and dreamt that the shades of the poets gathered at night to deliberate about whether Milton should be admitted. In the midst of the proceedings, as the poets and writers took their places, the dreamer's guide (who has identified himself as "the genius of the place") drew his attention to one figure in particular:

> But observe that Lady dressed in the loose *Robe de Chambre* with her Neck and Breasts bare; how much fire is in her Eye! What a passionate Expression in her Motions! And how much Assurance in her Features! Observe what an indignant look she bestows on the President [Chaucer], who is telling her that *none of her Sex has any Right to a Seat there*. How she throws her Eyes about, to see if she can find out any one of the Assembly who inclines to take her Part.

No! not one stirs; they who are enclined in her favour are overawed, and the rest shake their Heads; and now she flings out of the Assembly. That extraordinary woman is *Afra Behn*; but her Character does not deserve so much notice, as to divert you from remarking the Member who now walks up to his seat.[37]

If Stanley sees Strathmore as someone who belongs to the Middle Ages, the dream vision characterizes Behn as one who is rejected by the patriarchal embodiment of the Middle Ages. Chaucer's historical priority seems to validate his rejection of the idea of the woman writer, but the reaction of some of the assembly also seems to suggest a lack of consensus about Chaucer's peremptory judgment. Yet before the dreamer can entertain any serious doubt about the rectitude of the President's decision, the Genius Loci moves to have him take notice of another member of the assembly—Matthew Prior about whom the dreamer tells us that he "could observe nothing in the one that was slovenly, or in the other that was becoming."[38] Guthrie is thus redirected back to the nature of poetry as being defined not by dangerous passion or fire or, even more worrying, the partial nudity of the female form, but by the well-tailored figure of Prior.

So too, the harshness of the rejection by "father Chaucer" of any "of her sex" being admitted into the sacred assembly is seemingly mitigated by the fact that it is the voluptuous form of Behn in her *robe de chambre* who casts her eyes to see if any will take *her* part. Behn becomes the figure of the woman writer par excellence. Guthrie here is working with an old connection between the opening of a woman's mouth and the opening of her legs. As Francesco Barbaro stated, "It is proper . . . that the speech of women never be made public; for the speech of a noble woman can be no less dangerous that the nakedness of her limbs."[39] Peter Stallybrass suggests that "the signs of the 'harlot'" are her linguistic "fullness and her frequenting of public space."[40] Behn here is cast as the harlot whose body figures forth the danger of women's words especially the danger of women's words in the public sphere of the stage. At the same time she is silenced, forced to leave by the patriarch of poets and found to be wanting when compared with the "easy" and "genteel" figure of Prior.

It is then, not only Behn, but the woman who writes publicly and professionally who is being rejected by the sacred assembly. Even those who might speak in her favor are apparently "overawed" by the figure of Chaucer who, as President, is able to issue a summary judgment about the fitness of women writers to sit with their male counterparts. What is at stake here is the extent to which Poets' Corner has become a "public" space. Materially, of course, the assembly must acknowledge her burial within the precincts of the Abbey (and it is important to acknowledge here that the assembly of poets includes others—such as William Congreve—who lie outside Poets' Corner but within the Abbey). But even while acknowledging her right to enter the proceedings, she is not only denied membership, but is even denied a seat while others who are not reckoned a member are allowed to sit.[41] Her entrance, in fact, is an excuse to forbid the public space of commemoration to any of her sex. Crucially, then, the material space of the Abbey becomes a ground of contestation rather than an absolute determination or reflection of the sublime poetical pantheon.

The ghostly drama of Aphra Behn reflects what, in a sense, is obvious— that Poets' Corner is an inadequate (because material) representation of an imaginative space. Yet far from hampering the emotional appeal of the Corner, this inadequacy generates, as in the case of Behn, an imaginative reaction. It might be the "disturbance" that Queen Emma felt at the lack of a monument to Coleridge or the satisfaction that Stanley felt at Aphra Behn's inability to get beyond the East Cloister. But in either case (and whatever we might think of their reasoning), what is telling is the extent to which the encounters with the Abbey space are in some sense produced by the place before the encounter takes place. The Corner actually materializes thinking about poetry, making a legible history of literature in stone, but it also gestures to something else, much harder to get at, an affective, reactive response that can be produced by a kind of ghostly absence as well as lithic presence.

The delicate balance between enabling and disabling absence, hallowed and literary space, plays itself out in a drama involving Stanley in the final year of his life when George Eliot died. Unlike a number of other women who would later receive monuments in the Corner, Eliot had explicitly expressed her wish to be buried there. In a letter to Dean Stanley some three days after her death, the naturalist John Tyndall wrote: "It was, I am told the expressed wish of George Eliot to be buried in Westminster Abbey, and it has been hinted to me that I ought to aid in furthering the realization of this wish. Well, I can only say, that if you consent to give her shelter, the verdict of the future will be that Dean Stanley has enshrined a woman whose achievements were without parallel in the previous history of womankind."[42] Though Stanley had opposed the commemoration of Aphra Behn some eleven years earlier, he was seemingly not averse to burying Eliot in Poets' Corner. When contacted by Herbert Spencer about the possibility, Stanley replied that he would need "strong representations" before making such a decision. It is possible that he was simply putting Spencer off, but his earlier relationship with George Henry Lewes, Eliot's lover, his letter to Benjamin Jowett, and the testimony of Huxley (see below) suggests that he was seriously considering allowing her burial.[43]

Yet if he was serious about burying Eliot in the Abbey, it very quickly became clear that there would be opposition both from those who remembered the scandal of her relationship with Lewes and even like-minded agnostic friends like T. H. Huxley. After receiving Spencer's telegram asking him to intervene with Stanley, Huxley (a friend of Stanley's) replied:

> I had just been talking to Morley, and agreeing with him that the proposal for a funeral in Westminster Abbey had a very questionable look to us, who desired nothing so much as that peace and honour should attend George Eliot to her grave. It can hardly be doubted that the proposal will be bitterly opposed, possibly . . . with the raking up of past histories, about which the opinion even of those who have least the desire or the right to be pharisaical is strongly divided and which had better be forgotten. With respect to putting pressure on the Dean of Westminster, I have to consider that he has some confidence in me, and before asking him to do something for which he is pretty sure to be violently assaulted, I have to ask myself whether I really think it a right thing for a man in his position to do. Now I cannot say I do. However much I lament the circumstance, Westminster Abbey is a Christian Church and not a Pantheon. . . . How am I to tell the Dean that he ought to read over the body of a person who did not repent of what the Church considers mortal sin, a service not one solitary proposition of which she would have accepted for truth while she was alive?[44]

Huxley's opposition to burial in the Abbey is in some ways surprising given his friendship with Eliot. But in other ways his opposition makes perfect sense. At one point in the letter he expresses surprise that Eliot would want to be buried in the Abbey, suggesting that "one cannot eat one's cake and have it too." And as a close friend of Stanley's, he could have respect for his beliefs even if he himself did not believe in them. Perhaps most telling, in terms of the space of Poets' Corner, is Huxley's assertion that the Abbey is a church and not a pantheon, or place in which the illustrious dead are buried. This, of

course, is too easy an opposition, for as we have seen, the church and the pantheon not only coexist, but in some sense define one another. If Huxley did not
appreciate this, then Stanley did. For at the dean's death, Huxley revealed the
following to a friend: "The last time I had a long talk with him was about the
proposal to bury Eliot in the Abbey, and a curious revelation of the extraordinary catholicity and undaunted courage of the man it was. He would have
done it had it been pressed upon him by a strong representation."[45] As suggested in Huxley's second letter, Stanley understood all too well that there
was a kind of clash between the greatness of the artist and the moral qualities
to which the artist might be held. There was, in this case, no obvious decision
precisely because the space had produced its own logic and the dean was the
guardian of place's special qualities.

Yet if Byron and Eliot were denied burial in Poets' Corner, regret ultimately led to the erection of commemorative monuments long after their
deaths (Byron in 1969 and Eliot in 1980). So too, the retroactive commemorations of women in the South Transept in the twentieth and twenty-first centuries suggest attempts to make good an absence that, at the very least, seemed
inadequate. A tablet was given by the Brontë society in 1939 that commemorated Charlotte, Emily, and Anne Brontë many decades after their deaths. Jane
Austen received a mural stone in 1967.[46] Frances Burney was commemorated
in 2002 and Elizabeth Gaskell in 2010 (both in glass window panels). As suggested above, there was undoubtedly more than a little misogynistic hypocrisy involved in historical decisions about who could be buried in the South
Transept, and these late additions actually seem to confirm rather than re-
dress the suspicion that the Corner embodies an antiquated masculine or moral
fantasy about what a canon of literature "should" look like. Yet if the belatedness of the Abbey's response threatens to evacuate the affective power of the
Corner, the monumentalization of regret reenacts the peculiarly paradoxical
nature of the space. Just as the Corner's monuments memorialize poets by calling attention to the extent that they are inadequate memorials, so the belated
memorialization of the deserving actually reveals the extent to which this memorialization is *in time*. The beautiful disorder of Poets' Corner is a kind of
living ruin, at once a lithic record of how political, moral, and gendered concerns shaped a nation's approach to aesthetics and a self-conscious response
to its own ruined self.

CHAPTER 5

Poetic Exhumation and the Anxiety of Absence

There is still another sentiment, honourable in itself and not inconsistent with those which I have specified, though still more conditional upon the sufficiency of the reasons conducing to the act: namely, the desire, by exhumation, to set at rest a reasonable or important issue respecting the person of the deceased while he was yet a living man. Accordingly it is held justifiable to exhume a body recently buried, in order to discover the cause of death, or to settle a question of disputed identity: nor is it usually held unjustifiable to exhume a body long since deceased, in order to find such evidences as time may not have wholly destroyed, of his personal appearance, including the size and shape of his head, and the special characteristics of his living face.

—C. M. Ingleby, *Shakespeare's Bones*

For the most part this book has been concerned with literary inhumations— making the case that in order to understand how literature was thought of, and what its implications were for larger society, we have to excavate Poets' Corner—metaphorically exhume the poetic bodies buried beneath the Abbey's masonry. But what of those bodies that are literally exhumed? If the location of the poet's corpse is symbolically important, the dislocation of the poetical body might be considered crucial to any understanding of the larger "place" of poetry. There have been very few exhumations in the Abbey, and thus their importance is magnified. Chaucer was dug up, as we have seen, in

order to be buried again, and this exhumation and reburial signaled an attempt
to reinstitutionalize Catholicism within the Abbey. The dramatist and historian Thomas May was exhumed and thrown into a common pit near St. Margaret's because of his ties to Cromwell. In each of these cases, the exhumation
came at a time of national transformation. The exhumations marked this fact
and had consequences for the refiguring of the space in the South Transept,
which in turn had an important effect on the national imaginary.

The exhumation of "Spenser" that I focus on in this chapter occurs at a
similar moment of transformation. Unlike the earlier exhumations, the motivating factor was not religion (though religion plays its part). Rather the exhumation reflected ongoing concerns about class and its role in the formation
and continuation of the nation. Perhaps unsurprisingly, the great absent presence of Poets' Corner, William Shakespeare, haunts the disinterment—setting
the terms for the paradoxical logic that ultimately leads to the final burial in
Poets' Corner in the latter part of the twentieth century.

*   *   *

Exhumations of famous men had become something of a rage in the eighteenth and early nineteenth centuries. As Ingleby points out in his manifesto
on Shakespeare's bones, Schiller, Raphael, Milton, Swedenborg, and Burns
were all supposedly disinterred. The reasons for the exhumations varied, but
as Ingleby suggests, the rationales for the various exhumations tended to be
epistemological in nature. Even when, in the case of Schiller, the disinterment
was carried out in order to place him in a more exalted resting place, the process by which Schiller's bones were identified offer a fascinating example of
forensic detective work. In the case of Ingleby, however, his goal was not to
translate the bones of Shakespeare, nor to question the identity of the poet,
but to exhume the skull in order to establish the authenticity of various representations of Shakespeare's visage. It remains a bit unclear what Ingleby wished
to learn by discovering what Shakespeare looked like. And there were those
who felt that such idle curiosity demonstrated a kind of disrespect for what
they called humanity. Capel Lofft, for instance, averred:

> It were to be wished that neither superstition, affectation, idle
> curiosity, or avarice, were so frequently invading the silence of
> the grave. Far from dishonouring the illustrious dead, it is rather
> outraging the common condition of humanity, and last melancholy

state in which our present existence terminates. Dust and ashes
have no intelligence to give, whether beauty, genius or virtue,
informed the animated clay. A tooth of Homer or Milton will not be
distinguished from one of a common mortal; nor a bone of Alexander
acquaint us with more of his character than one of Bucephalus [his
horse]. Though the dead be unconcerned, the living are neither
benefited nor improved: decency is violated, and a kind of instinctive
sympathy infringed, which, though it ought not to overpower
reason, ought not without it, and to no purpose, to be superseded.[1]

Lofft's two-pronged critique of exhumation walks a thin line between superstition and reason. Reason, he claims, tells us that the body is nothing but
"dust and ashes." Hence, disinterring the body in order to measure it (as
Ingleby wishes) or gain some intelligence about the person's genius or virtue
is impossible. Without animation, the body is merely clay. Yet, if this is so,
then there could be no basis for preventing the disinterring of the body, for it
would be nothing more than exhuming the earth in which the body is buried. In order to overcome this problem, Lofft relies on abstract virtues such as
"decency" or "instinctive sympathy" to prevent the invasion of the grave. In
other words, even as he critiques the superstition that leads to the taking of
relics, he seems to acknowledge that it is the "common condition of humanity" to believe that honor should be granted to the dead.

Ingleby, of course, takes issue with Lofft's notion that the body has nothing to tell us, claiming, "I cannot allow that neither dust and ashes, bones, nor
teeth, have any intelligence to give us; nor yet that by the reverential scrutiny of
those relics the living be neither benefited nor improved."[2] He makes no claims
about the sanctity of the body, but his belief that one can read something of the
person in the remains, and his references to those portions of the body that remain as relics suggest that the body, though apparently unanimated, remains a
potent signifier of the person it was. Ingleby is less than clear in telling us what
it is that the body can reveal to us, but a seemingly casual reference to Ezekiel
may give a clue to his beliefs about the dry bones of great men.

In taking issue with Lofft, Ingleby claims that in the hunt for the remains
of Schiller, the skull "spoke" and "claimed to be that of Schiller."[3] His invocation of Ezekiel 37 here is metaphorical and rhetorical in that its central question, "Can these bones live?" is not only answered in the affirmative in the
Old Testament, but, in Ingleby's invocation, refigures questions of literal animation into figural reanimation in the nineteenth century. The skull "speaks"

only insofar as a number of experts are able to divine that the skull must have been Schiller's by close observation (particularly, as we discover, because of its beautiful teeth). The dead body, then, lives insofar as meaning about the person it was can be derived from it. Ingleby does not explicitly endorse the physiognomical or phrenological pseudosciences that were so prevalent in the nineteenth century, but his belief that the visage of the dead can relate something of the character of the living is part of a more general nineteenth-century belief system. In E. T. Craig's *Shakespeare's Portraits Phrenologically Considered*, for instance, Craig claims that the Droeshout portrait reveals "ample endowments of the higher sentiments. The imaginative and imitative faculties are represented as very large," along with "ideality, wonder, wit, imitation, benevolence, and veneration."[4] Like Lofft's criticism of exhumation, then, Ingleby's justification walks the line between a kind of rationality that condemns superstition and an almost occult belief in the ability of the body to render forth the invisible.

All of this interest in the body as legible pallet of interior invisible virtues materialized genius in ways that were problematic. Genius in its original "incarnation" was the result of divine inspiration. In his *Conjectures on Original Composition* (1759), Edward Young illustrates the meaning of genius by opposing it to mere learning: "Learning we thank, Genius we revere; That gives us pleasure, This gives us rapture; That informs, This inspires; and is itself inspired; for genius is from heaven, learning from man."[5] Learning in other words is fine in its place, but genius is to be reverenced and apparently has the power to "rapture" us to "heaven." To materialize genius is to bring it to earth. Once on earth, genius is often spoken of as universal, yet it is localized in a body. As Coleridge would later claim, genius "must embody in order to reveal itself."[6] Whether it is a body of work, or "a living body," we must be able to read the signs of genius.[7] In order to read genius, we must be able to quantify it. And, in fact, a year before Young's work was published, a "Poetical Scale" was published in both the *Literary Magazine* and the *London Chronicle* that rated poets on a twenty-point scale of genius. Perhaps unsurprisingly, Shakespeare received the highest score—nineteen out of twenty.[8] This quantification, of course, only revealed what was thought but offered no basis aside from discernment and taste on which to base such a ranking. The measurement of the cranium, on the other hand, offered a material means by which to measure not only beauty, goodness, and intelligence but ultimately genius.[9] It was, as Barbara Stafford argues, "the material manifestation of the world beyond the senses."[10]

Ultimately, then, we might see this interest in exhumation as an attempt to explain inspiration. Art had been explained as a kind of communion with

the divine, but as the divine receded (or at least seemed to recede) in the nineteenth century, there was not only a renewed interest in spiritualism, but in the
idea that extraordinary qualities must be sunk within the body and could be
discovered there if only we had the codes to read the signs aright. The "place"
of poetry was, then, identified as existing within the body and, as this occurred, the poet became not only representative of genius, but became genius itself. As Jonathan Bate suggests of Shakespeare (the great exemplar of
genius), "Through the very process of shaping a new sense for the word 'genius,' Shakespeare forced it back to its oldest sense, that of a tutelary deity.
Once claimed as the national poet, he was identified as the 'Genius of our
Isle.' . . . [He] became the guarantor of the new 'imagined community' of the
nation state."[11]

We might characterize the exhumations that I discuss in this chapter as
manifestations of a desire to discover the origins of originality and with them
the occulted origins of the nation state. What the genius of poetry offered,
then, was not merely the historical origin of a particular country or race, but
a transcendent origin that was paradoxically materialized in the body of the
poet. This process of getting back to the body and quite literally digging up
the poetical history was an attempt to address the inadequacies of explanation that characterizes art. In the century where (as Théophile Gautier put it),
"Le ciel a perdu sa puissance. / Le Christ est mort, le siècle a pour Dieu, la
science," the great hope was that science could uncover the origins of art and,
by extension, rationalize that which defined national identity.[12]

In the Abbey's history, one of the clearest examples of this cultural connection of the body with genius was in the exhumation of "Geoffrey Chaucer" in 1889. Responding to an article by Havelock Ellis entitled "Genius and
Stature," Henry Troutbeck, a medical doctor and the son of the precentor and
minor canon of Westminster, wrote in to the *Nineteenth Century* to report:

> I notice that the name of Chaucer does not occur in the list of
> "men of genius" given in Mr. Ellis's interesting article in the
> current number of *The Nineteenth Century*, and indeed, so far as
> I can ascertain, there is no record of his stature extant. Perhaps,
> Mr. Ellis might be interested to know that I had the privilege of
> examining Chaucer's bones when they were exposed in the digging
> of Browning's grave some years back. From measurements of the
> principle long bones remaining intact, I calculated that his height
> must have been about 5 feet 6 inches.[13]

As I have argued elsewhere, Troutbeck's letter seems an attempt to place "Chaucer" on the scale of what Ellis called the "anthropometry of genius."[14] In Ellis's system, great men seemed either to be short (below 5' 4") or tall (above 5' 9"). It is, as Ellis claimed "mediocrity alone that genius seems to abhor."[15] Troutbeck's suggestion that Chaucer was absolutely average in height, of course, problematizes Ellis's "scale," but it also reinforces the idea that the symptoms of the visible body might have something to say about the internal qualities of genius. Troutbeck makes good the absence of Chaucer within the English tradition of genius and naturalizes his genius as profoundly English. This genial Chaucer, in other words, at once challenges Ellis's conclusions about abnormality and genius and remains squarely within a tradition that posits the connection of the bodily attributes with mental or spiritual qualities—a tradition embodied, for instance, in the work of the influential Italian criminologist Cesare Lombroso who only six years earlier asserted a definitive link between genius and pathology in *The Man of Genius.*[16]

This larger concern with locating the "presence" of genius in the body results from an anxiety about the nature, status, and location of poetic inspiration. By extension the idea that genius resides in the body seems to confirm the importance of the poetical graveyard that is the South Transept of Westminster Abbey. But some forty years after the exhumation of Chaucer another exhumation occurs that seems to reorient thinking about the Corner and makes present a central absence that had given shape to the idea of Poets' Corner. That this exhumation involved the second poetical body to be buried in Poets' Corner and the identity of England's greatest literary figure suggests that Poets' Corner was seen not only as graveyard but, like the body itself, a place within which secrets were buried. In this case, the hidden location of Shakespeare's genius is revealed not in his body, which is absent from the Corner, but in part of his corpus that was buried with the poetical corpse of one of his contemporaries. For those who advocated for the exhumation, English culture and by extension national identity was animated by the potential resolution to a great literary mystery—who was Shakespeare?

Exhuming Spenser

On the evening of 2 November 1938, there was, as the *Evening Standard* put it, "Secret Digging at Poets' Tomb" (fig. 15).[17] This digging, as it turned out, was an attempt to exhume the English poet Edmund Spenser, buried since 1599.

The circumstances surrounding this purported exhumation are, to say the least, remarkable—for the exhumation was undertaken at the behest of the Bacon Society, whose stated aim was to prove that the author of Shakespeare's works was Francis Bacon. One might well wonder why and how a fringe intellectual movement had convinced the dean and chapter of Westminster Abbey to unearth corpses from beneath the transept masonry. After all, as the dean of Westminster (W. F. Norris) wrote to the Bacon Society when he was first asked about opening the grave in 1937: "To open a tomb is [a] very serious matter indeed and must be amply justified. I see, of course, that what you desire would be interesting to a certain number of people: but I am afraid that is not an adequate ground. I could not seriously *consider* the project unless it were urged upon me by the leading Literary men of the day as a matter of first class importance—and even then there are others whose advice I should seek."[18] What is so fascinating about Norris's response is that exhumation almost exactly recapitulates the process by which (in the nineteenth and twentieth centuries) inhumation took place in the Abbey. At the death of a well-known figure, leading literary figures would often urge the burial, or would be consulted about the worthiness and suitability of the candidate. As this was to be an exhumation, however, there was no motivating factor—no desire to memorialize or mourn. What there was, however, was a well-thought-out campaign by the Baconians that, unlike burial (which had to be relatively quick), could be conducted over a long period of time.

The Bacon Society was interested in the possibility that there was an elegy written by Shakespeare in Spenser's grave. This belief seems to have proceeded from popular press interest in a statement by William Camden in the early part of the seventeenth century that Spenser "was interred at Westminster, near to Chaucer, at the charge of the earl of Essex, his hearse being attended by poets, and mournful elegies, with the pens that wrote them, were thrown into the grave."[19] The logic was that since Shakespeare was a well-known poet at the time, and since he had connections to Essex (who was responsible for the funeral), he must have been present to throw his elegy into the grave.[20] This popular interest in a seventeenth-century annalist might well be surprising had not the Bacon Society apparently seeded public interest by planting a letter in the *Daily News*.[21] In fact, in a telling letter to Dean Norris, Henry Seymour (a member of the Society) intimates that it is public interest that has led him to ask that the tomb be opened saying that if Shakespeare's elegy was recovered, it "would surely become a precious treasure of our National

Evening Standard

To-morrow's Weather—
Unsettled.
See PAGE THREE.

Lighting-up Time
To-night 5.1 p.m.

No. 35,623   LONDON, WEDNESDAY, NOVEMBER 2, 1938   ONE PENNY

Premier Reveals Munich Pledge by Dictators

NO TERRITORIAL AIMS IN SPAIN

From Our Parliamentary Representatives

HOUSE OF COMMONS, Wednesday.

WHILE MR. CHAMBERLAIN WAS AT MUNICH, BOTH HERR HITLER AND SIGNOR MUSSOLINI "ASSURED HIM MOST DEFINITELY" THAT THEY HAD NO TERRITORIAL AMBITIONS IN SPAIN.

The Prime Minister made this disclosure in the Commons to-night in moving the House's approval of the Government's intention to bring the Anglo-Italian pact into force.

He said, too, that during the Munich conversations Signor Mussolini volunteered the information that he intended to withdraw 10,000 men, about half the Italian infantry forces in Spain. Since then these men had been withdrawn.

STAG DASHES ALONG RAILWAY

A FULLY grown stag dodging trains and shunting engines, trotted more than a mile along the Great Western Railway line at Reading to-day and slid down a steep embankment to the signal works yards near the centre of the town.

Workmen drove it into a stare shed, where it stood at bay. The animal charged one man, leapt over him and tore a hole in his jacket with its antlers.

A G.W.R. official told the Evening Standard: "We shall keep the stag here till arrangements are made for its removal."

The police stated that they would like to transfer it to the town pound, but were afraid it might run amuck in the streets. Actually, under the regulations, the stag should be placed in the railway lost property office.

British Troops Kill Five Arabs

JERUSALEM, Wednesday.

British troops who to-day began a search of the village of Mazraa Sharkiya, north of Ramallah, encountered a gang of Arabs, of whom five were killed and two wounded.

A cordon was thrown round the village at dawn by men of the West Yorkshire Regiment. The searching is continuing.
(Reuter messages).

Socialists Gain in London, Lose Lead in Six Provincial Towns

SOCIALISTS have gained in London and the Home Counties, but lost further afield, in yesterday's municipal elections in England and Wales.

Figures of the parties' losses and gains for London and the Home Counties are:

	Gains.	Losses.
Socialists	40	25
Conservatives and Ratepayers	24	33
Independent	12	18

The Socialists suffered severe set-backs in the provinces. They lost control of six boroughs—Burnley, Bristol, Leicester, Sunderland, Hull and Wakefield.

They suffered one of the biggest reverses at Chingford, where they lost five seats—all to the Ratepayers' Association candidates.

In the new borough of Erith, Socialists gained control in the district for the first time for 16 years. They gained eight seats where there was no change.

At Richmond (Surrey) the Mayor-elect, Councillor Val Wood (Ind.) was defeated by Mr B. W. Brickett (Ratepayers), by 583 votes to 504.

There were two recounts in the Lawrie Park ward at Beckenham.

The final state of the parties in 1332 municipal boroughs of England and Wales was:

	Gains.	Losses.
Conservatives	57	37
Liberals	14	16
Socialists	62	79
Independents	40	41

Results—PAGE TWENTY-THREE.

Bail Refused To Corrigan

The chief metropolitan magistrate, Sir Rollo Graham Campbell, this afternoon heard at Bow-street a renewed application for bail for Denals Michael Corrigan aged 46, of Park-lane, W. The application was refused.

Secret Digging At Poet's Tomb

By an Evening Standard Reporter

BENEATH a cloak of the darkest secrecy investigations at the site of Spenser's tomb in Westminster Abbey are being continued to-day.

Neither the Dean (Bishop de Labilliere) nor any of the officials have any statement to make about what stage has now been reached in the scheme to open the tomb, in an attempt to settle the Shakespeare-Bacon controversy; but there is intense activity in Poet's Corner.

Behind a double screen of canvas, work men are hammering away. Spades and picks have been carried behind the canvas and the chink of steel upon stone can be heard, and, now and again, grinding noises indicating the removal of stone slabs.

SWORN TO SECRECY

So careful are the arrangements to prevent the public catching even a glimpse of the operations behind the screen that, whenever a workman, coming or going, lifts the canvas all that can be seen is a second canvas effectively blocking the view.

All the workmen have been sworn to secrecy

The Dean spent an hour watching the operations. When he emerged he said: "I am sorry, but it is impossible to make any statement."

Reports that the grave had already been opened were current early to-day after lights had been seen in the Abbey during the night, while all the doors were locked and a policeman was on duty outside.

These, however, were denied

A search is to be made for a poem signed by Shakespeare which may be in Spenser's tomb. If one is found the manuscript will be compared with the known specimens of Bacon's writings.

DEATH OF AUSTRIA
Page Sixteen

"We have," he went on, "received from Signor Mussolini definite assurances first that the remaining Italian forces of all categories will be withdrawn when the non-intervention plan comes into operation; secondly, that no further Italian troops will be sent to Spain; thirdly, that the Italian Government have never for a moment entertained the idea of sending compensatory air forces to Spain in lieu of infantry forces now withdrawn.

"My mind is clear that the Spanish question is no longer a menace to the peace of Europe. Consequently there is no valid reason why we should not now take the step which obviously would contribute to the general appeasement.

Australia's Advice

"If any justification were required for the policy of the Government in closing our differences with Italy, it surely can be found in the action of Signor Mussolini when, at my request, he used his influence with Herr Hitler in order to make time for discussion which led up to the Munich agreement."

Mr. Chamberlain read a message from the Prime Minister of Australia, who said: "The Commonwealth Government are convinced that the Anglo-Italian agreement...
(Continued on PAGE FIVE)

CROOKED FINGER CLUE TO RIDDLE OF THE SANDS

By an Evening Standard Reporter

THE most significant clue so far discovered in the mystery of the woman's arm found on the beach at Perranporth, Cornwall, became known to-day.

It was disclosed that one of the fingers of the hand is crooked. It was not the action of sea or rocks that caused the deformity. Whoever the woman was, she must have been walking about for several years with a noticeably crooked finger.

The possibility that the arm was not buried on the beach, but was washed in from the sea during the heavy storm which raged just before it was found, is still being considered. Chief-Inspector Hatherill, of Scotland Yard, has visited coastguards along the rocky coast to learn from the men who have spent their lives watching the sea how the complicated tides run.

AUSTRALIAN WOMAN

It has not been forgotten that one missing woman is Miss Ethel May Idiens, an Australian, who was returning from a visit to her brother at South Cerney, near Cirencester. She was travelling home by way of Canada in the C.P.R. liner Empress of Britain. She disappeared and her body was never recovered.

New information, which may lead to renewed digging on the beach, has been given to the police by Mrs. Beryl Lee Booker, a breeder of great danes.

Inspector Hatherill to-day took a long statement from her.

Afterwards, at her house on the outskirts of Perranporth, she told me:

"One day I was taking out a bitch and her 11-month-old puppy. We crossed the sand-dunes and I noticed the dogs digging in the sand at their foot.

"I called them, and the puppy, came up carrying a large piece of flesh weighing, I should say, about two and a half pounds.

"I knew nothing about the arm then—it had been kept secret, and I had not heard the rumours in the village—so I took the flesh away from the puppy and buried it in the sand below high-water mark."

Asylum Murder

POLICE investigating the murder of Arthur Izzard, the 34-year-old patient of Chartham, Kent, Mental Hospital, who was found dying in a lane from head injuries on October 22, to-day traced the writer of an anonymous letter which provided them with a valuable clue.

By conducting a house-to-house inquiry in Chartham they were able to establish the writer's identity.

Superintendent J. A. Stuchfield and Detective-inspector J. F. Sharp, who are in charge of the investigations, are confident that they are near the end of their quest.

Figure 15. The exhumation of "Spenser" was front page news in 1938 competing with the troubling news from Europe. Copyright British Library.

literature."[22] This recourse to the language of national patrimony is, of course, calculated to appeal to the literary patriotism of the dean. Indeed, one might see that it would be difficult for the dean to resist the exhumation if there were sufficient support for it.

But the distance between the Society's appeal to the dean and what the Bacon Society hoped for became articulated in an essay in *The Era* which appeared some eighteen days after the new dean, Dr. Paul Fulcrand Delacour de Labilliere, had agreed to open the tomb (Norris had died in 1937). Though the Baconians dissociated themselves from prematurely releasing the information, the article entitled "Shakespeare Poem Discovery?" neatly summarized the hopes of the Bacon Society:

> A new signed poem by Shakespeare and a final answer to the
> Shakespeare-Bacon controversy are expected to be discovered when
> Edmund Spenser's tomb in Westminster Abbey is opened
> shortly . . . As one of the foremost poets of his time Shakespeare
> was almost certainly present at the funeral, so that a signed
> poem in his own handwriting may be among those disclosed
> when the tomb is opened. Even if the manuscript had rotted
> with time the scraps of writing would be of the greatest importance
> to Shakespearian scholars in deciding the question of the claim to
> Shakespeare's authorship of the writings.[23]

One might see in the disjunction between the Bacon Society's private hopes and the public appeal to the dean, an attempt to trick the authorities into opening the tomb. But the aims of the Bacon Society (which had existed for over fifty years), "to encourage the study of the works of Francis Bacon . . . [and] . . . to encourage the general study of the evidence in favour of Francis Bacon's authorship of the plays commonly ascribed to Shakespeare," were far from secret. There is, in other words, every reason to believe that the dean understood all too well what the Bacon Society was after.[24] So why did the dean agree to the exhumation? Though it was unlikely that the dean was a secret Baconian, the possibility of discovering a Shakespearean manuscript must have been intriguing. But this remote possibility seems unlikely to have been the determining factor in allowing the exhumation. More likely was the fact that the previous dean (Dean Norris) had already laid down the ground rules for the opening of the tomb (that it be urged by "leading Literary men of the day"). And, in fact, the Bacon Society seems to have garnered the support of a number of men and one woman. As R. L. Eagle (the prime mover of the project) put it:

> In April 1927 [*sic*], the "Daily News" followed up a letter which
> I wrote to the editor on this subject, by approaching the Dean (the
> Very Rev. W. S. Norris) who replied, "it would depend entirely on
> how the proposal was presented. We might consider it if we were
> approached by a committee of well-known literary men." Interviews
> with some distinguished Shakespeareans resulted with the following
> in favour:
> Sir Johnston Forbes-Robertson. Mr. John Buchan, Mr. Robert Lynd,
> Miss Sybil Thorndike, Mr. A. E. W. Mason, Mr. Alfred Noyes,
> Mr. Baliol Holloway.[25]

Though three of these "distinguished Shakespeareans" were well-known Shakespearean actors (Miss [later Dame] Sybil Thorndike, Mr. Baliol Holloway, and Sir Johnston Forbes-Robertson), the other four had very little to do with Shakespeare. Mason and Buchan were, among other things, well-known novelists. Lynd was a journalist, and Noyes was a popular poet who held the chair of modern English literature at Princeton for a time. What all seven shared, however, was a connection with the public. And it is this connection with the public that seems to problematize the entire rationale for the exhumation.

For, if it was the idea that Shakespeare might be Bacon that appealed to the Baconians, the English people, and even the American public (reports of the exhumation and controversy were disseminated on Paramount newsreels and ABC radio), the reason for this appeal seemed uncongenial to what might be called a popular reception of "Shakespeare." Francis Bacon (eventually Lord Bacon) was a well-known essayist and also Lord Chancellor under James I— hence a member of the cultural elite. Shakespeare, on the other hand, was popularly perceived (erroneously) as a relative unknown who came from an undistinguished family. He was, therefore, outside of what one Baconian called "a small group of highly cultured men of letters." The idea that the author of Shakespeare's plays might be a member of the "cultural elite" rather than a man of the people, then, played into conservative class fantasies about the conditions that were necessary for the production of great works of art—conditions far removed from the general public and especially from the Baconians who requested the exhumation in the first place.

What is so compelling about the rationale for the exhumation, then, is that a group of nonprofessional "scholars" (led by the former advertising director for the *Daily Mail*) convinced the dean and chapter to open the tomb. The desire to have the "populist" Shakespeare be the "elite" Bacon can be seen as the fulfillment of conservative ideal of what Stefan Collini has called the Whig interpretation of literary history—the belief that English literature was a "crucial vehicle for establishing and negotiating the relevant sense of national identity."[26] The Baconians were interested in promoting this conservative and culturally elitist idea of England's greatest poet because they saw themselves as conservators of a past that was increasingly under attack by the advocates of literary Modernism.[27]

In many ways the Baconians' ideas were an expression of Ruskin's and Morris's social aesthetic (which located in art a "medieval" ability to establish communal hence organic order). Indeed, even in the 1930s this belief in the power of art to organize society continued. W. R. Lethaby (Westminster's surveyor of the fabric and a disciple of Ruskin and Morris) asserted that, within art, existed an order that should be reflected in civilization.[28] Frank Pick, the chief executive of the London Underground, argued that art might replace the lost religious bonds that purportedly held society together: "I think art might be converted and become a religion of society. It is a social bond and that is what religion means."[29] The rationale for the exhumation, then, finds its origin both in nationalistic ideas about the golden past of the English Renaissance and in fantasies about the well-ordered medieval past. As Sir John Manners characterized it, "Each knew his place—king, peasant, peer or priest—/The greatest owned connexion with least,/ From rank to rank the generous feeling ran, /And linked society as man to man."[30]

Yet if the Baconians were ultimately advancing a conservative cultural agenda, they did so using the very modern tools of twentieth-century advertising. Indeed, the members of the cultural elite were consistently outflanked at every turn by the Baconians who managed to ascribe the "publicity" that they were most probably disseminating to the dean's secretary:

> My attention has been called to the enclosed cutting from the Era of
> August 18th. and on enquiries being made it was ascertained that
> the signature M.R. represented one of the staff of the Era—Miss
> Rowlands, who would not give the source of her information, but
> said that she had telephoned the secretary of the Dean. The Society
> is very concerned about the matter because a promise was given to

the Dean that no communication was to be made to the Press
without his consent. Would you be so good as to assure the Dean
that this promise has been carried out to the letter by those
concerned, i.e. Mr. B.G. Theobald, R.L. Eagle, and the writer.
There will, no doubt be enquiries from other newspapers, and
I would suggest that no information should be given either
confirming or denying the story.[31]

Smith's denials notwithstanding, there is every reason to believe someone of
the Baconians or someone connected with them was informing the newspapers. Smith had actually worked for the *Daily Mail*. As we saw above, the entire project had been set in motion by R. L. Eagle's anonymous letter to the
Daily News. In addition, Douglas Hamer (a Spenserian who was invited to
the exhumation) claimed to have information that the newspaper accounts
"were all built up from material supplied by Mr. Valentine Smith, and were
sensational in the extreme."[32] In fact, what this narrative makes clear is that the
Baconians understood that even as they took the position that Shakespeare
was an aristocrat, they could use the power of mass culture, exemplified in
the popular press, in order to get the dean to accede to their request. In addition, Smith's insinuation—that it was the secretary who had let the cat out of
the bag and that the Abbey should keep mum about the story—undoubtedly
irked the Abbey authorities who were, in a sense, under a state of siege by the
newspapers.

In his unpublished recollections, Lawrence Tanner takes time to recall
the lengths to which the press attempted to get this story:

We have been subjected to an appalling amount of publicity over
this opening and I believe that the Press have had people (127)
watching the Abbey for the last week. Certain it is that just after
work started tonight Bishop thought that he would put a notice on
the Poets' Corner Door (just by the grave) warning the Vergers not
to open it tomorrow. When he went to put it up he found a man
(whom he had noticed earlier in the day in the Abbey) lying
between the two doors. At first he thought he was dead as he gave
no sign of movement however much we shook him. So they carried
him out and put him on a chair where he still gave no sign of life.
However they thought he might be in a fit and one of the workmen
smacked his face industriously and indeed so hostily [*sic*] that

Bishop had to tell him to desist. After a glass of water he revived a
bit and told a rambling story of having found the door locked and
then having fainted. Eventually after taking his name (King?)
let him go. He could not have seen anything from where he was
lying but it remains to be seen if it will all be out in the papers
tomorrow. If he got his "scoop" it will have been at a great deal of
personal discomfort to himself! The papers are quite capable of
this.[33]

In his letter to F. C. Wellstood (secretary to the Shakespeare Birthplace Trust),
Sir Charles Peers complained that "the whole matter, I think I should say, has
taken a rather undesirable turn owing to the unfortunate publicity given to
it in the newspapers."[34] And Hamer recalls that other ruses were used to get
the story of the exhumation: "My observations of the behaviour of journalists in the abbey—including two bedizened young women who tried to get
into conversation with some of us entering the opening in the tarpaulins—
determined me never to have any dealings with journalists. I think they are
best kept out, and so any who have any connection with the press. Their
loyalties are to the press not to their word of honour, spoken or written. The
dean had obtained from the Bacon Society an undertaking that no communication would be made to the press."[35] Tanner's story about the uncon-
scious man and the undisguised delight that he takes in the rough treatment
of him by one of the workmen indicates a not merely latent hostility to the
idea of publicity. And the Spenserian Hamer's peculiar complaint about "bedizened young women" suggests that he sees these journalists as twentieth-
century versions of Spenser's Duessa—temptresses whose sole purpose is to
mislead. For these men, the newspapers should operate as nothing more than
propagators of official information. They acknowledged that public interest
in the exhumation was high, but felt little inclination to satisfy this public
interest.

The exhumation of "Spenser" demonstrated, if anything that the medieval modernist idea of a unified society was a kind of mirage. One of the
prominent members of the cultural elite at the exhumation, Hamer, who
was also lecturer in English at University of Sheffield, not only dismissed
the possibility that the grave was Spenser's, but, in his unpublished "An Account of an Opening of a Grave," was completely dismissive of what he clearly
considered meddling amateurs. In recommending against continuing the
search, he says,

They were ignorant men of little education and much credulity. The leader, Mr. Valentine Smith, who was, I think, the Secretary of the society, and certainly the dominating personality among the three of them, was or had been Advertising Manager for *The Daily Mail* for thirty years. This was itself no proof of intellectual capacity, or evidence of integrity, and the conversation of these three men at the graveside only indicated the unintellectual basis of the Baconian Theory. They just hadn't any inkling of the meaning of evidence or of straight thinking: anything and everything could be twisted to support their theories. The only thing they did not do was to hint that we others had abstracted the pens and poems on vellum from the grave overnight in order to destroy their case. Every other insinuation, however, was made.[36]

Hamer's characterization of the Baconians as "ignorant men of little education" and his suggestion that an "advertising manager" could hardly be expected to engage in "straight thinking" reflects what Collini characterizes as "a profound cultural pessimism . . . [among] many many members of the educated class" and "anxiety about the techniques employed in advertising, the potential power of new media like film and radio, and a wider unease at the cultural consequences of greater social equality."[37] The Baconians, on the other hand, clearly distrusted the dean and chapter. When they discovered that the Abbey had "pre-excavated" the grave almost a month before the actual exhumation, they sent off an indignant letter both reminding the dean that he had promised that they could be present and suggesting that only a full excavation of the grave in their presence would satisfy them.[38] In other words, as Hamer's account suggests, they suspected that the evidence could be tampered with if they were not present. Part of their concern is undoubtedly generated by the very nature of the Baconian theory in which a good part of Elizabethan and Jacobean England was involved in a large conspiracy to cover up the true author of "Shakespeare's" works. That they would extend this conspiracy to the dean and chapter is perhaps not surprising. Yet part of their suspicion seems justified. Hamer's suggestions about the motives of the Baconians would seem ample evidence of this, but a letter sent to the dean by R. P. Howgrave-Graham (the photographer of the event and future assistant keeper of the muniments), if a bit more more measured about two of the Baconians, confirms the less than charitable view of the Baconian project and the means used to further it,

[On]e man present, who I understood was of the Society, was [not] to be so described and I should shrink from association [with h]im in further work and should wish you to be forewarned [about] his possible immediate activities.

[At an ear?]ly stage he was suggesting to me that I [profit?] by my photographs and he wa[s] busy throughout getting exact particulars and addresses [of] those present and speaking of particular newspapers. When Sir Charles Peers and Mr. Tanner went out for [a] short time he propounded rather coarsely, and with a half pretence of jocularity to cover real intention, a scheme for opening the recent exhumation to the pu[blic] at 6° a head "for Abbey funds." "You'd have a q[ueue] to Victoria and the public would love it!"—he said. I said, "I feel sure that neither St. Peter nor St. Edward the Confessor nor the present Dean would approve." The others present agreed warmly and on the return of Sir Charles and Mr. Tanner he propounded the plan "we have concocted" in still more jocular vein. I said I objected to the pronoun "we." Mr. Tanner didn't hear, I think, but the other Baconian said warmly "Hear. Hear!"[39]

Howgrave-Graham's invocation of the "feelings" stirred by the event suggests a reverence that is shattered by the commercial scheme of Valentine Smith (who is, of course, the man in question). His suggestion that "the public would love it" casts Poets' Corner as a mere tourist attraction. Howgrave-Graham's invocation of St. Peter (the patron of the Abbey) and St. Edward (its founder) attempts to return the South Transept to a kind of premodern hallowed space. The uncovering of a poetic body is seen by Howgrave-Graham, at least, as part of this legacy and tradition—not part of the commodification of space.

Ultimately the exhumation was a disappointment for all concerned as it became apparent that the grave that they dug was not that of Edmund Spenser. It, in fact, is a bit unclear why the Abbey authorities initially decided to dig where they did—in front of Spenser's monument. Sir Charles Peers made it clear in several personal letters that he did not believe Spenser to be buried in front of his monument.[40] Douglas Hamer knew that it was not Spenser's grave and even Tanner expressed doubts about the location of the exhumation (fig. 16).[41] Further the final statement by the dean to the BBC makes it clear that they were unable to dig in front of the memorial because the masonry was solid.[42] In fact, they were so near the Drayton monument that Peers and

Figure 16. The grave actually contained three inhumations, hence the collapsed lid. The coffin was eighteenth century and they had extended the
search so far from Spenser's monument that Lawrence Tanner theorized in
his unpublished "Recollections" that they had actually uncovered Matthew
Prior (126). Copyright Dean and Chapter of Westminster.

Hamer thought they had uncovered Drayton (they were mistaken as Drayton had been buried in the North Aisle).[43]

The whole history of the exhumation is, then, eventually one of distrust
and failure. In metaphorical terms—Spenser, who, of course, had his own project to resurrect Chaucer's medieval poetics—became a figure for the failure
of the attempt to exhume the quiet hierarchies of the Middle Ages. The result
is perhaps best outlined by the keeper of the muniments at Westminster, who
in a newspaper article put it this way, "I suppose," said Mr. Tanner, "that a
good deal of public interest was aroused in connection with the recent opening of the ground in our effort to find Spenser's tomb. I can best sum up the
result of the work by saying that all that has happened is that we have now
lost Spenser."[44] In fact, what the exhumation really pointed to was the loss of
a nostalgic social body that had been created in the nineteenth-century work-
shops of Ruskin, Morris, and Arnold. Unlike the productive melancholia that
(as we saw in Chapter 2) attended the loss of Spenser and led to a kind of

reanimation of the poetic in Poets' Corner, this failed attempt to find Spenser portended a clash of cultures. The modern relevance of literary culture would no longer be limited to the quiet "companionship" between author and reader that might enable an ordered civil society (and was given institutional form by visits to the Corner). Instead, the general public increasingly saw the cultural capital of the literary as part of the national patrimony, and, if the story of "Spenser's exhumation" is any measure, something that was available to all. This democratization of culture ultimately empowered those who historically had little influence over more transcendent and abstract notions of aesthetics. The potential for this power had always existed, but in the late nineteenth and early twentieth centuries, the materialization of politics in the bodies of poets enabled a kind of revolution through which mass culture was finally able to lay claim to the genius of England.

Absent Shakespeare and the Final Burial

The search for the lost elegy of Shakespeare might be seen as a failure, but what it uncovered was the extent to which the "well-ordered" social body of England had itself been lost (if it ever had been present to begin with). The desire for a culturally conservative literary history yielded to a struggle over who should voice that cultural history and how that voice would be expressed. In the context of this clash over expression, it's fair to ask whether a national consciousness could continue to coalesce around the singular space of Poets' Corner. In other words, could the Corner now be seen as a classic *lieu de mémoire*, a place that commemorates the life of literature only to signal the extent to which literary culture is passing away? In order to answer this question, we need to return to the beginning of Poets' Corner and understand how it relates to its "end." Anxieties about absence, of course, had been expressed long before the loss of Spenser and the flood of cenotaphs in the twentieth century. And these absences, as I have suggested, in some sense enlivened the space even as modern attempts to supplement these absences have led to a disabling regret.

In particular, it is William Shakespeare's absence that creates the "idea" of the space. As I've argued, it is erection of the Scheemakers statue of Shakespeare that marked the great expansion of the corner in the eighteenth century. And even the search for Shakespeare's elegy can be seen as an attempt to locate his corpus in the Corner. Shakespeare, then, becomes the *sine qua non* for the

Corner, for it is quite literally his absence that generates the life of Poets' Corner. This sense of enlivening absence is pictorially realized in a piece of nineteenth-century technology marketed under the name "Spooner Protean Views." The dioramic print presents a pleasant daytime view of Poets' Corner. But when a light is held up behind it, the scene changes to night and the "shades" of Shakespeare, Scott, and Byron appear (figs. 17 and 18). At the time of the production of the print (ca. 1840), neither Scott nor Byron was memorialized in the Corner.[45] The suggestion is that Poets' Corner is haunted by these writers precisely because they are not there. The fact that Shakespeare attends the spirits of those who have no material presence in the Corner (even though a statue was raised to him in 1740) signals how the feeling of his absence materialized itself in the gloom of the Abbey despite the existence of a marmoreal substitute.

The failure of the Scheemakers statue to dispel the ghost of Shakespeare should not be surprising. Even after Pope enabled the commemoration of Shakespeare in the Abbey, writers fantasized about disinterring Shakespeare and burying him in the Abbey. The statue was seen as an inadequate substitute for Shakespeare because, as we saw in Chapter 2, his omission from the Corner was in some sense the founding absence. This absence excited a desire that would be revisited over and over again with each new visitor. And, as *the* originary absence, it stood behind all reactions of visitors who searched in vain for monuments to Coleridge, Milton, Byron, and George Eliot. As I have suggested, this deferral of desire for a long time ensured an insistent vitality for the space—expressing loss, but also giving the public a place to locate absence and hence revive their relationship with the author.

Yet if the logic of the Corner has always operated in a paradoxical manner—inadequacy of memorialization being used to memorialize, belatedness of memorialization signaling how memorialization is in time, or corporeal absence generating presence—we must acknowledge that one event in particular, involving that originary absence of Shakespeare, as being symbolic of this change in the nature of Poets' Corner. In 1989 Laurence Olivier's funeral was held in Westminster Abbey. Marjorie Garber has persuasively argued that

> Olivier's death, quite simply, was celebrated, or mourned, or commemorated, as if it were the death of Shakespeare himself—only this time, much more satisfyingly *with* a body. At a memorial service in Westminster Abbey, where, famously, Shakespeare is

Figure 17. The frontlit view of Spooner's "Poets' Corner." Used by permission of the Folger Shakespeare Library.

not buried . . . the casket . . . "was surmounted with a floral crown . . . studded with flowers and herbs mentioned in Shakespeare's works: from lavender and savory to rue and daisies." . . . That impossible event in literature history, a state funeral for the poet-playwright who defines Western culture, doing him appropriate homage—an event long-thwarted by the galling absence of certainty about his identity and whereabouts—had now at last taken place. Through a

Figure 18. The backlit view of Spooner's "Poets' Corner." Used by permission of the Folger Shakespeare Library.

mechanism of displacement, the memorial service for Olivier became a memorial service for Shakespeare.[46]

Such a claim is satisfying on a number of levels. The service seems to repair the breach in the Corner by providing not merely an effigy, but a body—even if displaced. It locates in Olivier an avatar of Shakespeare and, thus, in some sense identifies him as a kind of reincarnation of the poet. And, though

Garber could not have known this when she wrote the article, it also provides a body to bury in the corner as Olivier's ashes were laid to rest near Shakespeare's statue in 1991. If, as I have argued, Shakespeare's body is the enabling absence that in some sense generates poetic presence in the South Transept, does Olivier's body make good that absence? In other words, does the actor's burial finally put the poetical shades to rest?

The initial answer is no. For if this is the way that the "story" of Poets' Corner ends, one has to admit that we have seen this type of story before. In the eighteenth century it was (as Michael Dobson has argued) David Garrick who purportedly embodied Shakespeare. One midcentury poem has Shakespeare addressing Garrick from Elysium, complaining the Scheemakers statue in the Abbey is inadequate to his memorialization,

> What can avail the sculptor's curious art,
> Embodying rich the animated stone,
> Though high exalted in the sacred dome,
> Where all our venerable sages sleep,
> Where monarchs, with their poets, lie inurn'd?

Fortunately, however, Garrick exists to animate or perhaps reanimate the bard,

> THOU art my living monument: THEE
> I see the best inscription that my soul
> Could ever wish, perish, vain pageantry despis'd!
> SHAKESPEARE revives in GARRICK breathes again![47]

Playing on Jonson's famous recollection of Shakespeare: "Thou art a monument without a tomb / And art alive still, while thy Booke doth live," the author substitutes Garrick for Shakespeare's "book," hence certainly drawing attention to the ways in which acting is the living manifestation of the playwright, but also drawing attention to the ways in which only Garrick is able to embody him.

So, too, when Garrick died in 1779, a series of eulogies associated or even equated Garrick with Shakespeare: "When Shakespeare died, he left behind / A mortal of an equal mind. / When Garrick play'd, he liv'd again."[48] As he was buried almost directly in front of the Shakespeare statue, his corpse in some sense provided the absent corpse of the playwright with the statue as a kind of headstone. His own monument would not be erected until 1797 and

until then, as Sheridan put it, "SHAKESPEAR's Image from its hallow'd Base /
Seem'd to prescribe the Grave, and point the Place."[49] Garrick's body, then,
having been the reincarnation of Shakespeare would appear to repair the absence or loss felt in the Corner, which had (as the 1752 poem suggested) only
the "sculptor's curious art." Yet this burial seems not so much to provide a
pleasing conclusion to the plot of Poets' Corner. Instead it quite literally conjures up the spirit of Shakespeare who appears in a 1785 work by Samuel Jackson Pratt before the grave of Garrick. After a series of Shakespearian
characters have progressed to his grave, "all *alone* he [Shakespeare] stood before *his* GARRICK's shrine. / Rest, rest, perturbed spirits, then, he said, / To *me*
belongs th'estimable dead."[50] In this poem it is the presence of Garrick that
calls attention to the absence of Shakespeare who *must* appear to claim Garrick
as his own.

Olivier's burial, then, seems like yet another failed attempt to make good
the central absence of Poets' Corner. Yet if Olivier's burial replays Garrick's,
there is a central difference. Olivier's was not only the most recent burial in
the South Transept; it may also be the last one. The history of the Corner is
in some sense at an end with the final burial. We have come full circle as the
absence that in some sense inaugurated the life of Poets' Corner has been
eliminated, and the completeness for which the corner has strived has been
achieved. In this reading Poets' Corner would have achieved a kind of quiescence and now is free to recede into a historical curiosity—a quaint monument
to the cultural products of a waning empire. This reading also suggests that
the usefulness of Poets' Corner as a kind of material index to the canon of
English literature is at an end. Without any more burials, the raison d'être for
Poets' Corner no longer exists. The dynamism or organic capacity for growth
(in Stanley's terms) is over—a state of affairs that is signaled not only by the
real end of burials but by the metaphorical burial of the one famously absent
corpse, finally making the Corner complete.

Coda

Is Poets' Corner, for lack of a better word, dead? Some eight years after the burial of Olivier an incident occurred in one of the satellites of England's Poets' Corner that suggests a possibility for the continued relevance for the Westminster space. The American Poets' Corner was originally conceived in 1984 as an American version of the English Poets' Corner located in Westminster Abbey—something that (according to Daniel Haberman, the first poet-in-residence at the cathedral and the driving force behind the Corner) "served to remind all peoples of that nation's literary heritage."[1] The American corner would be different, however, because "as America has a democratic tradition, it was determined that a committee of electors should be chosen to vote for the two deceased American writers to be annually elected for memorialization in the Poets' Corner, rather than the English method of having the dean of Westminster Abbey do the selecting."[2] This profoundly American connection of "literary heritage" with democracy replaces the English connection of corporeal presence with "literary culture."

Necromancy and the American Poets' Corner

One might well argue that is precisely the absence of the body and the presence of the monument that ensures that the corpse—the site of decay and dissolution—will not intrude. And, in fact, the smooth-rubbed Buckingham, Virginia, slate plaques which stand in for sepulchers connote a kind of cleanness appropriate to what the *New Yorker* called "a boneless American Counterpart to Westminster Abbey."[3] To get away from the body is to leave behind materiality and to strive for transcendence. This transcendence is, of course, a marker of the status of poetry itself—a kind of aesthetically pure and profoundly unmaterialistic thing. One could even go so far as to argue (as Terry Eagleton has) that "this reverence for the aesthetic reflects the way in which art, or at least a certain exalted notion of it, is forced in the modern age to stand in for a religious transcendence which has fallen on hard times."[4] Such a position would seem to be supported by the fact that the poetic quotation on the Corner wall is from Psalm 45—"My heart is inditing a good matter; my tongue is the pen of a ready writer."

Yet, like the missing bodies of the poets, what is missing in the poetic quotation may tell us more about what the Corner is meant to transcend than a recollection of an Arnoldian aesthetic. This lyric initially seems an appropriate expression of a fairly straightforward aesthetics of composition. "Indite" here can mean to write, but in this context it probably has the earlier meaning of "to dictate." Hence the tongue is giving voice to the matter that has been dictated from the heart. But the quotation on the wall is only the beginning and ending of verse one. Between the first and second clause is a separate clause which reads, "I speak of the things which I have made touching the king." In other words, between the "inditing" and the "writing" is a reference to the regal subject of the psalm—historically, the Davidic king. Formally, however, the reference to the subject matter interrupts the transmission of "matter" from heart to tongue. It identifies writing as something that is ultimately connected not with democracy but with monarchy.

I do not mean to suggest that the elision of the monarchical subject matter was a consciously conspiratorial move on the part of the cathedral officials. One could perhaps see that the intrusion of a specific subject matter rather ruins the effect of the quotation. But it is interesting that the representation of the first verse of Psalm 45 (from the King James Bible) omits any suggestion that there might be a gap between the two clauses with the use of a semicolon. It's almost as if the two processes of composition and recitation are sutured up *by indicating a break between them.* This suturing between composition and recitation ultimately uncovers the work that the monument is supposed to do. For not only are composition and representation collapsed, but biblical history is, as it were, buried. And accompanying the suppression of the Davidic king is a suppression of the monarchical roots of the American Episcopal Church—the formation of a national religion.

To return briefly to Dean Stanley's claim about Westminster Abbey, we might remember that he brought together "the race of distinguished men . . . in the hearth of our *national* religion." The critic, Robert Gorham Davis, reacting to this connection of nationality with religion wrote some four years after the inception of the corner to the incoming honorary chairman, saying, "I know that the Poets' Corner, which seems to be very successful, imitates a similar corner at Westminster Abbey in London, but of course England has an established church, whereas opposition to such a church was one of the many provoking causes of our American revolution and is incorporated in the Constitution."[5] Davis's anxiety is based at least partially on the collapse of national and religious distinctions that ultimately undergirds a profoundly American literary heritage. In other words, it is the distinction between nation and religion that, in Davis's mind at any rate, enables a national literary heritage. It would be easy to dismiss Davis's comments as the objections of one captious critic had not the honorary chairman responded in terms which would seem to complement rather than contradict Davis's assertion. Mrs. Edward T. Chase writes that "the American Poets' Corner in New York was never intended to 'imitate' the one in Westminster Abbey, although it was inspired by the same idea: paying homage to the nation's great writers and thereby honoring the importance of significant literature in our culture. . . . There is certainly nothing to prevent other institutions from honoring poets or other creative people in any way they chose. However, it was the Cathedral of St. John's inspired initiative, preceded by that of no other institution, secular or religious. And in our country, of course, the institutions of the republic of letters are entirely separate from those of the Republic as government."[6] This final statement, an attempt to divorce "letters" from government, might be seen as a complement to Davis's attempt to separate religion from literature. As becomes clear from the rest of the letter, she allows that no particular religious persuasion is needed to appreciate the Corner, but she does assert a kind of religious unreligiousness—"things of the spirit which transcend any specific faith *or* lack of religious commitment."

But if the Corner is dependent on a kind of repression of the connection between the republic of letters and the republic of government, what of Daniel Haberman's assertion that it is the democratic nature of America which determined that the poets themselves would be "elected" to the corner? The requirements for consideration are purportedly only two—that "they must be American and they must be dead." Yet in 1999, after the electors had chosen two writers for commemoration—Ezra Pound and F. Scott Fitzgerald—the dean used his veto for the first time to disallow the commemoration of Pound. The dean said that he did so because of Pound's "destructive prejudices and anti-Semitism."[7] The impulse for his rejection, however, came from within the congregation of the cathedral. The dean had originally planned to accept the electors' recommendations when Marsha Ra, a warden of the cathedral's congregation who had converted from Judaism, led a protest against Pound's inclusion in the Corner citing his anti-Semitic views as a disqualifying factor. As she put it, "He was giving anti-Semitic radio broadcasts while my relatives were being gassed."[8]

The reaction of many electors to the dean's veto was expressed by Donald Hall: "I believe that the dean is within his rights. I clearly nominated him [Pound] knowing that some or many people would object. But if the literature is the criteria, he belongs there, and in fact his absence is utterly ludicrous."[9] Hall's argument proceeds from the formalist belief that (as the poet-in-residence, Mr. Hoffman, stated) the "achievements of his work" needed to be "distinguished from the prejudicial opinions." Yet as Marsha Ra suggested, "The belief in art for art's sake is neither Christian nor Jewish. . . . We are not a temple to the Muses."[10]

What is so intriguing about this conflict is how the carefully wrought connection of art, religion and democracy that is enabled by a kind of "boneless" celebration of death is undone by the intrusion of the corpses of the Holocaust. Once Ra tells us that fifteen of her cousins were murdered by the very politics that Pound espoused, the monument's magic is seemingly undone. The dean must act as his English predecessors did in disallowing the commemoration. The similarities between the national religion of Westminster and the American religion of St. John's are exposed. And the ability of the monument to elude the messy materiality of the body is forsworn. In other words, the repression of death, the body, politics, and religion in order to celebrate a transcendence of these things in American literature is now disabled by the history of the American Poets' Corner itself. For no matter how many names might be added to the monument, there will always be one which is *not* inscribed, one which is *not* celebrated. This absent presence (elected but uncommemorated) will point to and uncover what the monument does not wish to reveal—its own history. Yet oddly enough, it may be at this moment that the American Poets' Corner becomes something more than a series of plaques in a building at 112th and Amsterdam.

For though the monument "embodied" a number of repressions from the outset, these were abstract repressions already encoded in the prehistory of the monument. The decision *not* to celebrate Pound, on the other hand, is a conscious repression that engenders an ambivalence about the commemoration of art. To return to Westminster' Poets' Corner for a moment—the thing that

makes the English Corner an effective monument to literature is the presence
of the body. The repression, or ambivalence, that generates the "presence" of
the poets is the absence to which the corpse points. In the American Poets'
Corner that particular repression is superfluous because, of course, the bodies
themselves are absent. Hence, the monument (in 1984 at least) left no work,
no enabling repression for the viewer to carry out. It was a sign without a
sepulcher, whose deictic function (to point to a transcendent corpus of American letters) was coextensive with the meaning that visitors to the monument
were to carry away with them. But when, in 1999, there was a rupture between
the "democratic" impulses of the monument and what the dean called "an
aesthetic theology," the disjunction of politics and religion which always un-
derwrote the uniqueness of the American corner was realized.[11] This perfor-
mative repression—the discorporation of Pound from the body of writers
commemorated in the Corner—creates a kind of nontranscendent body
which (implicated in the politics of anti-Semitism) carries the taint of death.
As may be clear, this repression actually focuses the gaze of the visitor on the
vision of a transcendent corpus of American literature. Pound's absent presence, then, something that is there and not there—a spectral presence which
now haunts the Corner, takes the place of the corpse, and gives the monument a perhaps unexpected power which proceeds more from the dismember-
ing than the remembering of the American poetic body.

The Future of Poets' Corner

Given the different resonances of the American Poets' Corner, it might seem
unrealistic to look to St. John the Divine for the future of the original Poets'
Corner. After all, the space is quite different. It does not possess the history of
the Collegiate Church of St. Peter. Decisions about who should be commemorated are made in a very different fashion. Yet the conception of the American Poets' Corner as a "boneless counterpart" to the Abbey's South Transept
enables, at least, analogical thinking about the two Corners. And the analogy
is rooted in the original idea behind Poets' Corner. Further, recent controver-
sies involving the Abbey suggest that even without the bones of the poet, the
space occasions animated discussions about who belongs in the "pantheon"
and who does not.

In 2003, Jill Balcon, widow of the poet C. Day-Lewis (who had been poet
laureate from 1968 to 1972), petitioned the dean to erect a plaque to her hus-

band. Despite the fact that Seamus Heaney, A. S. Byatt, P. D. James, and Melvyn Bragg (among others) signed a petition supporting erection of the plaque, Jill Balcon's request was denied. The denial of her petition became public and the dean issued a press release stating in part that "there seems to be a view around that anyone who is Poet Laureate is automatically memorialized in the Abbey. That has not been the case. . . . We have to take a very strict view of the literary contribution of the candidate. People try to recommend candidates not for specific reasons but for a whole range of reasons that one might call general worthiness."[12] A columnist for the *Times Literary Supplement* characterized this statement as "short on tact" (which perhaps it was) but then admitted that "there is no disputing the decline of Day-Lewis's reputation."[13] The columnist seems to buy into the idea of "general worthiness," as espoused by the dean.[14] And it is this worthiness that most people think of when they consider who should be found in Poets' Corner.

But what this worthiness is, or how it is discovered is perhaps less clear than one might wish. The dean's invocation of "literary contribution," however, suggests an economic model in which "contributions" are made in order to increase literary "worth." And it is the size of the contribution that indicates the worthiness of being buried or memorialized in Poets' Corner. In short, one could make the argument that the controversy over the commemoration of the poet was not so much based on a model of transcendent sublime aesthetics as on a materialistic model, one that, even in the absence of the material corpse has evoked the language of materiality. In some ways Poets' Corner, of course, is merely the material version of an abstract place that exists in the collective mind of a particular culture. In this abstract place we imagine a kind of congress of poets and writers who deserve to be there. Historically this place even has a name—Mount Parnassus (or in some traditions Mount Helicon), the home of the muses and the poetic immortals. As might be obvious, however, Parnassus and Poets' Corner are not perfect reflections of one another. What we see in the dean's attempt to justify his decision about the exclusion of Day-Lewis are the ways in which concrete space and abstract place are in tension with one another.

This tension resolves itself into three related problems all of which have to do with the uneven ways in which these spaces impinge upon one another. First, as a material space, Poets' Corner cannot be subject to the same kind of revision that a purely imaginary space can be, and so one sometimes ends up with people commemorated in this space who might seem less than worthy. As the columnist Robert McCrum irreverently notes, "Poets' Corner contains memorials to some very weird poetical birds."[15] The eighteenth-century poet Christopher Anstey, for instance, is little known and less read and thus might well be seen as a curious addition to the Corner. But there is no provision for going back and correcting the supposed "mistakes" of one's predecessors, nor would this seem to be a very good recipe for providing a place that is supposed to represent a kind of universal and long-lasting notion of who is considered a great poet. The history of Poets' Corner, then, is made up of a series of "plot twists" that are written in stone. Just as important, however, as the plots that are included are the various plots that are excluded. A number of poets and writers who might be seen as worthy of burial (Milton, George Eliot, Shakespeare) and commemoration were initially excluded from the Abbey. These omissions are somewhat more easily rectified than the commemoration of an unworthy writer and indeed all three writers are now commemorated in the South Transept though it is, curiously enough, their absences that appear to define the space of Poets' Corner.

And this brings me to the second recent example of controversy in the Abbey. In 2002 a window lozenge was installed in the window above Geoffrey Chaucer's tomb. The honoree was Christopher Marlowe, who had (according to a coroner's report discovered at the Public Records Office in 1925) been murdered in 1593 and (according to the *Register of Burials in the Parish of St. Nicholas, Deptford*) been buried in an unmarked grave. There was no real debate over whether Marlowe deserved the honor. But there was a good deal of debate about how the poet was to be remembered. The lozenge is relatively simple, containing Marlowe's name and his birth and death dates. Unusual, however, is the presence of a question mark before the death date of 1593. As Stanley Wells has said, "The fact is that Marlowe's death is one of the best recorded episodes of English literary history."[16] So why did the question mark appear? A spokesmen for the Abbey said, "Nobody is 100 percent sure of the date of his death, so the question mark was put in."[17] The head of the Marlowe Society, Colin Niven, had a somewhat different take, telling the *Daily Telegraph*, "I put the question mark there to keep the debate going."[18] The so-called debate to which Niven makes reference is over the authorship of Shakespeare's works. Some members of the Marlowe Society argue that the poet was not murdered in 1593 but staged his death (or had it staged). After remaining in hiding for a while, they argue, he emerged to write a number of poems and plays and convinced the actor William Shakespeare to take credit for them.

This scenario, of course, is highly unlikely. But what is so interesting is not that there are people who believe that Shakespeare was Marlowe (or, as we have seen, that Shakespeare was Francis Bacon). What is curious is the way in which the cultural authority of the Abbey is exercised through this memorialization. In this particular case, the academicians were fairly united in their dismissal of the Abbey's act of memorialization. But there was something of a split in the popular press. The BBC, the *Telegraph,* and the Australian newspaper the *Age* put out stories that more or less attempted to give a balanced view of the controversy.[19] Individual columnists like McCrum of the *Guardian*, on the other hand, dismissed the question mark as a publicity stunt that trivialized Marlowe's accomplishments.[20] Whether or not the Abbey meant to "keep the controversy going" by putting a question mark in front of the death date, it is pretty clear that this was its effect.[21] And it is quite possible that this "debate," while from an academic view regrettable, actually keeps the Corner alive as an idea of a kind of metaphorical space of literature.

The final problem is less tractable and it is here, I think, that we find the real problem of the Corner—relevance. As Michael Caines put it, "There cannot be many tourists who look on the lavish monuments to Drayton, Spenser and Cowley or their eighteenth-century counterparts (anyone for Prior or Rowe?) with more than a blank appreciation for the quaint acts of the English sculptors."[22] Those who are being memorialized no longer activate the same emotions that they did when they were contemporary. Of the five poets that Caines mentions, only Spenser could be called "widely read." One might well argue that such poets ought to be read, but whether or not this is a contemporary cultural failing or a failure of our educational system is not really the point. The existence of Poets' Corner as a place of pilgrimage, or what we would even call a tourist attraction, is threatened by the ignorance of the larger public about its own literary history.

Indeed, the only moment that Caines detects any vitality in the space is when one of the tourists recognizes that she is standing on Alfred Tennyson's tombstone, " 'Tennyson!' a woman hisses loudly, pointing at her feet and then, inexplicably, at Abraham Cowley's urn. The wreath itself [recently placed on the grave by the Tennyson Society] attracts a lot of pointing and camera-work, and the Corner comes back, as far as it can, to life."[23] For this particular woman and those with her, it is the dual aspects of commemoration and corporeal presence that invigorate her visit to Poets' Corner. But curiously it is also doubt and absence that keep the Corner meaningful, for it is in the attempt to repair absence and the corresponding attempt to resolve doubt that the visitor and the reader find meaning. In this way the reading of the Corner continues, seemingly driving toward an end even as we are kept in suspense about the ultimate meaning of the plot. If this particular plot is in danger of losing its relevance, it is because the space itself is only the material extension of an idea. Once that idea ceases to exist in the collective cultural consciousness of the nation, the place of poetry in some sense ceases to be. It can no longer perform the function of reminding us what we have lost, how we can repair that loss, and how this sense of loss generates a literary presence that in turn informs a cultural sense of who we are.

The mission of Poets' Corner, if we can call it that, has then perhaps changed. It has always been a conservative place, by which I mean that it has always retained its relevance by sustaining, or perhaps reviving, a relationship between writer and reader that was always past. And that renewed relationship has always been based on the sense of *heimischness* or "homeliness" that is activated in the visitor. When Poets' Corner worked to mobilize what Pope called "public love," it was always by a profoundly private or solitary relationship with the author. Increasingly, however, the space seems not homely to visitors, but strange. Christopher Howse is only the most recent critic to declare that the Corner celebrates mostly forgotten poets and goes so far as to characterize the place as a "marmoreal Madame Tussauds, except there at least they melt down the wax effigies once the celebrity factor has worn off."[24] Of course, from its founding, the space has always occasioned criticism both for who was and was not commemorated there. But the point of attack in late modernity seems to be the very worth of conservation. The Corner, thus, becomes not merely a place that celebrates poetry, or reenacts the relationship of author and reader, or even enables the public to lay claim to their cultural patrimony; it becomes a kind of defense against those who, like the reformers in the sixteenth century, would dispose of the past in the interests of a relentlessly modern ideology.

Ted Hughes, the last poet to receive a stone in Westminster Abbey (6 December 2011), was characterized at his funeral in the Abbey as a "guardian spirit of the language and the land."[25] The speaker of these words, Seamus Heaney, casts Hughes at his death as a kind of conservator who would live on to guarantee the continuing relevance of English and the land that gave it birth. The poet here is protector, a constant (if traditional and invisible) companion who ensures continuity to an increasingly fractured Anglophone community. "He would," Heaney adds, "be as much at home being compared to

Caedmon, the first English poet, as he would with [Wilfred] Owen and his doomed men in the trenches of the Somme."[26] By invoking the idea of home, Heaney gives voice to a nostalgic vision of poetic continuity that echoes what Hawthorne and Irving claimed in the nineteenth century. But here it seems less like the productively melancholic observations of friendly poets, and more like a writer who is making the case that to lose one's poetic heritage is to sacrifice the unspoken ways in which that heritage guarantees the cultural continuity that is England.

POETS' CORNER GRAVEPLAN

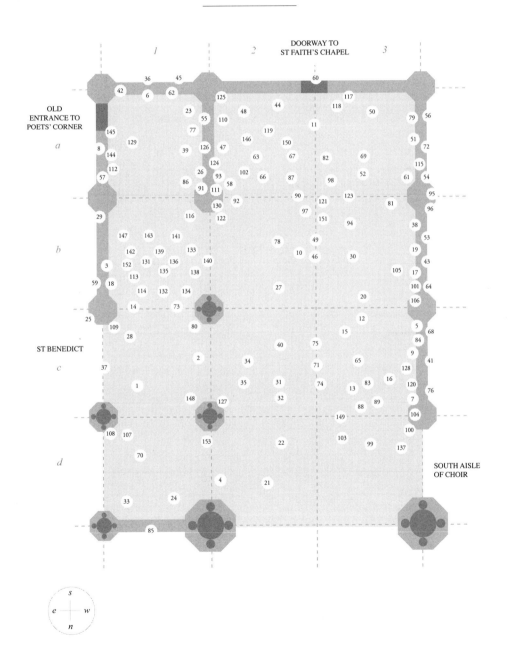

1   *2*   DOORWAY TO ST FAITH'S CHAPEL   *3*

OLD ENTRANCE TO POETS' CORNER

a

b

ST BENEDICT

c

d

SOUTH AISLE OF CHOIR

s
e — w
n

POETS' CORNER ALPHABETICAL BURIAL AND MONUMENT LIST

Name	Date	Number	Location
Robert Adam	1792	71	c3
Joseph Addison	1809	81	b3
Christopher Anstey	1807	80	c1
Duke of Argyll (See John Campbell)			
Matthew Arnold	1891	112	a1
Matthew Arnold	1989	144	a1
Peggy Ashcroft	2005	150	a2
Family Atkyns	1750	51	a3
W. H. Auden	1974	134	b1
Jane Austen	1967	130	a2
Dr. Harry Barker	1740	46	b3
Isaac Barrow	1677	19	b3
Samuel Barton	1715	31	c2
Sir John Betjeman	1996	148	c1
Martha Birch	1703	25	c1
Peter Birch	1710	28	c1
William Blake	1957	127	c2
Samuel Bolton	1668	16	c3
Barton Booth	1772	57	a1
Mary Eleanor Bowes	1800	78	b2
Anne Brontë	1947	125	a2
Charlotte Brontë	1947	125	a2
Emily Brontë	1947	125	a2
Robert Browning	1894	114	b1
William Burnaby	1706	27	b2
Robert Burns	1885	110	a2
Richard Busby	1702	24	d1

Samuel Butler	1721	36	a1
Lord Byron (See George Gordon)			
Caedmon	1966	129	a1
William Camden	1627	7	c3
John Campbell (Duke of Argyll)	1749	50	a3
Major General Sir Archibald Campbell	1791	69	a3
Major General Sir Archibald Campbell	1795	72	a3
Thomas Campbell	1844	90	a2
Thomas Campbell	1848	92	b2
Robert Cannon	1722	40	c2
Major Henry Carr	1690	21	d2
Lewis Carroll	1982	139	b1
Reverend Henry Francis Cary	1868	97	b2
Dr. Isaac Casaubon	1634	9	c3
Sir William Chambers	1796	74	c3
Geoffrey Chaucer	1400	3	b1
Thomas Chiffinch	1666	12	c3
John Clare	1989	145	a1
Samuel Taylor Coleridge	1885	111	a2
Abraham Cowley	1667	14	b1
Abraham Cowley	1675	18	b1
Sir Richard Coxe	1623	5	c3
William Craig	1720	35	c2
Mary Ann Cross (See George Eliot)			
Richard Cumberland	1811	82	a3
Sir William Davenant	1668	15	c3
Charles Lutwidge Dodgson (See Lewis Carroll)			
Abbot Richard de Kedyngton	1315	1	c1
Charles de St. Denis	1703	26	a1
Charles Dickens	1870	98	a3
Michael Drayton	1631	8	a1
John Dryden	1721	37	c1
George Eliot	1980	138	b1
T. S. Eliot	1967	131	b1
Adam Fox	1977	137	d3
David Garrick	1779	63	a2
David Garrick	1797	76	c3

Name	Date	Number	Location
John Gay	1736	44	originally a2 (transferred to triforium)
William Gifford	1826	88	c3
Oliver Goldsmith	1777	60	a2
Adam Lindsay Gordon	1934	122	b2
George Gordon (Lord Byron)	1969	133	b1
John Ernest Grabe	1727	41	c3
Thomas Gray	1778	62	a1
George Grote	1871	99	d3
George Grote	1871	100	d3
Stephen Hales	1761	53	b3
George Frederic Handel	1759	52	a3
George Frederic Handel	1762	54	a3
Thomas Hardy	1928	121	b3
Robert Hauley	1378	2	c1
William Heather	1926	120	c3
John Henderson	1785	67	a2
Elizabeth Heylin	1747	49	b2
Mary Hope	1767	56	a3
Gerard Manley Hopkins	1975	135	b1
Dr. Anthony Horneck	1697	22	d2
Ted Hughes	2011	152	b1
John Ireland	1842	89	c3
Henry Irving	1905	119	a2
Henry James	1976	136	b1
Samuel Johnson	1784	66	a2
Samuel Johnson	1939	124	a2
Ben Jonson	1728	42	a1
John Keats	1954	126	a2
John Keble	1873	101	b3
Rudyard Kipling	1936	123	a3
D. H. Lawrence	1985	141	b1
Edward Lear	1988	143	b1
William Leo	1645	11	a2
Jenny Lind-Goldschmidt	1894	115	a3
C. S. Lewis	2013	153	(d1)

(*continued*)

Nicholas Litlyngton	1873	102	a2
Henry Wadsworth Longfellow	1884	109	c1
Richard Lucas	1715	32	c2
Thomas Babington Macaulay	1860	94	b3
Thomas Babington Macaulay	1866	96	b3
Right Honorable James Stewart Mackenzie	1801	79	a3
James Macpherson	1796	75	c3
Frederic William Maitland	2001	149	c3
Stephen Marshall	1880	105	b3
John Masefield	1967	132	b1
William Mason	1799	77	a1
Thomas May	1880	106	b3
Thomas May	1880	105	b3
John Milton	1737	45	a1
Gilbert Murray	1957	128	c3
Queen Anne Neville	1485	4	d2
Laurence Olivier	1991	146	a2
John Osbaldston	1666	13	c3
William Outram	1679	20	b3
William Outram	1721	38	b3
Thomas Parr	1634	10	b2
Philadelphia Percy	1791	70	d1
John Philips	1710	29	b1
Sir John Pringle	1782	64	b3
Matthew Prior	1721	39	a1
Hannah Pritchard	1772	58	originally a2 (transferred to triforium)
Lieutenant George James Riddell	1783	65	c3
John Roberts	1772	59	b2
Elizabeth Robinson	1777	61	a3
Sir Thomas Robinson	1777	61	a3
Nicholas Rowe	1743	48	originally a2 (transferred to triforium)
Founders of the Royal Ballet	2009	151	b3
John Ruskin	1903	118	a3

Name	*Date*	*Number*	*Location*
Sir Walter Scott	1897	117	a3
Thomas Shadwell	1700	23	a1
William Shakespeare	1740	47	a2
Granville Sharp	1816	86	a1
Percy Bysshe Shelley	1954	126	a2
Richard Sheridan	1816	87	a2
Barbara Simpson	1795	73	b1
Robert South	1716	33	d1
Robert Southey	1845	91	a2
Edmund Spenser	1620	5	a1
William Spottiswoode	1883	107	d1
Dame Mary Steele	1718	34	c2
Countess Strathmore			
(See Mary Eleanor Bowes)			
William Strong	1880	105	b3
Archibald Campbell Tait	1884	108	d1
Sir Robert Taylor	1789	68	c3
Alfred Lord Tennyson	1892	113	b1
Alfred Lord Tennyson	1895	116	b1
William Makepeace Thackeray	1865	95	a3
Connop Thirlwall	1875	103	d3
Connop Thirlwall	1876	104	c3
Dylan Thomas	1982	140	b1
James Thomson	1762	55	a2
Dr. Thomas Triplett	1670	17	b3
Anthony Trollope	1993	147	b1
William Twisse	1880	105	b3
William Vincent	1815	85	d1
War Poets	1985	142	b1
Bishop Edward Wetenhall	1713	30	b3
Bishop Edward Wetenhall	1733	30	b3
Dr. Edward Wetenhall	1735	43	b3
William Wordsworth	1854	93	a2
Jane Wowen	1758	31	c2
John Wowen	1760	31	c2
James Wyatt	1813	83	c3
James Wyatt	1813	84	c3

This listing is based on the updated 1870 graveplan for the South Transept of the Collegiate Church of St. Peter, Westminster, popularly known as Westminster Abbey. As is apparent from even a cursory look at the plan, there are a number of stones that are so old or so worn that no name could be seen even in 1870.[1] In addition a number of burials have taken place in the South Transept but have remained unmarked. We have a general idea of where some of these burials took place, and I have given a partial list at the end of this longer chronological listing. Unfortunately, because of incomplete and damaged records and the sheer age of the Abbey, we will never know everyone who is buried there.

The philosophy underlying this listing is to give some sense of how the South Transept in general and Poets' Corner in particular developed over the course of approximately six hundred years. Thus I have listed the burial stones and monuments not by the death dates of those they memorialize, but by the probable dates of their inscription and erection. When this date is not clear, I have used the date of the sculpture or the date that the fee or fine for the monument was paid. Occasionally, however, all we have is the death date. A number of individuals have both gravestones and monuments. I have indicated this by reference to date. The numbers following each reference locate the stone or monument on the graveplan included in this volume. This listing would have been impossible without the guidance of the Abbey library staff, in particular the Abbey librarian Tony Trowles. I am also deeply indebted to the loose-leaf list of monuments put together by John Physick (updated by Christine Reynolds) located in the Abbey library.

1315
Abbot Richard de Kedyngton alias Sudbury. Died 9 April 1315. The 1870 graveplan says that he was buried under the lower pavement before the altar and

then moved here, but it is unclear what Poole's source was for this conjecture (1).[2]

1378
Robert Hauley, knight. Murdered 11 August in the Choir and buried here. The stone was cut either in 1881 or 1887. The brass is gone but the indent is still visible (2).

1400
Geoffrey Chaucer, English poet. Died ca. 25 March 1400. Buried in front of St. Benedict's Chapel and translated here in 1556 (3).

1485
The 1870 graveplan indicates a stone to Queen Anne (Neville), but the reading is doubtful. In addition we know that she is buried near the door in the screen leading into the Confessor's Chapel in an unmarked grave (4).

1620
Edmund Spenser, English poet. Died 1599 and buried somewhere in the South Transept. Monument raised by Anne Clifford, countess of Dorset. It was replaced in 1778 with a copy (6).

Ca. 1623
Sir Richard Coxe, taster to Queen Elizabeth and King James. Also Steward of the Household. Died 13 December 1623. Buried here (5).

Ca. 1627
William Camden, antiquary, headmaster of Westminster School, author of the first "guidebook" to the Abbey. Died 9 November 1623. Buried here 19 November 1623.[3] His monument was probably erected no later than 1627 as William Heather, his executor died then.[4] The monument was restored ca. 1780 by the University of Oxford (7).

Ca. 1631–45
Michael Drayton, English poet. Died 1631. Buried near the north wall "not far from the little dore openeth into one of the Prebend's houses."[5] His mon-

ument was erected by the countess of Dorset who, if John Aubrey is to be believed, died in 1645 (8).[6]

1634

Dr. Isaac Casaubon, scholar and critic. Died 10 July 1614 and buried (according to the Register) "at the entrance of St. Benedict's Chapel." There is no trace of the gravestone any longer, but the Abbey still possesses a rubbing of the stone that reads, "NEAR THIS SPOT WAS BURIED ISAAC CASAUBON WHOSE MONUMENT IS OPPOSITE 1614. AND WAS ALSO HIS FRIEND JOHN SPOTTISWOOD ARCHBISHOP OF ST ANDREWS 1639." The monument was erected in 1634 by Thomas Moreton, Bishop Durham. Casaubon was a close friend of Lancelot Andrewes, dean of Westminster from 1601 to 1605. Mrs. Casaubon died either 8 or 10 July 1635 and was buried with her husband (and apparently Archbishop Spottiswood) in front of St. Benedict's Chapel (9).

1635

Thomas Parr. Died 15 November. Supposedly 152 years old. The stone was re-cut in 1967 (10).

1645

William Leo (*sic;* his surname is Loe), clergyman and preacher. Died by 21 September. The stone is worn, but the Abbey possesses a rubbing of it that says: "WILLIAM LEO / PREBRY. OF WESTMINSTER / AND POET. / 1645." The Abbey monument book put together by John Physick says that "this is obviously a modern stone. He is in Chester but he is not in our list as a Prebendary of Westminster. He was a Prebendary and Sub-Dean of Gloucester." The *DNB* says that he is buried here (11).

1666

Thomas Chiffinch, Keeper of the Privy Closet and Comptroller to the Royal Excise under Charles II. Brother of William Chiffinch. Died 8 April and buried here (12).

John Osbaldston, Page of the Bedchamber to Charles II. Died 1 March. Buried 3 March. James Wyatt was also buried here. See 1813 (13).

1667
Abraham Cowley, English poet. Died 28 July. Buried 3 August 1667. See also 1675 (14).

1668
Sir William Davenant, Poet Laureate. Died 7 April and buried here 9 April. The inscription repeats the sentiment of Ben Jonson's stone, "O Rare Sir William Davenant." The stone was replaced in 1866 (15).

Samuel Bolton, prebendary. Chaplain in Ordinary to Charles II. Died 11 February and buried here (16).

Ca. 1670
Dr. Thomas Triplett, prebendary to Westminster Abbey. Died 18 July 1670. Buried here (17).

1675
Abraham Cowley, monument raised by the duke of Buckingham. For tombstone see 1667 (18).

1677
Isaac Barrow, scholar. Died 4 May 1677. Buried here 7 May. The inscription says that "friends" erected the monument. He was living in a prebendal house (Stanley believes that it was the old prebendal house called "the Tree"). John Physick in the Abbey Monuments Book theorizes that this may be why he was buried here. Stanley, however, emphasizes his connection with Westminster School (19).[7]

1679
William Outram, prebendary, Canon of Westminster Abbey. Died 23 August, buried here 25 August. Jane, his wife, was buried here ca. 4 October 1721. See also 1721 (20).

1690
Major Henry Carr, Gentleman Usher and Daily Waiter to King Charles II and King James II. Died 25 August and buried here (21).

1697

Dr. Anthony Horneck, prebendary of Westminster, Chaplain in Ordinary to King William and Queen Mary. Buried on 4 February. His wife Jane, son William, and daughter Elizabeth are buried here as well (22). His monument may have been raised at the same time.

Ca. 1700

Thomas Shadwell, English poet. Died 19 November 1692. Buried at Chelsea. Monument raised by his son who (in the inscription) refers to himself as "Johannes Shadwell M.D.," a degree he received in 1700 (23).

1702

Richard Busby, prebendary, headmaster of Westminster School. Died 1695. Monument executed ca. 1702. Buried in front of the steps going up to the Sacrarium (24).

1703

Martha Birch, wife to Peter Birch, prebendary (see 1710). Tablet. Died 25 May 1703 (25).

Charles de St. Denis, Sieur de St. Evremond, French wit and writer. Died 9 September and buried 11 September near Thomas Parr's stone. The monument was erected and funeral services paid by Peter Birch, prebendary, despite the indignation of Francis Atterbury (later dean) at St. Evremond's agnosticism. Birch paid the funeral expenses because of the friendship between St. Evremond and Birch's father-in-law Edmund Waller, the poet. The monument was formerly on the west side of the screen to the chapel of St. Blaize, which extended across the South Transept until the eighteenth century. See the engraved plan by John Dart (26).

1706

William Burnaby, English dramatist and translator. Died 8 November and buried here (27).

1710

Peter Birch, prebendary and Subdean. Died 2 July 1710 and buried here. His first wife Martha has a tablet in the South Transept (see 1703) (28).

John Philips, English poet. Died 1708. Monument in place by 4 September 1710 (29).

1713
Bishop Edward Wetenhall, bishop of Cork, Kilmore, and Ardagh. Died 12 November 1713. His son is buried beside him. See 1733 (30).

1715
Samuel Barton, prebendary of Westminster. Died 15 August 1715.[8] Buried with him near the tablet is his daughter Jane Wowen, died 9 December 1758, and her husband John Wowen, died 1 June 1760 (31).

Richard Lucas, prebendary. Died 29 June. Buried here (32).

1716
Robert South, prebendary. Died 1716. Monument. Buried in front of the steps going up to the Sacrarium (33).

1718
Dame Mary (Prue) Steele, second wife of Richard Steele. Died 26 December and buried here (34).

1720
William Craig, prebendary. Died 19 February. Also buried with him is his wife Mary who died 1 January 1745 (35).

1721
Samuel Butler, English poet. Died 25 September 1680. Buried in St. Paul's, Covent Garden. The monument once extended to the floor but has been considerably reduced and moved from its original position (see John Gay's monument, 1736) (36).

John Dryden, Poet Laureate. Died 1 May 1700. Buried in the South Transept 13 May in or near Chaucer's original grave. His monument was erected by the duke of Buckingham and unveiled on 23 January. Buckingham's widow replaced the bust in 1731 with one by P. Scheemakers. The upper part and back of the monument were taken down in 1848 (37).

William Outram, prebendary, Canon of Westminster Abbey. Died 23 August, buried in the South Transept 25 August 1679. Jane, his wife, was buried with him ca. 4 October 1721. The monument with its monumental urn might have been raised earlier, but the inscription commemorating Jane Outram could only been completed after her death (38).

Matthew Prior, English poet and diplomat. Died 18 September. Buried "at the feet of Spenser" according to Dean Atterbury. The bust had been given to Prior by Louis XIV and was placed on his monument in accordance with Prior's will. The monument was certainly in place by 1723 when it appears in John Dart's *Westmonasterium* (39).

1722
Robert Cannon, dean of Lincoln and prebendary of Westminster. Died 28 March and buried here. A tablet to his memory is in the South Aisle of the Nave (40).

1727
John Ernest Grabe, ecclesiastical scholar. Died 3 November 1711. Buried in the parish church of St. Pancras. The fee for the monument was paid in 1727. The memorial was erected by Robert Harley, earl of Oxford and Harley (41).

1728
Ben Jonson, English poet. Monument. Buried in the North Aisle. Died 6 August (42).

1733
Dr. Edward Wetenhall, eldest son of Edward Wetenhall, D.D. Died 29 August and buried just south of his father, Bishop Wetenhall. Both the 1870 graveplan and the Abbey website record the existence of a stone, but it was not possible to verify its existence or legibility. See 1713 (30).

1735
Dr. Edward Wetenhall, eldest son of Edward Wetenhall, D.D. Died 29 August 1733 and buried in the South Transept. The monument was raised by his daughters Anna and Philippa. The fee for the monument was paid in 1735 (43).

1736

John Gay, English poet and dramatist. Died 9 December 1732. Buried 23 December in the South Transept. Monument erected by the duke and duchess of Queensbury.[9] To make room for the monument, Samuel Butler's bust was removed to its present position (Chapter Book, 31 October 1733) (44). Moved to the triforium. See 1743.

1737

John Milton, English poet. Died 1674. Buried at St. Giles's, Cripplegate. Bust erected by auditor William Benson (45).

1740

Dr. Harry Barker, prebendary. Died and buried here in September (46).

William Shakespeare, English playwright and poet. Died 23 April 1616. Buried at Stratford-upon-Avon. Monument unveiled 29 January (47).

1743

Nicholas Rowe, Poet Laureate, and Charlotte, his daughter. Nicholas Rowe died on 6 December and was buried "in the aile where many of our English poets are interred, over against Chaucer" on 19 December 1718.[10] The Chapter Book of the Abbey states "On Oct. 29th 1742 ordered that leave be given to put a Monument in the South Cross of the Abbey between Shakespeare and Mr. Gays for Mr. Rowe the Poet on the payment of twenty guineas." But the Treasurer's account says that the monument was not erected until 1743. In 1936 wall paintings were discovered behind Rowe's and John Gay's monuments and they were moved to the triforium (48).

1747

Elizabeth Heylyn, wife of Rev. Dr. John Heylyn, prebendary of Westminster. Died 9 June and buried here. It is possible that he and their daughter were buried here as well. He died 11 August 1759 and she died 28 March of the same year (49).

1749

John (Campbell) second duke of Argyll and first duke of Greenwich. Died 4 October 1743. Buried in Henry VII's Chapel (50).

1750

The Atkyns Family. A monument raised by Edward Atkyns to four of his ancestors (Edward, died 1669; Robert, died 1709; Edward, died 1698; Robert, died 1711) "who have so honourably presided / in the Courts of Justice in Westminster Hall." The fee was received 1746, 29 May, but Rupert Gunnis dates it to 1750, the same year that Edward died (20 January) (51).[11]

1759

George Frederic Handel, composer. Died 14 April 1759. See also 1762 (52).

1761

Dr. Stephen Hales, D.D., botanist and physiologist. Died 4 January. Buried at Teddington. The fee was paid 19 May 1761. Raised by Princess Augusta, mother of George III; Hales was her private chaplain (53).

1762

George Frederic Handel, composer. Died 14 April 1759. He is buried under his gravestone in the South Transept (see 1759). The monument was unveiled 10 July. The fee was paid by Roubiliac, who also executed the monument (54).

James Thomson, English poet. Buried in Richmond Parish Church, Surrey (55).

Ca. 1767

Mary Hope. Died 25 June 1767. Buried at Norton. Monument raised by her husband, John Hope (56).

1772

Barton Booth, actor. Educated at Westminster School. Died 1733. Monument raised by his widow, Hester. Buried at Cowley, Middlesex (57).

Hannah Pritchard, actress. Died August 1768. Buried at Twickenham—her funeral fees paid by Lord Nuneham. Permission at chapter 16 June 1772 to erect a monument. Now in the triforium. See Johnson's monument (1939) for why her monument was displaced (58).

John Roberts, Secretary of the Right Honourable Henry Pelham, Minister of State to King George the second. Monument erected by his sisters, Susannah, Rebecca, and Dorothy (59).

1777
Oliver Goldsmith, English poet, dramatist, writer. Died 4 April 1774. Buried in Temple Churchyard, London. The fine for the monument was received from Joseph Nollekens (who also executed the monument) in September 1777 (60).

Elizabeth, baroness of Lechmere, and Sir Thomas Robinson, Bt. She died 10 April 1739 and was buried here. He died 3 March 1777 and was buried in Merton Church, Surrey. Fine for the monument and half burial fees were paid on 22 February 1753 by Robinson, but the inscription suggests that the monument was not erected until after his death. The monument was cut down in 1894 in order to accommodate the monument to Jenny Lind-Goldschmidt (61).

1778
Thomas Gray, English poet. Died 1771. Buried at Stoke Poges. Fine for monument paid 23 June (62).

1779
David Garrick, actor. Died 20 January. Buried here 1 February. His wife Eva died 16 October 1822 at the age of 99. She was buried here 25 October. See also 1797 (63).

Ca. 1782
Sir John Pringle, Bt. Died 18 January 1782. Buried at St. James, Westminster. Physician to the Army, the Princess of Wales, the Queen, and King George III. Monument erected by his nephew and heir Sir James Pringle (64).

1783
Lieutenant George James Riddell, son of Sir James Riddell, Bt. Died 22 April. Also buried here is Dame Sarah Riddell, second wife of Sir James Riddell. She died 5 June 1817. The stone has been recut (65).

1784
Samuel Johnson, English writer and critic. Died 13 December. Buried 20 December. A monument was intended, but was finally transferred to St. Paul's.[12] But see 1939 (66).

1785

John Henderson, actor. Buried here 3 December. In 1821 the remains of his wife were deposited "upon his coffin, at scarcely a foot in depth" (67).[13] The stone is too worn to read.

1789

Sir Robert Taylor, architect. Died 26 September 1788. Buried in St.-Martin-in-the-Fields. Fee for the monument paid August 1789 (68).[14]

1791

Major General Sir Archibald Campbell. Died 31 March 1791. See also 1795 (69).

Philadelphia Percy, illegitimate daughter of the Duke of Northumberland. Died 6 November 1791. Buried here 24 November. Her younger sister died on 2 November 1794 and was buried on the 24th (70).

1792

Robert Adam, architect of the King's Works. Died 3 March and buried here. According to John Physick's Monument Book in the Abbey library, Joseph Nollekens designed a monument for Adam for the Abbey but this was never carried out (71).[15]

1795

Major General Sir Archibald Campbell. Died 31 March 1791. Buried in the South Transept (see 1791). His nephew, Lieutenant General James Campbell, Bt. (died 6 June 1819), was buried here (72).

Barbara Simpson. Died 2 March and buried here. Wife of James Simpson, formerly His Majesty's Attorney General for South Carolina (73).

1796

Sir William Chambers, architect of the King's Works and surveyor general of His Majesty's Works. Died 8 March and buried here 18 March (74).

James Macpherson, Scottish poet, historian and "translator" of the so-called Ossianic cycle of poems. Died 17 February. Buried here 15 March in accordance with his will (75).

1797

David Garrick, actor. Died 20 January 1779. Buried in the South Transept with his wife, Eva (d. 16 October 1822). This monument was erected in 1797 by a friend, Albany Wallis. See also 1779 (76).

1799

William Mason, English poet. Died 7 April 1797. Buried at Aston, Yorkshire (77).

1800

Countess Strathmore (Mary Eleanor Bowes). Died 28 April and buried here May 10. Ancestor of Queen Elizabeth II. She is the author of a play, *The Siege of Jerusalem,* and *The Confessions of the Countess of Strathmore,* which served as the basis for Thackeray's *Barry Lyndon* (78).

1801

Right Honorable James Stewart Mackenzie, Lord Privy Seal of Scotland. Died 6 April 1800. On 10 February 1801 leave was given to erect the monument and on 30 October Nollekens paid the fine (and also executed the monument). Mackenzie was the nephew of the Duke of Argyll, alongside whose monument his resides (79).

1807

Christopher Anstey, English poet. Died 3 August 1805. Buried at St. Swithin's, Bath. The fine for the monument was paid 6 May 1807 (80).

1809

Joseph Addison, English critic and writer. Died 17 June 1719. Buried in the North Aisle of Henry VII's chapel on 26 June, possibly to be near his patron Montagu, earl of Halifax. On 15 November, 1806 the dean and chapter gave their permission for a monument to be erected in the South Aisle of Henry VII's chapel for a fine of 100 guineas. An earlier idea of putting his monument on the tomb of Thomas of Woodstock was apparently frustrated.[16] This monument was erected in the South Transept in April (81).

1811

Richard Cumberland, English dramatist. Died 7 May. Buried here 14 May (82).

Ca. 1813

James Wyatt, architect of Westminster Abbey and surveyor general of His Majesty's Works. Died 4 September 1813. Buried either in or close to John Osbaldston's grave 28 September (83). There is also a mural monument to Wyatt that might be of the same vintage (84).

1815

William Vincent, dean of Westminster. Died 21 December 1815. Tomb (85).

1816

Granville Sharp, pamphleteer and abolitionist. Died on 6 July 1813 and buried in Fulham Churchyard. Monument erected 1816 by the African Institution of London (86).

Richard Sheridan, English dramatist. Died 7 July. Buried here 13 July. The stone, recut in 1956, reads: "THIS MARBLE IS THE TRIBUTE OF HIS ATTACHED FRIEND PETER MOORE" (87).

1826

William Gifford, critic and poet. Died 31 December and buried here. His friend Dean Ireland was buried with him. See 1842 (88).

1842

John Ireland, Dean of Westminster. Died 2 September 1842. Buried with his friend William Gifford on 8 September. See 1826 (89).

1844

Thomas Campbell, English poet. Died at Boulogne 15 June. Buried 3 July (90). See also 1848.

1845

Robert Southey, Poet Laureate. Died 4 March 1843. Buried at Crossthwaite church in Cumbria. Educated at Westminster School. The fine for the monument was paid 12 May 1845. The tablet to Hannah Pritchard was lowered to accommodate the memorial (see the letter of Robert H. Inglis to the chapter clerk G. G. Vincent, WAM 66363) (91).

1848

Thomas Campbell, English poet. Monument (92). See also 1844.

1854

William Wordsworth, Poet Laureate. Died 23 April 1850. Buried at Grasmere, Cumbria. Fine for monument paid 24 June 1854. Sir Gilbert Scott "had protested, though not publically, against Wordsworth's Statue, and that, strangely enough, it had been the product of a Committee, of which Ruskin and Beresford Hope were nominal members. *They did not, however act*—so much for Committees of Taste" (WAM 57685). Monument originally stood under the southwest tower with John Keble's monument and Matthew Arnold's statue. Removed to its present position in 1932 (93).

1860

Thomas Babington (Macaulay), first baron Macaulay. Died 28 December. Buried 9 January. See also 1866 (94).

1865

William Makepeace Thackeray, novelist and essayist. Died 24 December 1863. Buried at Kensal Green Cemetery, London. Fine for the bust was paid in April (95).

1866

Thomas Babington (Macaulay), first baron Macaulay. Died 28 December. Buried in the South Transept 9 January, 1860. The fine for the marble bust was paid on 21 December. The monument is signed George Burnard S 1866 (96).

1868

Reverend Henry Francis Cary, author and translator of Dante. Died 14 August 1844 and buried here. But (according to Stanley) the inscription was not added until 1868 (97).

1870

Charles Dickens, English novelist. Died 9 June. Buried here 14 June. Despite Dickens's wishes that he be the subject of no "monument, memorial or testimonial," by public demand it was decided that he would be brought to the Abbey for burial.[17] The ceremony was attended by the dean and only about twelve individuals and kept secret from the public. Afterward, however, the grave remained open until 16 June. A bust was offered in 1906, but declined (98).

Ca. 1871

George Grote, historian. Died 18 June 1871. Bust. Buried in the South Transept (99) with his friend Connop Thirlwall (see 1875) (100).

1873

John Keble, English poet and one of the triumvirate of the Oxford Movement. Died 29 March 1866. Buried 6 April at Hursley, where he was the vicar. The fine for the monument was paid 27 March 1873. The monument originally stood under the southwest tower as a larger monument; only the bust remains. Author of *The Christian Year* (101).

Nicholas Litlyngton, abbot of Westminster. Died 1386. The stone (cut in 1873) states, "buried near this spot in the Ancient Chapel of St. Blaize" and lists Owen Tudor, monk of Westminster and uncle of King Henry VII (probably Edward Bridgewater, son of Owen Tudor monk of Westminster from 1468/69–1471/72), as well as William Benson, last abbot and first dean of Westminster, 1549 (102).[18]

1875

Connop Thirlwall, historian, bishop of St. David's. Died 27 July 1875 and buried here with his friend George Grote (103).

1876

Connop Thirlwall, historian, bishop of St. David's. Bust. Died 27 July 1875 and buried with his friend George Grote (see 1871/75) (104).

1880

A monument was erected in 1880 of gray fossil marble stone at floor level that reads: "Near This Spot Were Buried / William Twisse D.D. 1646 / Prolocutor of the Westminster Assembly. / Thomas May 1650 Translator of Lucan, / and Secretary to the Long Parliament. / William Strong 1654— Stephen Marshall 1655 / Parliamentary Preachers. / These Were Removed by Royal Warrant 1661." All four were buried in a pit in St. Margaret's Churchyard (105).

Thomas May, English poet and historian, also had a monument that was erected in 1652 and destroyed at the restoration. The epitaph is preserved in Crull's *The Antiquities of St. Peters, or the Abbey Church of Westminster* (1772),

Appendix, 22–23. The monument to Dr. Thomas Triplett (1670) now occupies its place (106).

1883
William Spottiswoode, president of the Royal Society, printer to Her Majesty. Died 27 June and buried here. He is a direct descendant of John Spottiswoode, archbishop of St. Andrews—now buried in St. Benedict's Chapel. No stone is visible, but see the entry on Casaubon's monument (1634) (107).

1884
Archibald Campbell Tait, archbishop of Canterbury. Monument unveiled 13 November 1884 (108).

Henry Wadsworth Longfellow, American poet. Died 1882. Bust (109).

1885
Robert Burns, Scottish poet. Died 21 July 1796. Buried in Dumfries. The earl of Rosebury unveiled the bust on 7 March 1885. The bust was paid for by means of a shilling subscription coordinated by a committee in Glasgow (110).

Samuel Taylor Coleridge, English poet and critic. Died 25 July 1834. Buried in St. Michael's, Highgate. The monument was unveiled by James Russell Lowell, U.S. Minister to the Court of St. James, on 7 May 1885. The fine for the monument was given by an American (111).

1891
Matthew Arnold, English poet. The bust was formerly in St. George's Chapel (beneath the southwest tower). It was unveiled on 31 October 1891 and moved in 1967. Died April 15 1888. Buried at Laleham, Middlesex (112). See also 1989.

1892
Alfred Lord Tennyson, Poet Laureate. Died 6 October 1892 and buried 12 October. See also 1895 (113).

1894
Robert Browning, English poet. Died 12 December 1889. Buried here 31 December. Fee for the stone received 1894 (Funeral fee book). The lines "His

wife / ELIZABETH BARRETT BROWNING / is buried in Florence. /1806–1861" were ordered to be added at chapter, 12 November 1906 (114).

Jenny Lind-Goldschmidt, singer. Died 2 November 1887. Buried in Great Malvern, cemetery, Worcester. The monument was unveiled by Princess Christian (third daughter of Queen Victoria) 20 April. The top part of the marble to Lady Elizabeth Lechmere and Sir Thomas Robinson was cut down to fit Lind in (see 1777) (115).

1895
Alfred Lord Tennyson, English poet. Died 1892. Bust (as a young man). Buried in the South Transept. See 1892 (116).

1897
Sir Walter Scott, Scottish poet. Died 21 September 1832. Buried at Dryburgh Abbey. Funds for the bust were raised by public subscription. One fifth of the cost was paid by Americans. The bust was unveiled by the duke of Buccleuch on May 22 (117).

1903
John Ruskin, English critic. Died 20 January 1900. Buried in the churchyard of St. Andrew's in Coniston. Burial was offered by the dean and chapter but declined due to the fact that Ruskin wished to be buried where he died. The bronze roundel was unveiled 8 February 1902, but the memorial may have been in place earlier as the sculptor (Edward Onslow Ford) died 23 December 1901 (118).

1905
Henry Irving, actor. Died 14 October. Buried 20 October. First record of the burial of ashes in the abbey (119).

1926
William Heather, chorister and lay vicar in the Abbey choir, Gentleman of the Chapel Royal, founder of the Music Professorship at Oxford 1626. Died 1627 and "buried near this spot." His wife is buried here as well. The stone was inscribed on the tercentenary of the foundation of the Heather chair and unveiled on 18 June. See also Camden's memorial (1627) (120).

1928
Thomas Hardy, English novelist. Died 11 January. His will stated that he was to be buried at Stinsford, Dorset beside his parents. Nonetheless his ashes were buried in the Abbey on 16 January. His heart was removed before cremation and buried in Stinsford in a service simultaneous with that at Westminster. It is unclear when the stone was laid (121).

1934
Adam Lindsay Gordon, steeplechase rider and Australian poet. Died 24 June 1870. Buried at Brighton Cemetery, Melbourne. Bust unveiled 11 May 1934 (122).

1936
Rudyard Kipling, English writer. Died 18 January. Ashes buried here 23 January 1936. The original stone is at Bateman's in Sussex, Kipling's home (123).

1939
The Brontës. See 1947.

Samuel Johnson. A mural monument was erected in which a bust by Nollekens (1777) was placed. This was placed where Hannah Pritchard's monument had been—hers was moved to the triforium. On 17 March 1790 dean and chapter gave permission for a monument in the north aisle but this does not appear to have been executed. The fine was to be 25 guineas. Dean Stanley says that it was moved to St. Paul's. See 1784 (124).

1947
Charlotte, Emily Jane, and Anne Brontë. English novelists. Emily Jane Brontë died in 1848 and Anne died in 1849. Charlotte Brontë died in 1855. They are buried in the Church of St. Michael and All Angels, Haworth. The tablet was given by the Brontë Society and unveiled during July 1947. It had been erected on 9 October 1939 but because of the war no ceremony was held. It was formally handed over after evensong on 19 July 1947 (Abbey Chronicle) (125).

1954
John Keats and Percy Bysshe Shelley, English poets. Keats died 23 February 1821. Shelley died 8 July 1822. Both are buried in the Protestant Cemetery, Rome. A memorial to Keats was first proposed at chapter, 28 March 1939. A

decision on a memorial to Shelley was postponed on 27 September 1943. The two small oval tablets incised with the names "Keats" and "Shelley" were erected by the Keats-Shelley Memorial Association. The monument was unveiled 10 June (126).

1957
William Blake, English poet. Died 12 August 1827. Buried in Bunhill Fields, Finsbury. Statue unveiled on 24 November 1957 by Sir Geoffrey Keynes, chairman of the Blake Trust, on the occasion of Blake's bicentenary (127).

Gilbert Murray, classical scholar. Died May 20 1957. His ashes were buried here on July 5 (128).

1966
On 10 June a stone was unveiled that read, "IN THE 900TH YEAR OF THE ROYAL / FOUNDATION OF THE MONASTERY / The Dean and Chapter / of the Collegiate Church of St. Peter in / Westminster placed this memorial to / CAEDMON / who first among the English made verses" (129).

1967
Jane Austen, English novelist. Died 18 July 1817. Buried in Winchester Cathedral. The mural stone was unveiled 17 December. An earlier request (1939) for a memorial was refused on the grounds that there was already one at Winchester (130).

T. S. Eliot, Anglo-American poet. Died 4 January 1965. Buried in East Coker. Stone unveiled 4 January 1967 (131).

John Masefield, Poet Laureate. Died 12 May. Memorial service with committal of ashes 20 June (132).

1969
George Gordon (Byron), sixth baron Byron, English poet. Died at Missolonghi, Greece 19 April 1824. It is said that his heart is buried there. He is buried at Hucknall Torkard, Nottinghamshire. Previous requests for memorialization in the Abbey had always been refused. This stone was finally unveiled 8 May 1969 given by the Poetry Society (133).

1974
W. H. Auden, Anglo-American poet. Died 29 September 1973. Buried at Kirchstetten, Lower Austria. The stone was unveiled 2 October (134).

1975
Gerard Manley Hopkins, English poet. Died 8 June 1889. Buried at Glasnevin Cemetery, Dublin. Stone unveiled by duke of Norfolk 8 December (135).

1976
Henry James, Anglo-American novelist. Died 28 February 1916. Buried in Cambridge, Massachusetts. Stone unveiled 17 June (136).

1977
Adam Fox, canon of Westminster. Died and buried here. Stone given by the Skinner's Company (137).

1980
George Eliot (Mary Ann Cross), English novelist. Died 22 December 1880. Buried at Highgate Cemetery. Stone unveiled 21 June (138).

1982
Lewis Carroll (Charles Lutwidge Dodgson), English writer. Died 14 January 1898. Buried at Guildford, Surrey. The round design of the monument is meant to represent a rabbit hole. Unveiled 17 December (139).

Dylan Thomas, Welsh poet. Died 9 November 1953. Buried at Laugharne, South Wales. Stone unveiled 1 March (140).

1985
D. H. Lawrence, English novelist and poet. Died 2 March 1930 at Vence, France. His ashes were moved to New Mexico in 1936. The stone was unveiled by George Lazarus, president of the D. H. Lawrence Society, on 16 November (141).

On November 11 the Poet Laureate Ted Hughes unveiled a memorial stone to the War Poets: Richard Aldington, Laurence Binyon, Edmund Blunden, Rupert Brooke, Wilfrid Gibson, Robert Graves, Julian Grenfell, Ivor Gurney,

David Jones, Robert Nichols, Wilfrid Owen, Herbert Read, Isaac Rosenberg, Siegfried Sassoon, Charles Sorley, Edward Thomas. Graves was still alive when the stone was unveiled (142).

1988
Edward Lear, English writer. Died 29 January 1888. Buried in San Remo. Stone unveiled by Sir Hugh Casson 6 June (143).

1989
Matthew Arnold, English poet. Monument unveiled on 28 February 1989. He is the only person to have two memorials in the Abbey. The Abbey website suggests that this monument was commissioned because the original bust (which was unveiled in 1891 in the southwest tower chapel and moved to a window ledge in 1967) is difficult to see. See also 1891 (144).

John Clare, English poet. Died 20 May 1864. Buried in Helpston, Cambridgeshire. Monument unveiled June 13 (145).

1991
Laurence Oliver, actor. Died 11 July 1989. Ashes buried on 16 September. The stone was unveiled 23 September 1991 by Sir John Gielgud. Olivier was the last to be buried in Poets' Corner (146).

1993
Anthony Trollope, English novelist. Died 6 December 1882. Buried in Kensal Green Cemetery, London. Stone unveiled by Prime Minister John Major 25 March (147).

1996
Sir John Betjeman, Poet Laureate. Died 19 May, 1984. Buried in St. Enodoc's in Trebetherick. Cartouche unveiled 11 November (148).

2001
Frederic William Maitland, English jurist and historian. Died 19 December 1906. Buried in the English cemetery at Las Palmas in the Canary Islands. Stone unveiled 4 January (149).

2005

Peggy Ashcroft, actress. Died 14 June 1991. Her ashes were scattered around the ancient mulberry tree at New Place, Stratford-upon-Avon. Her stone was unveiled by Sir Peter Hall on 7 June (150).

2009

"THE ROYAL BALLET. THE FOUNDERS" and in the center their names: Ninette de Valois, Frederick Ashton, Constant Lambert, Margot Fonteyn. Stone unveiled on 17 November (151).

2011

Ted Hughes O.M., O.B.E., poet. Died October 28, 1998. His stone was unveiled on 6 December by Nobel Laureate Seamus Heaney (152).

2013

C. S. Lewis, writer, scholar, and Christian apologist. Died 22 November 1963. Stone unveiled on November 22 (153).

Buried in the South Transept, but without any visible marker

1396

John Shakel, knight. Apparently buried next to his former partner and "martyr to the rights of sanctuary" Robert Hauley (see 1378).

1616

Francis Beaumont, English dramatist. Died 6 March. Buried in front of St. Benedict's Chapel near where Dryden would be laid to rest.

Richard Hakluyt, English travel writer. Died 23 November. Educated at Westminster School and prebendary. Probably buried somewhere in the South Transept.

1627

John Beaumont, English poet. Brother of Francis Beaumont. Died 19 April. Buried in front of St. Benedict's Chapel near where Dryden would be laid to rest.

1669

John Denham, English poet. Died 10 March. Buried near his friend Abraham Cowley.

Sir Robert Stapleton, English poet and translator. Died 11 July. Buried in the South Transept near the western door 15 July.[19]

1673
Robert Moray, first president of the Royal Society. Died 6 July. Buried near William Davenant.

1761
Joshua Ward, famous quack doctor. Died 21 December. Buried 26 December near William Camden.

NOTES

Westminster Abbey Muniments is abbreviated WAM.

PREFACE

1. Hawthorne, "Up the Thames," 610.

2. Burial or commemoration in Poets' Corner is closed to those of Great Britain's former colony, with one exception. Henry Wadsworth Longfellow was commemorated here in 1884, though not without a fair amount of controversy. For a full treatment of the commemoration, see Lathem, *England's Homage to Longfellow*.

3. Nora, "Between Memory and History: *Les Lieux de Mémoire*," 12.

4. Ibid.

5. Huyssen, *Present Pasts: Urban Palimpsests and the Politics of Memory*, 2.

6. Ibid.

7. Hutson, "Fortunate Travelers: Reading for the Plot in Sixteenth-Century England," 86.

8. Sidney, *A Defense of Poetry*, 53.

9. Hutson, "Fortunate Travelers," 96.

10. Foucault, 26.

INTRODUCTION

1. The legislation also grew out of a desire to forestall abuses by the vergers who were charging visitors fees on top of those they paid to enter the Abbey. WAM, RCO Box 4, 1851–58: "Returns of Fees charged for admitting individuals to see the monuments at Westminster Abbey and St. Paul's printed by order of parliament. Dated 7 August, 1843. For several years, up to Midsummer 1841, a fee of 3d. was paid by each individual for admission to Poet's Corner and the Nave and 1s. more for admission to Chapels and the North Transept; and thus up to Midsummer 1841, 1s. 3d. was paid by each individual for admission to the whole of the Abbey. From Midsummer 1841 to the present time, there has been a free admission to Poet's Corner; a fee of 3d. has been charged to each individual for admission to the Nave and North Transept, and admission to the whole of the Abbey has been 6d. The monuments are explained by guides appointed for the purpose, and no farther remuneration is on any account to be received."

2. Carlyle, *On Heroes, Hero-Worship and the Heroic in History*, 94.

3. Ibid., 97.

4. Ibid.

5. Ibid., 94.

6. Bond, *Spectator* 1: 108–109.

7. Baker, "Travel Advisory; Recovering the Calm at Westminster Abbey."

8. Harkin, "Modernist Anthropology and the Tourism of the Authentic," 655. For a critique of Harkin's notion see Trigg, "Walking Through Cathedrals: Scholars, Pilgrims, and Medieval Tourists."

9. In addition to Cromwell himself and Admiral Robert Blake, twenty others were also exhumed from the more general spaces of the Abbey though not all were buried behind the prebendal houses in St. Margaret's. See "The Warrant for the Disinterment of the Magnates of the Commonwealth" in Stanley, *Historical Memorials of Westminster*, 601 and accompanying note.

10. Fitzgerald, *Poems on Several Occasions*, 24–25.

11. Fuller, *The Church-History of Britain*, 152.

12. Verdery, *The Political Lives of Dead Bodies*, 27.

13. Geary, *Living with the Dead*, 202.

14. Brown, *The Cult of the Saints*, 11.

15. Ibid., 10.

16. See, for instance, Duffy, *The Stripping of the Altars*, 475.

17. See Prendergast, *Chaucer's Dead Body*, 45–57.

18. See Chapter 2.

19. Castronovo, *Fathering the Nation*, 110.

20. See Chapter 2.

21. Jonson, quoted in Hinman, *The Norton Facsimile: The First Folio of Shakespeare*, 9.

22. Dart, *Westmonasterium*, 1: xxxviii.

23. Ibid.

24. Ibid.

25. Libra, "Westminster Abbey, As It Is and As It Was," 22.

26. Morris, *Architecture and History and Westminster Abbey*, 35.

27. Stanley, *Historical Memorials of Westminster*, 351.

28. Eliot, "Tradition and the Individual Talent," 31–32.

29. Connell, "Death and the Author: Westminster Abbey and the Meanings of the Literary Monument," 559.

30. Stanley, *Historical Memorials of Westminster*, 351.

31. What Canon Fox seems to suggest is that as an object of contemplation, Poets' Corner is indeed, as the anonymous nineteenth-century author above suggests, an eyesore. The puzzle is, how can such an "informal" object of contemplation lead to a contemplation of formal beauty? Fox's response to the Corner—that it is informal, irrational, and disordered, but nonetheless an appropriate space to appreciate "the great English art"—is born, I think, of the stark contrast between the space of Poets' Corner and the temporal construction of the Corner. Fox, "Poetry Is the Great English Art," 3.

32. See Lerer, *Chaucer and His Readers*, 149.

33. This claim goes back at least to Augustine, but see Freccero, "The Fig Tree and the Laurel: Petrarch's Poetics," 27.

34. Benjamin, *One Way Street and Other Writings*, 52.

35. Flatley, *Affective Mapping*, 18.

36. Qtd. in McCoy, *Alterations of State*, 56.

37. Brown, *A Description of Mr. D—n's Funeral*, 8.

38. The phrase is Žižek's from *For They Know Not What They Do*, 261.

39. Anon., "Evermore," *New Yorker*, 21.

CHAPTER 1. WESTMINSTER ABBEY AND THE INCORPORATION OF POETS' CORNER

1. The idea came to him, he says, when he wondered "what an Indian would think of such a motley Herd of People, and what a diverting Amusement it would be to him to examine with the Traveler's Eye all the remarkable things of the mighty City." Brown, "A Walk Around London and Westminster, Exposing the Vices and Follies of the Town," 3: 315.

2. Henri Lefebvre once famously remarked that one might be able to read space that has already been produced, but codes "worked up from literary texts" could never tell us about the genesis of a space (Lefebvre, *The Production of Space*, 7). In the absence of an origin, Lefebvre's point of departure was the idea that an already produced space can be read precisely because that which encodes the space is already in place to be read. As will become clear, I think that Lefebvre's claim gives voice to an epistemology of despair. If space is always already encoded by the time we approach it, it resists what he calls "decryption." Its status as space remains like the psychologist's black box. I would suggest that the only way to understand truly or remember Poets' Corner is in some sense to inhabit it precisely because it was a space that was designed to enable memory and defeat time. But even before we consider how to inhabit Poets' Corner, we need to come to terms with how the space surrounding the South Transept originally came to be.

3. Freud, "Constructions in Analysis," 23: 259.

4. Indeed, I argue this in "Spenser's Phantastic History: *The Ruines of Time* and the Invention of Medievalism."

5. Burkert, *Greek Religion*, 206–207.

6. Certeau, *The Practice of Everyday Life*, 118. The anthropologist Katherine Verdery has argued that dead bodies can help place political claims, as when the Minister of Foreign Affairs for Serbia and Montenegro claimed that "Serbia is wherever there are Serbian Graves." The speaker was Vuk Draskovic. Qtd. in Verdery, *The Political Lives of Dead Bodies*, 95.

7. Harrison, "Hic Jacet," 396.

8. Geary, *Living with the Dead in the Middle Ages*, 221–242.

9. Ibid., 235–236.

10. Stanley, *Historical Memorials of Westminster Abbey*, 340. The only other remaining shrine is St. Wite's in Whitchurch Canonicorum.

11. Qtd. in ibid., 45.

12. Barlow, *The Life of King Edward*, 113.

13. As we will see, this claim became especially important much later when the Abbey produced charters that also contained the story (though these charters were late fabrications).

14. "Sex namque et xxx annis rex delituerat Eadwardus in tumulo, eumque iuxta condicionem mortalitatis nostre arbitrati sunt nonnulli humanitas in cineres defluxisse. Quidam uero pio mentis desiderio quoddam diuinum presagiebant in eo cuius membra, quia uirginei

kebab.

pudoris dampna non senserant, in quadam resurrectionis gloria corpus manere dubitabant." Bloch, *La Vie de S. Édouard Le Confesseur par Osbert de Clare*, 121. The translation is taken from Robinson, *Gilbert Crispin: Abbot of Westminster*, 24.

15. Ibid., 24. "Cum uero eam solidam sentiret in carne, heros obstupuit de miraculi nouitate. Temptauit tamen pilum aliquem si sponte sequeretur suauiter detrahere, ut de sancti regis reliquiis huiusmodi copia preualeret habundare. Astans uero et considerans hec domnus abbas Gillebertus: 'Quid' inquit 'est, presul amabilis, quod agis? Qui in terra uiuentium perpetuam cum sanctis Dei possidet hereditatem, quare temporalis eius glorie queris minuere porcionem? Relinque, uir insignis, talia presumere, et noli tantum principem in regni sui thalamo pregrauere.' Iam uero Gunnulfus totus in lacrimis resolutus: 'Probe, uenerabilis abbas, locutus es' ait. 'Set noueris quod me nulla presumptionis audacia ad hoc precipitauit. Ardor namque sancte deuotionis quo in amore gloriosi regis incalui monuit ut uel unum ex barba niuea pilum contingerem, quod ad eius memoriam sollempniter exceptum auro precioso preciosius possiderem. At quia spes effluxit nec ad uotum michi cedere potuit, que sua sunt ut Dominus habeat in pace, et superni iuris non spolietur concessa celitus libertate. Requiescat in palatio suo et incorruptus et virgo, donec tripudio gratulabundus occurat aduentui iudicis, recepturus in hac carne perhennem gloriam beate immortalitatis.'" Bloch, *La Vie de S. Édouard Le Confesseur*, 121.

16. Barlow, *The Life of King Edward*, 132–133.

17. According to Aelred's *Life* (ca. 1070) when Lanfranc, Archbisop of Canterbury, attempted to depose Wulfstan, Bishop of Worcester, Wulfstan said that he would only give up his pastoral staff to Edward. He drove the staff into the lid of the sarcophagus and said, "Take this, my master," he said, "and deliver it to whom thou will." When none of the assemblage (including the bishop of Rochester and Lanfranc himself) could withdraw it, Lanfranc rescinded the deposition and Wulfstan withdrew the staff from the sarcophagus. See Barlow, *The Life of King Edward*, 118n and 133n.

18. Geary makes this point vis-à-vis the body of Helen of Athyria and Troyes. To have the whole body (as opposed to some piece of it) was to possess something that distinguished the resting place of the relic from other churches and religious houses that also possessed relics of the true cross, the holy blood, etc. *Living with the Dead in the Middle Ages*, 227–228.

19. Barlow, *The Life of King Edward*, 113.

20. The term *gloriosus*, however, was approved. See Barlow, *The Life of King Edward*, 130.

21. Mason, *Westminster Abbey and Its People, c. 1050–c. 1216*, 311.

22. None of the surviving lists of *festa ferianda* issued by the bishops of the thirteenth century and later periods include it. See Harvey, *Westminster Abbey and Its Estates in the Middle Ages*, 43.

23. Ibid., 44.

24. For a lively rendering of the "Becket story," see John Butler, *The Quest for Becket's Bones*, 1–33.

25. Ultimately, the body was returned to Trinity Chapel, and a tomb was built very much like the one in the manuscript illumination of Edward's tomb.

26. One need only recall that Chaucer's pilgrims actually leave the environs of London near Edward's shrine in Westminster in order to proceed to Canterbury. Interestingly, on this journey we are promised a tale of St. Edward (presumably Edward the Confessor) by the Monk. Yet he immediately changes his mind and decides first to relate a number of "tragedies," or reversals of fortune. The Knight stops him apparently before he finishes telling all the "hundred tragedies" that he knows and so "the lyf of Seint Edward" is never told. Chaucer, *The Riverside Chaucer*, VII: 1970–1971.

27. The coronation ceremony insisted on the sovereign's connection to Edward. See Stanley, *Historical Memorials of Westminster Abbey*, 41–47.

28. Ibid., 132.

29. The body was, however, missing the heart which was sent to rest with his ancestors at Fontevrault.

30. See Strohm's illuminating essay for a discussion of the delay, "The Trouble with Richard: The Reburial of Richard II and Lancastrian Strategy," *Speculum* 71 (1996): 87–111.

31. Agamben, *Homo Sacer: Sovereign Power and Bare Life*, 100.

32. So says the coronation rite in the *Liber Regalis*. See Stanley, *Historical Memorials of Westminster*, 47.

33. C Lefort, *Democracy and Political Theory*, 250.

34. Ibid., 249.

35. Ironically, his decision might be seen as a kind of analogue of Henry II's penance before Becket's tomb, for Henry's grave would always be secondary to Becket's which was, after all, a monument to the Church's triumph over the state.

36. Stanley, *Historical Memorials of Westminster*, 340. The poet quoted is Aaron Hill in a letter to Alexander Pope. The occasion of the letter was the death and burial of Hill's wife.

37. Ross, "Just When Did 'British Bards Begin t'Immortalize'?" 386. Stanley, *Historical Memorials of Westminster*, 283. Fitzgerald, "Upon Poets' Corner in Westminster Abbey," 24–25.

38. Libra, "Westminster Abbey, As It Is and As It Was," 22.

39. Indeed, the body indicated the "thereness" of that most important of places, the altar, as every church altar was to contain a relic. (Geary, *Living with the Dead in the Middle Ages*, 202).

40. The poet William Basse seems to be the first to think of the South Transept as a kind of specialized poetical space. See his poem "On Mr. Wm. Shakespeare, he died in April 1616," It circulated widely in manuscript in the seventeenth-century and was printed five times (see Chapter 2). It is quoted in E. K. Chambers, *William Shakespeare: A Study of the Facts and Problems*, 2: 226.

41. See Fitzgerald, "Upon the Poets' Corner in Westminster Abbey," 24–25.

42. Apparently, the prince had allowed them to keep the count despite his rank. The crown, however, apparently maintained an interest in him. See Dahmus, *The Prosecution of John Wyclyf*, 74.

43. See Edouard Perroy, "Gras profts et rançons pendant la guerre de cent ans: l'affaire du Comte de Denia," 575. None of the chronicles mention Chamberlain. As Ralph Hanna notes, the documentary evidence adduced by Perroy often accords ill with the chroniclers' representations of what happened (*London Literature*, 242).

44. Wyclif claims that the English government had apparently arranged for the release of some English knights still being held in Spain and needed Alphonso to secure its plan. See Workman, *John Wyclif; A Study of the English Medieval Church*, 315.

45. Ibid.

46. Haydon, *Eulogium*, 3: 342, 343.

47. Some sources have it that he ran around the Chancel and was finally slain before the Shrine of Edward the Confessor (Workman, *John Wyclif*, 316). This makes for a more colorful tale and could be true. But it also seems suspiciously close to the events of 1381 when a similar outrage involved John Mangett, marshall of the Marshalsea. He was caught by the forces of Wat Tyler and torn away from the Shrine. See Brayley, *The History and Antiquities of the Abbey Church of St. Peter, Westminster*, 266.

48. Thomas Walsingham, *Historia Anglicana*, 1: 377–378.

49. Specifically, Walsingham (no friend to Gaunt) claimed that the prisoner was wanted in order to advance Gaunt's own claim for the throne of Castile. See Walsingham, *Historia Anglicana*, 1: 376; Thompson, *Chronicon Angliae*, 210–211.

50. See Dahmus, *The Prosecution of John Wyclyf*, 75.

51. Walsingham, *Historia Anglicana*, 1: 379; Thompson, *Chronicon Angliae*, 210.

52. Of course, Walsingham reports this. But Wycliff's own writings seem to suggest that the rumor (if not the substance) was real. See Poole, "Review of *Johannis Wyclif, Tractatus de Ecclesia*," 574.

53. Strachey, *Rotuli parliamentorum; ut et petitiones, et placita in parliamento*, 3: 35–37;

54. Wyclif himself says that he had prepared a case exonerating the duke, and the arguments advanced in Parliament are expanded in Wyclif's arguments in his *De Ecclesia* in which he extensively discussed the Hauley/ Shakel case. See Dahmus, *The Prosecution of John Wyclyf*, 76–77. For a full treatment of Wyclif's position and some reasons why Walsingham would fail to mention Wyclif, see Elizabeth Allen's treatment of the Hauley/Shakel affair in " 'As mote in at a munster dor': Sanctuary and Love of This World."

55. Strachey, *Rotuli parliamentorum*, 3: 37. Again, though Wycliff is not mentioned by name here, it is generally understood that, as he was at Parliament, and as the argument is his, it is most probably he whom the rolls are talking about.

56. Haydon, *Eulogium*, 3: 346. For a version of the story from Aelred's life of Edward the Confessor see Stanley, *Historical Memorials of Westminster Abbey*, 21–22. The story is first alluded to in the charters purportedly from the Confessor.

57. This was a bit odd as in 1355 Abbott Langham had made the same claim using the same charters, and the court had found, in fact, that sanctuary extended *only* to felony.

58. Walsingham, Thomas. *The Saint Albans Chronicle: The Chronica Maiora of Thomas Walsingham*, 1: 237.

59. Line 1721 of the poem outlines Daniel's description of the sin (the unholy use of the temple vessels) that leads to the condemnation of Belshazzar (Andrew, *The Poems of the Pearl Manuscript*). For a reading of this line that links it with sexual transgressions earlier in the poem see Keiser, *Courtly Desire and Medieval Homophobia*, 262.

60. Spearing, *Readings in Medieval Poetry*, 148.

61. Walsingham, *The Saint Albans Chronicle*, 237.

62. Ibid.

63. Ibid., 243.

64. The rationale he gives for the removal of Parliament is that "they" (presumably Gaunt and the council) "thought that the bishops and the common people of the realm, especially the people of London, would not dare to resist or oppose their will expressed in so distant a place" (ibid., 247). One would not want to rule this political explanation out, but one would also have to admit that the place where Parliament usually met in London, the Chapter House of Westminster Abbey, was not really available, as the entire precincts of the Abbey were considered polluted.

65. Haydon, *Eulogium*, 342.

66. Ibid., 344.

67. Durandus, *Rationale Divinorum Officiorum*, 102.

68. Ibid., 105.

69. Qtd. in Hayes, *Body and Sacred Place in Medieval Europe 1100–1389*, 13.

70. Durandus, *Rationale Divinorum Officiorum*, 67–68. Translation by Hayes, *Body and Sacred Place in Medieval Europe 1100–1389*, 13.

71. Walsingham, *The Saint Albans Chronicle*, 237.

72. As reported in the *Liber Niger Quaternus*. See Robinson, "An Unrecognized Westminster Chronicler, 1381-1394."

73. Flete, *The History of Westminster Abbey*, 137. Special thanks to Matthew MacGowan who helped with the translation and suggested the emendation of *dabis* to *diebus*.

74. Stanley, *Memorials of Westminster Abbey*, 393.

75. Camden, *Reges, Reginae, Nobiles, & alij in Ecclesia Collegiata B. Petri Westmonasterij sepulti . . .* , I1a.

76. Brayley, *The History and Antiquities of the Abbey Church of St. Peter, Westminster*, 2: 150.

77. Camden, *Reges, Reginae, Nobiles . . .* , I2r. Thanks to Matt McGowan who aided in the translation.

78. Wyclif, of course, claims that Hauley drew his sword first and thus was the one who really violated the holiness of the sanctuary. Camden gives a different reading of the final line some five years later in his *Remains Concerning Britain*, most crucially altering the final word *enses* (swords) to *hostes* (enemies). The altered line might then read "I who in my misfortune experienced the enemy bringing evil here for the first time." On the basis of *lectio difficilior*, I think the earlier version more probable.

79. Fuss, "Corpse Poem," 30.

80. He was probably buried in Westminster because his house was within the precincts of the Abbey. See Derek Pearsall, "Chaucer's Tomb: The Politics of Reburial," 52-53. Pearsall asserts that Chaucer may have taken the house to gain the honor of burial in the Abbey precincts.

81. Pearsall makes a case for Chaucer's desire to be buried here despite the lack of such documentation, ibid., 53-54.

82. Richard II, in fact, seems to be the king who began this practice. See Stanley, Historical Memorials of Westminster Abbey, 204. The phrase "regum receptaculum" is from Walsingham, *Historia Anglicana*, I: 378.

83. Pearsall, *The Life of Geoffrey Chaucer*, 207.

84. But see Strohm, *Chaucer's Tale*, 135.

85. See Finnel, "The Poet as Sunday Man: The Complaint of Chaucer to His Purse," 150. So extensive are the actions against Chaucer in the years 1388-1399, in fact, that they receive a separate chapter in the *Chaucer Life Records*.

86. See my "Politics, Prodigality, and the Reception of Chaucer's 'Purse.'" Pearsall says, "There are no grounds whatever for the notion that he was seeking sanctuary for himself, to escape pursuit for actions of debt" (*The Life of Geoffrey Chaucer*, 275).

87. The clause was a standard for Westminster leases. Translation from Finnel, "The Poet as Sunday Man," 150.

88. This particular quotation is from the *Ancient State, Authoritie, and Proceedings of the Court of Requests,* 2 October 1596 (see Spurgeon, *Five Hundred Years of Chaucer Criticism*, 1:143). See 1: 99, 1:128 for the other orders.

89. MacMichael, "Sanctuary at Westminster," 14.

CHAPTER 2. MELANCHOLIA, MONUMENTAL RESISTANCE,
AND THE INVENTION OF POETS' CORNER

Note to epigraph: Derrida, *Spectres of Marx: The State of the Debt, the Work of Mourning, and the New International*, 9.

1. The poet John Gower, for instance, had a house within the precincts of St. Mary Overie and was originally buried in the priory church. His tomb has since been moved but can still be seen near its original site in Southwark Cathedral.

2. Lethaby, "Chaucer's Tomb," 137; Pearsall, "Chaucer's Tomb: The Politics of Reburial."

3. Pearsall, 62.

4. Prendergast, *Chaucer's Dead Body: From Corpse to Corpus*, 45–69.

5. I rely on Joshua Scodel's concise analysis of the contradictory function of funeral "monuments" for the next two paragraphs (*The English Poetical Epitaph*, here 22).

6. Scodel, *The English Poetical Epitaph*, 22.

7. "Prohibiting Destruction of Church Monuments," in Hughes and Larkin, *Tudor Royal Proclamations*, 2: 146.

8. Ibid., 2: 146–147.

9. Qtd. in Farmer, "Fulke Greville and John Coke: An Exchange of Letters," 221.

10. "Satyr II. 1 (Vanitie)," qtd. in Scodel, *The English Poetical Epitaph*, 19.

11. The elegy to Thomas Ravis also invokes the two types of "immortality" and critiques "perjur'd stone." See the discussion in Scodel, *The English Poetical Epitaph*, 19.

12. See Freud, "Mourning and Melancholia" and Loewald, "Some Considerations on Repetition and Repetition Compulsion." Freud suggests that unlike mourning, in which the mourner loosens the psychological bonds that have connected him or her with the lost object, melancholia leads to a pathological connection with the object.

13. Biddick, *The Shock of Medievalism*, 55; Castronovo, *Fathering the Nation: American Genealogies of Slavery and Freedom*, 111.

14. Contemporary clinical definitions of melancholia as pathological along with modern (and Renaissance) dismissals of phantasy as an aberration, naturalize humanistic and positivistic recoverings of the past while ignoring the possibilities of a conscious and constructive melancholia (possibilities that have recently received a good deal of attention). See, for instance, Flatley, *Affective Mapping*; Ng and Kazanjian, eds., *Reading Loss: The Politics of Mourning*.

15. Simpson, *Reform and Cultural Revolution*, 17.

16. Bale, qtd. in ibid.

17. Levine, *Humanism and History*, 78.

18. For a more extensive treatment of this "rewriting," see Prendergast, "Spenser's Phantastic History," 175–196. See also Summit, "Monuments and Ruins."

19. Spenser, *The Shepheardes Calender* in *Yale Edition of the Shorter Poems*, 112. Moroney, "Spenser's Dissolution," 116–117, attempts to reconcile these competing visions of the effects of the Reformation by pointing to the Spanish setting of Arthur's acts. Her assertion is that Arthur's acts are politically justified, while the Blatant Beast's rampage through England reveals a destruction of England's patrimony.

20. Spenser, *The Ruines of Time* in *The Yale Edition of the Shorter Poems*, 238.

21. Agamben quotes Hugh's *De medicina animae* in *Stanzas*, 13.

22. Aristotle, *Problems*, 953a. Judith Schiesari has emphasized that such melancholy is not only a male purview but that "the eroticized nostalgia that recuperates loss in the name of an imaginary unity . . . . gives to the melancholic man . . . a privileged position within literary, philosophical, and artistic canons," *The Gendering of Melancholia*, 11.

23. Prendergast, *Chaucer's Dead Body*, 134–135.

24. Quoted in Agamben, *Stanzas*, 24.

25. Romano Alberti, *Trattato della nobiltà dell pittura* (1598). Qtd. in ibid., 25.

26. Qtd. in Agamben, *Stanzas,* 20.

27. Agamben, *Stanzas,* 21.

28. Jewel, *A Reply to Harding's Answer,* vol. 2, art. 14, 10th division, 659–661. See Nohrnberg, *Analogy of "The Faerie Queene,"* 107–108, for commentary on this passage

29. Nashe, *The Anatomie of Absurditie,* 11.

30. Ascham, *Of Imitation,* 1:3.

31. Sidney, *A Defense of Poetry,* 85.

32. Ibid., 53.

33. For a discussion of Spenser's invocation of the notion of "true-seeming" and its relationship to phantastical history see Prendergast, "Spenser's Phantastic History."

34. Horace, 216.

35. Ibid., 217.

36. Spenser, *The Yale Edition of the Shorter Poems,* 679.

37. Protestant writers were not, of course, of one mind about the worth of preserving the past. In fact, it is precisely because the medieval past was in the process of being destroyed by the dissolution of the monasteries and other Tudor "reforms" that antiquarians tended to see some value in that past (see Aston, "English Ruins and English History").

38. Weever, *Epigrammes,* 101.

39. Rambuss reads in Weever's words a critique of Spenser's indulgence in the publication of the *Complaints* and the temporary abandonment of his "imperial" project *The Faerie Queene* (*Spenser's Secret Career,* 92). Yet if he critiques the *Ruines* here, he must have come around, as he has frequent recourse to it in his *Ancient Funerall Monuments.*

40. Camden, *Reges, Reginae, Nobiles,* 34v.

41. "Vix enim ibi secessum & scribendi otium nactus, cum á rebellibus è laribus eiectus & bonis spoliatus, in Angliam inops reuersus, statim expirauit, & Westmonasterii prope Chaucerum impensis Comitis Essexiae inhumatus." Camden, *Tamus Alter,* 1720.

42. Lane, *Triton's Trumpet,* qtd. in Spenser, *Works of Spenser,* I: lxxxvii.

43. Qtd. in Herford and Simpson, *Works of Ben Jonson,* 1: 137.

44. Fuller, *The Histories of the Worthies of England,* 219–220.

45. Phillips, *Theatrum Poetarum: Or a complete Collection of the Poets,* 35–36.

46. Harvey, *Foure Letters and Certaine Sonnets,* 7.

47. The pathological turn of Phillips's story would seem to reappear in a slightly different version that made its way into the "Life" attached to the 1679 edition of the *Faerie Queene.* Structurally, the drama is much the same. Yet here, the anonymous author suggests that the incident took place not in front of the queen, but Philip Sidney.

48. Spiers, *Note-Book and Account Book of Nicholas Stone,* 54. The countess of Dorset also erected a monument to her tutor, Samuel Daniel, a member of the Wilton circle and an admirer of Spenser's. This indeed would have seemed to have been a monument rather than a tombstone for most reports place Spenser's grave close to Chaucer's 1556 tomb on the eastern wall of the South Transept, while the monument raised in 1620 is in the middle of the south wall. Given the words in the epitaph, the expectation would, rightly, be that Spenser's body lay under this particular stone at this particular spot. It is possible, of course, that the body is there and that by "near to" Chaucer the sources meant in the same transept. But later evidence seems to rule out this particular possibility. As I will discuss at greater length in Chapter 5, the space in front of the monument was excavated in 1938, but the coffins found there came from a date later (perhaps eighteenth century) than the Spenser burial. Alternatively, there may have been a temporary marker that migrated from the original burial spot.

49. "HEARE LYES (EXPECTING THE SECOND / COMMINGE OF OVR SAVIOVR CHRIST / JESUS) THE BODY OF EDMOND SPENCER, / THE PRINCE OF POETS IN HIS TYME; / WHOSE DIVINE SPIRIT NEED NOE, / OTHIR WITNESSE THEN THE WORKS / WHICH HE LEFT BEHINDE HIM, / HE WAS BORNE IN LONDON IN / THE YEARE 1510, AND / DIED IN THE YEARE / 1596." The transcription of the 1620 memorial is taken from Dart, *Westmonasterium*. The tomb was restored by private subscription in 1778, at which time the dates were altered from 1510 to 1553 and from 1596 to 1598.

50. This is undoubtedly the result of a misunderstanding of an earlier source that reports that Essex paid for Spenser's funeral. It may also have something to do with the legend of Essex's aid coming too late, for an analogous story has Essex providing the funds for Spenser's funeral only after he was reminded to do so by Lodowick Lloyd (fl. 1573–1610) poet and compiler, a sergeant at arms to Elizabeth I and James I. As John Lane put it, "Ne had that cost vppon [him] binn imploid, / But for my lovinge frend *Lodowick Lloyd.*" (Qtd. in Spenser, *Works of Spenser,* I: lxxxvii.) Essex was apparently so busy preparing for his invasion of Ireland that he forgot that there was no money to pay for his old friend's funeral.

51. Camden, *Reges, Reginae, Nobiles, & alij,* 34v. The translation, with the oft-repeated first rhyming couplet is from Dart, *Westmonasterium,* 75–76.

52. For the difficulties in understanding where Chaucer was buried, see Prendergast, *Chaucer's Dead Body.*

53. Spenser was seen as the spiritual heir of Chaucer. As Francis Thynne, the son of Chaucer's early modern editor (William Thynne), puts it, "The famous Chaucer yealds his Lawrell crowne / Unto thy sugred penn, for thy renowne," in Thynne,, *Emblemes and epigrammes,* 71.

54. "To the Reader," in *A Continuance of Albions England* (1606), A2r.

55. Spenser, *The Works of Edmund Spencer: A Variorum Edition,* 10: 531–532.

56. In the entry for 4 May 1602 Manningham reports that William Towse told him: "When hir Majestie had given order that Spenser should have a reward for his poems, but Spenser could have nothing, he presented hir with these verses: 'It pleased your Grace upon a tyme / To graunt me reason for my ryme. / But from that tyme untill this season / I heard of neither ryme nor reason.'" Manningham, *The Diary of John Manningham,* 78.

57. Browne, *Britannia's Pastorals,* 1: 226. One might well echo Judson's desire for a less poetic recitation of this story (*The Life of Spenser,* 206). But see *Revue Celtique* 48 (1931): 447.

58. Shakespeare, *Complete Works,* lviii. There are many versions of this poem (see below); this one is taken from the 1640 edition of Shakespeare's works.

59. Folger MS V.a.232, p. 32 has the title of the poem as "An Epitaph Prepared for Shakespeare, if hee had been buryed at Westminster," Wells and Taylor, eds., *William Shakespeare: A Textual Companion,* 163.

60. Stanley, *Historical Memorials of Westminster Abbey,* 286.

61. *Songs and Lyrics from the Plays of Beaumont and Fletcher,* Fellowes, ed., 38.

62. Cicero, *Pro Archia Poeta* X 24–32, qtd. in Cicero, *The Orations,* 2: 421.

63. Shakespeare, *The First Folio of Shakespeare,* prep. Hinman, A4r.

64. Marlowe was buried in Saint Nicholas's Churchyard, Deptford. Kyd was buried in the churchyard of the former St. James Church, London (now the Huddleston Community Center). And Lyly was buried in the Church of St. Bartholomew the Less, London.

65. See, for instance, the comment by Jasper Mayne's publisher in 1639. Helgerson, *Self-Crowned Laureates,* 145.

66. Sidney, *A Defense of Poetry,* 69.

67. Helgerson, *Self-Crowned Laureates,* 154.

68. Qtd. in Short, "Ben Jonson in Drayton's Poems," 158.

69. Goldsmith, 302.

70. Brown, *The Works of Mr. Thomas Brown*, 3: 314.

71. Sir John Beaumont (brother of Francis) has to be counted the fourth poet, as he died in 1627. Only one of his works (*The Metamorphosis of Tobacco*) was published in his lifetime. He is purportedly buried (like his brother) near St. Benedict's Chapel under a nameless stone.

72. In the 1660s a vicar of Stratford, John Ward wrote, "Shakespear, Drayton, and Ben Jhonson [*sic*] had a merry meeting, and itt seems drank too hard, for Shakespear died of a feavour there contracted" (Chambers, *William Shakespeare,* 2.250).

73. The evidence that Lady Anne Clifford, countess of Dorset, raised the monument to Spenser is based on the testimony of Nicholas Stone (the sculptor, effigy- and monument-maker). Spiers, *Note-Book and Account Book of Nicholas Stone*, 54. The evidence connecting her with the erection of Drayton's monument is somewhat contradictory. Aubrey, in *Brief Lives,* claims that Lady Anne erected the monument in 1631, but then asserts (in a letter to Anthony Wood) that the countess who ordered the monument was "governess to Prince Charles, now our King." If true, then this is a different countess of Dorset—Mary Curzon, who was the wife of the fourth Earl, Edward Sackville, brother-in-law of Lady Anne Clifford. For an argument that the latter is responsible for raising the monument see Jean Wilson, "The Patron of the Monument to Michael Drayton in Westminster Abbey."

74. Fuller, *The Church-History of Britain*, 152.

75. Heylyn, *Examen Historicum,* 69 [item 84].

76. Aubrey, *Brief Lives*, 1: 224. It is quite possible, however, that Aubrey got this information from Heylyn, as he probably wrote after Heylyn's work had been published.

77. Fuller, *The Appeal of Iniured Innocence*, 2: 42.

78. Even if, as we will see in Chapter 5, Spenser's monument probably does not mark his grave.

79. As a number of critics have pointed out, the etymology of the word *monere* means "to remind." See, for instance, Castronovo, *Fathering the Nation*, 109–111.

80. In fact, Stanley speaks to this uncertainty in the nineteenth century, saying, "It is uncertain whether he is buried in the Nave or in this spot [beneath his monument]," *Historical Memorials of Westminster*, 287. The official guide to the Abbey is silent about his burial spot.

81. Derrida, *Spectres of Marx*, 9.

82. Connell, "Death and the Author," 563.

83. See above.

84. Connell, "Death and the Author, 563.

85. Scodel, *The English Poetic Epitaph*, 164.

86. Herrick, *The Hesperides*, 910.

87. Scodel, *The English Poetic Epitaph*, 165.

88. Aubrey, *Brief Lives*, 172.

89. The current triangular stone is not original, but was replaced when the Nave was re-paved in 1821. The original stone, however, was found in the stoneyard of the Clerk of the Works and placed in the north wall of the nave near the grave by Dean Buckland (Stanley, *Historical Memorials of Westminster*, 289).

90. Aubrey tells us that he lived "in Westminster, in the house under which you passe as you goe out of the church yard into the old Palace" (*Brief Lives*, 172). Stanley locates it between the Abbey and St. Margaret's (*Historical Memorials of Westminster*, 288). See Bayley, "Ben Jonson in Westminster," 112.

91. Sir Edward Walker, garter King of Arms at the time, qtd. in Dobson, "Frank Buckland and Rare Ben Jonson," 298.

92. This monument was erected quite late—sometime in the eighteenth century but before 1728, by the earl of Oxford. See *Westminster Abbey*, 95.

93. Stanley suggests as much (*Historical Memorials of Westminster*, 289).

94. Crull, *The Antiquities of St. Peter's*, II: 45. The original stone was "broken up, but was replaced in 1866" (Stanley, *Historical Memorials of Westminster*, 291).

95. Aubrey, with his taste for salacious gossip, suggests that Davenant was Shakespeare's illegitimate son. See Shoenbaum, *Shakespeare's Lives*, 62.

96. Aubrey, *Brief Lives*, 195.

97. His body (along with three others) was taken to Tyburn and hung. He was then decapitated and his head was placed on top of Westminster Hall.

98. The quotation is from Sprat, *An Account of the Life and Writings of Mr. Abraham Cowley*, A12r—A12v.

99. Stanley, *Historical Memorials of Westminster*, 291.

100. See Chapter 1 for the importance of Hauley's death and burial. Suggestively, Cowley left money for debtors in his will.

101. The literal translation of the epitaph as well as the amplification can be found in Henry Campkin, 267–268. Also included is a "burlesque" of the epitaph that suggestively opposes the "rotting corpse" with Cowley's soaring body. It ends by stating "Whilst thou dost soar aloft leave coyrs behind / to be interrd in antient monast'ry / And to the chimeing rabble safely joyn'd / [To] Draiton, Spencer and old Jeoffrey." But we cannot be sure it is not a nineteenth-century forgery. See, Kinney, http://etext.lib.virginia.edu/kinney/small/urn.htm.

102. Thomas Higgons, *Upon the Death of Mr. Cowley* in Kinney http://etext.lib.virginia.edu/kinney/small/elegies.htm (accessed 3 January 2014).

103. Orrery, *Several Copies of Verses on the Death of Mr. Abraham Cowley and his Burial in Westminster Abbey* in Kinney, http://cowley.lib.virginia.edu/small/elegies.htm accessed 3 January 2014.

104. Ibid.

CHAPTER 3. LOVE, LITERARY PUBLICITY, AND THE NAMING
OF POETS' CORNER

Note to epigraphs: From Ode 1. 4. 13–17 in Bond, 108; P.S., *Notes and Queries* (1851): 381.

1. Craske, "Westminster Abbey," 60.

2. Ibid., 64.

3. Craske, *The Silent Rhetoric of the Body*, 29.

4. Reverend John Coates, "On the Monument of the Honourable Lady Frances Nightingale," ll. 36–39, qtd. in Craske, *The Silent Rhetoric of the Body*, 336.

5. Craske, *The Silent Rhetoric of the Body*, 33.

6. Qtd. in Bindman and Baker, *Roubiliac and the Eighteenth-Century Monument*, 35. The Nightingales are buried in the north ambulatory.

7. Ibid., 288.

8. Ibid., 289.

9. There is, however, a poetical burial between the Addison monument and the South Aisle. Sir William D'Avenant was buried in the grave of the man who stood against him for

poet laureate, Thomas May (quadrant c3). In 1661 Charles II ordered that May (along with other Cromwell sympathizers) be exhumed and thrown into a common pit near St. Margaret's. D'Avenant's burial here seems to have been an attempt to erase the history of spot rather than a conscious attempt to extend Poets' Corner (at this time occupying only the southeast corner of the transept). This particular spot seems to have been chosen as a burial ground for sympathizers, for William Twisse, William Strong, and Stephen Marshall were also buried here (and disinterred). See chronological list for 1880. It is a profound irony that the monument that extended the poetical space of Abbey was, in fact, Addison's. And it is a further irony that the monument, a full-scale statue of Addison either in classical dress or a dressing gown (depending on whom you asked), was itself a cenotaph rather than a tomb as Addison would satirize such productions in *Spectator* 26. Addison was buried in the Abbey, but in the North Aisle of Henry VII's chapel near his patron Charles Montague.

10. Bond, *The Spectator*, 1: 108.

11. Ibid.

12. Ibid.

13. Ibid., 1:109.

14. For a treatment of the problematic relationship between satire and commemoration in the Abbey and elsewhere see Craske, *The Silent Rhetoric of the Body*, 1–10 et passim.

15. *The Post Man, And the Historical Account, & c.* 750 (Saturday, May 11–Tuesday May 14 1700), 2.

16. *Post Boy* 792 (Sat. May 4–Tues. May 7, 1700), 2.

17. Pepys, *The Letters of Samuel Pepys*, 239.

18. Tom Brown, *Works*, 3: 228.

19. Pope, *The Twickenham Edition*, 3:228. The epitaph that ultimately appeared on Rowe's monument (erected by his widow in 1742) is based on Pope's suggested lines, but it remains unclear if Pope actually wrote it. This monument was removed to the south triforium in the 1930s when fifteenth-century wall paintings were found behind it. Though the 1742 monument was purportedly placed near the burial place of Rowe (as well as his daughter and eventually his wife), Samuel Johnson quotes Dr. Welwood to the effect that "he died the sixth of December, 1718, in the forty-fifth year of his age; and was buried the 19th of the same month in Westminster-abbey, in the aile where many of our English poets are interred, over against Chaucer, his body being attended by a select number of his friends, and the dean and choir officiating at the funeral" (*Lives of the English Poets*, 1: 69). The Chapter Book of the Abbey states "On Oct. 29th 1742 ordered that leave be given to put a Monument in the South Cross of the Abbey between Shakespeare and Mr. Gays for Mr. Rowe the Poet on the payment of twenty guineas." It would be hard for Rowe's monument to point the way to Dryden's tomb if it were in St. Faith's chapel (between Shakespeare's and Gay's monuments), so Pope's original epitaph only makes sense if he had expected that it would be erected over Rowe's corpse (along the east wall of the South Transept). Ironically then, it was Rowe who was buried beneath a nameless stone. For the details of the epitaph see Jackson, "Pope's Epitaphs on Nicholas Rowe," 76–79.

20. See Prendergast, *Chaucer's Dead Body*, 60–69.

21. "To the Memory of John Dryden, Esq." in Playford and Roper, *Luctus Britannici*, 18.

22. And see Trigg, *Congenial Souls*, 145–152 for an expansive treatment of this phrase.

23. Johnson, *Lives of the English Poets: A Selection*, 145.

24. Brown, *A Description of Mr. D—n's Funeral. A Poem*, 3.

25. Ibid., 10.

26. Fitzgerald, *Poems on Several Occasions*, 24–25.

27. See, for instance, his reaction to the fire at the Cottonian library: "Upon the Burning of the Cottonian Manuscripts at Ashburnham House" in *Poems on Several Occasion*, 71–74.

28. Certainly in the case of Pollio this is true as Virgil addressed his famous fourth eclogue to him. But even Caius Mecaenas's name was, at the time, synonymous with that of the wealthy patron of the arts.

29. Poole, "Westminster Abbey: A Study on Poets' Corner," 137.

30. Poole, "Westminster Abbey, The Lost Chapel of St. Blaize," 244.

31. Ibid.

32. It was sometime between 1723 and 1733 that the monuments finally spilled over into what had been the chapel of St. Blaize. Samuel Butler's bust, though it now stands over Spenser's monument in what was the original space of the Corner, stood for a time in front of the wall paintings representing St. Christopher and the incredulity of Thomas that were uncovered in 1936. It was moved in October 1733 in order to make room for John Gay's monument (which was subsequently removed to the triforium along with Nicholas Rowe's monument when the paintings were discovered). We are uncertain about when the bust first made its way to what had been St. Blaize's, but the Initial from John Dart's *Westmonasterium* (1723), shows Butler's monument on the south wall of the Transept near Chaucer's tomb, so Butler's monument must have been moved sometime after that but before 1733. Given the destruction of the east wall of the Chapel in 1723, it is possible that in addition to building the monument to Prior, the monument to Butler was moved at this time. Poets after this, of course, continued to be buried elsewhere in the Abbey. William Congreve, for instance, was buried in the Nave in 1729 apparently at the direction of his patroness, Henrietta Godolphin, the second duchess of Marlborough (Stanley, *Historical Memorials of Westminster*, 301–302). But it was clearly during this period that the modern idea of the Corner was crystallized.

33. See Chapter 2.

34. Goldsmith, *Persian and Chinese Letters*, 302.

35. Pope, *The Twickenham Edition*, 4: 349–350. There are three versions of the epitaph. See 4: 350–352.

36. Johnson, *Lives of the English Poets*, 3: 382.

37. Pope, *The Twickenham Edition*, 4: 247–248.

38. For an excellent discussion of Pope's involvement with Poets' Corner, see Brownell, *Alexander Pope and the Arts of Georgian England,* 339–361.

39. The inscription, as he printed it in a footnote, reads: "DRYDEN. / *Natus* Aug. 9. 1631 / *Mortuus* Maii I. 1701 / *Johannes Sheffield, Dux Buckinghamiensis, fecit.*" Pope, *The Twickenham Edition*, 6: 209. The monument itself reads somewhat differently. Notably, Dryden's dates are 1632 and 1700, read *posuit* for *fecit*, and the date of the erection on the monument (1720) is included.

40. "On the Old Bust," 95–96. See also Scodel, *The English Poetic Epitaph*, 293.

41. Ibid.

42. Sherburn, *Early Career*, 277.

43. "M. S. / SAMUELIS BUTLERI, / qui Strenshamiae in agro Vigorn. nat 1612: obit. Lond. 1680. / Vir doctus imprimis, acer. integer; / Operibus Ingenii, non item praemiis, faelix: Satyrici apud nos Carminis Artifex egregius; Quo simulatae Religioni Larvam detraxit, / Et Perduellium scelera liberrime exagitavit: Scriptorum in suo genere Primus & Postremus. / Ne, cui vivo deerant fere omnia, / Deesset etiam Mortuo Tumulus, / hoc tandem posito marmore curavit /JOHANNES BARBER Civis Londinensis. 1721." Qtd. in Brayley, *The History and Antiquities of the Abbey Church of St Peter*, 2:263.

44. Pope, *Dunciad* 4; in *The Twickenham Edition*, 5: 354.

45. Ibid., n. 119.

46. See, for instance, Pope's correspondence about Barber.

47. Spence, *Observations, Anecdotes, and Characters of Books and Men*, 161.

48. Spence claims that he heard the story from Warburton who got it from Pope. But then he says that he was "assured of it by others who knew both Mr. Pope and the Alderman well" (ibid.).

49. See Brownell, *Alexander Pope and the Arts of Georgian England*, 357.

50. The same John Barber who was responsible for the raising of the monument to Samuel Butler was the one who obtained the license. See Mack, *Alexander Pope*, 397.

51. Edmund Curll, a particular target of Pope, brought out a pamphlet which contained the expurgated material called "The Castrations" (Mack, *Alexander Pope*, 398).

52. See Goldgar, *Walpole and the Wits*.

53. Gay, *Poetical Works*, 76.

54. The phrase is Watt's. See "Publishers and Sinners," 18.

55. For an evenhanded treatment that explores the extent to which Curll was "a symptomatic but dynamic figure of the developing public sphere in early eighteenth-century Britain," see Baines and Rogers, *Edmund Curll*, 8, passim.

56. *Dictionary of National Biography*, 33: 947–948.

57. Qtd. in Mack, *Alexander Pope*, 479.

58. The lapse of the Licensing Act of 1662 in 1692 allowed the number of printers to grow in contravention of the original decree by the Tudors and the Star Chamber decree of 1627 (Watt, "Publishers and Sinners," 8).

59. Pope, *The Twickenham Edition*, 6: 395.

60. Qtd. in Dobson, *The Making of the National Poet*, 135. It should be noted, however, that John Rich, manager of the Covent Garden Theatre suggested a statue as early as 1726. See Brownell, *Alexander Pope*, 354.

61. Dobson, *The Making of the National Poet*, 147.

62. The quatrain appeared in April 1739. Ibid., 141.

63. Roach, "Celebrity Erotics," 213.

64. See the Introduction, 2.

65. Brownell, *Alexander Pope and the Arts of Georgian England*, 354.

66. William Benson was an architect who had raised a monument to Milton in 1737 and included an epitaph similar to Barber's (Scodel, *The English Poetic Epitaph*, 293 n.). His role in raising a monument to Milton would have been noxious to Pope as he was also a loyal servant of the Walpole government. Scodel believes that Pope's attacks on Barber and his silence about Sheffield can be explained by their difference in class. He quotes part of an anonymous epigram, "Respect to *Dryden* justly *Sheffield* paid; / . . . / But whence is *Barber*? That a name so mean / Should, join'd with *Butler*, on a tomb be seen!" The epigram is highly suggestive but perhaps is testament more to the need to explain Pope's silence about Barber than any views that Pope himself felt. There were a number of suggestions for what might be inscribed on the empty scroll, many of them critical of the Walpole government. The words that can be found on the statue's scroll are a mangled version of Prospero's speech from *The Tempest* IV: 1: 152–156. The dean apparently had it inscribed in order to defuse "the statue's potential for sedition" (Dobson, *The Making of the National Poet*, 146).

67. Indeed, he may have been involved in the erection of Sheffield's own monument in the north-east aisle of Henry VIII's Chapel in 1722 (Brownell, *Alexander Pope and the Arts of Georgian England*, 346).

68. Scodel, *The English Poetic Epitaph*, 292.

69. Tangible proof that friendship could override even Pope's satirical sense might be seen in one of the nonpoetical monuments that he oversaw at the Abbey. When he erected the monument to his friend James Craggs in the southwest corner of the Nave, he allowed verses to be inscribed on the monument that spoke to Craggs's "faith . . . honour," nobility and honesty. The inscription claims that he "lost no Friend" was "Ennobled by Himself, by All approv'd," despite the fact that he had disgraced himself in the South Sea scandal. The epitaph was widely parodied and ridiculed (see Brownell, *Alexander Pope and the Arts of Georgian England*, 346).

70. Goldsmith, *Persian and Chinese Letters*, 302.

71. Ibid.

72. Stanley, *Historical Memorials*, 202.

73. Craske, "Westminster Abbey," 58–59.

CHAPTER 4. ABSENCE AND THE PUBLIC POETICS OF REGRET

Note to epigraph: Stanley, "Unpublished Recollections," 74. WAM 64918.

1. Queen Emma was, in fact, on a tour to raise funds for an Anglican cathedral in Hawaii.

2. Leersen, "Monument and Trauma," 205.

3. Stanley, *Historical Memorials,* 318.

4. Watson, *The Literary Tourist*, 29–30; Matthews, *Poetical Remains*, 224–225.

5. Matthews, *Poetical Remains*, 32–34, 222–224, 307.

6. The phrase is Matthews's (ibid., 223).

7. Qtd. in Stanley, *Historical Memorials of Westminster Abbey*, 300.

8. Ibid., 319.

9. Hobhouse, *Recollections of a Long Life*, 3: 38. It is perhaps unsurprising that immediately following this sentiment Hobhouse narrates his notorious success in destroying Byron's (apparently scandalous) account of his own life.

10. Samuel Smiles, *A Publisher and His Friends*, 1:436.

11. Robinson, *John Clare by Himself,* 157.

12. The letter was originally addressed to the editor of the *Morning Post*. But when the *Post* did not publish it, "Sydney" sent it to the editor of the *Courier* with a cover letter. These letters, along with one written a week later, were collected and published in a pamphlet. Sydney, *Sydney's Letters*, 6–7.

13. Ibid., 9–13.

14. Stanley, *Historical Memorials of Westminster*, 351.

15. Ibid.

16. Ibid., 319.

17. Bradley and Bradley, *The Deanery Guide to Westminster Abbey*, 22.

18. Anon. "Monuments in the Abbey," *Times* (London), 18 January 1933. Arnold's bust was not, however, removed to Poets' Corner until 1967. See chronological listing for 1891.

19. The *Daily Express*, in a discussion of the transformation of the Chapel, characterized Stanley's project as "a kind of overflow from the south transept. He [Stanley] even styled this

place "Little Poets' Corner"—after the arrival of a terrible statute of Wordsworth and busts or tablets equally bad of Matthew Arnold, Keble and Kingsley" (30 July 1932).

20. See, for instance, Herbert Mansfield's letter to the *Daily Telegraph* where he agrees with an earlier assessment of the crowded quality of the monuments: "Sir—I have read Mr. Walter G. Bell's letter, and am in heartiest agreement with him. Much of the fine arcading of the Abbey has been wantonly destroyed by many of these hideous monuments" (29 December 1934).

21. Bond, *The Spectator*, 108.

22. Barron, "The Londoner," 19 January 1933.

23. For a treatment of the function of these effigies, see Harvey and Mortimer, ed., *The Funeral Effigies of Westminster Abbey*.

24. Watson, *The Literary Tourist*, 29.

25. Ibid., 29–30.

26. They were, it is true, sometimes removed to other portions of the Abbey, but this tended to happen (as in the case of the memorials to Butler and Rowe that were removed to expose the fifteenth-century wall painting) only when there was some driving need to remove them.

27. "Not only Nelson's tomb is now in the crypt, but many monuments have been moved there over time . . . many of the heroes have thus lost their positions in the narrative they once constituted" (Hoock, "Nelson Entombed," 136–137).

28. In fact, St. Paul's was originally almost devoid of decoration for theological reasons. See ibid., 119.

29. Ibid.

30. William Morris, *Architecture and History*, 37.

31. There were a number of other proposals. For these and a discussion of why such buildings were never built despite enormous popular interest see Anthony D. C. Hyland, "Imperial Valhalla."

32. Jonathan Glancy, "Top 10 Buildings that Remain Just a Dream—or a Nightmare," *Guardian* (1 November 2001).

33. Hyland, "Imperial Valhalla," 132.

34. The same might be said about Margaret Cavendish, who was buried in the North Transept with her husband, William Cavendish, duke of Newcastle.

35. Stanley, *Historical Memorials of Westminster*, 299.

36. Ibid., 341.

37. Guthrie, "The Apotheosis of Milton," 8: 469.

38. Ibid.

39. Barbaro, *On Wifely Duties*, 205.

40. Stallybrass, "Patriarchal Territories," 127.

41. For instance, Charles de St. Denis, Sieur de St. Evremond. See Guthrie, "The Apotheosis of Milton," 8, 521.

42. Qtd. in Haight, *George Eliot*, 548–549.

43. Haight suggests that Stanley was taken aback when he discovered that Eliot was not married to George Henry Lewes (*George Eliot*, 452). Stanley, *Letters and Verses*, 445.

44. Huxley, *Life and Letters*, 2: 19.

45. The letter is to Professor (later Sir) William Flower. Huxley, *Life and Letters*, 2: 31.

46. In both cases, however, the commemoration of these women was not only delayed, but belated. The Brontës had to wait to be officially commemorated until some eight years after their memorial had been donated because the war prevented any official ceremony in 1939. And

the Abbey had been petitioned for a Jane Austen memorial in 1939, but had denied the request because there was already a memorial at Winchester where she is buried. Her case suggested that something of a double standard existed well into the twentieth century.

CHAPTER 5. POETIC EXHUMATION AND THE ANXIETY OF ABSENCE

Note to epigraph: Clement Mansfield Ingleby, *Shakespeare's Bones*, 2.

1. Qtd. in Ingleby, *Shakespeare's Bones*, 28.

2. Ibid.

3. Ibid, 29.

4. See Barbara Stafford's discussion of how this system attempted to extract "semantic meaning from isolatable looks" and hence uncover more spiritual qualities of character by reference to the material qualities of the body (*Good Looking*, 38). Craig, *Shakespeare's Portraits Phrenologically Considered*, 5.

5. Young, *Conjectures*, 36–37.

6. Coleridge, *Coleridge's Shakespearian Criticism*, 233.

7. Ibid.

8. The scale was anonymously produced, but for potential connections to an earlier "Poetical Ballance" published by Mark Akenside; see Bate, "Shakespeare and Original Genius," 87.

9. Stafford, *Body Criticism*, 116.

10. Ibid., 118.

11. Bate, *The Genius of Shakespeare*, 185. The phrase is Elijah Fenton's, see 168.

12. Gautier, *La Comédie de la Mort*, in *Poésies Complètes*, 139

13. Troutbeck, *The Nineteenth Century* 42 (August 1897): 336.

14. It is clear why Troutbeck thought he had examined Chaucer's bones, but it remains unclear that the bones were actually that of Chaucer. See Prendergast, *Chaucer's Dead Body*, 117–125.

15. Ellis, "Genius and Stature," 93.

16. Lombroso, *The Man of Genius*.

17. *Evening Standard* (2 November 1938), 1.

18. WAM 61987. 21 July 1937.

19. "Westmonasterii propre Chaucerum impensis Comitis Essexiae inhumatus, Poëtis sunus ducentibus, flebilius carminibus & calamis in tumulum conjectis" (Camden, *Tomus Alter Annalium Rerum Anglicarum*, 172). It was perhaps Stanley's comment about Spenser's funeral that ultimately led to the Baconians' request. "What a funeral was that at which Beaumont, Fletcher, Jonson, and, in all probability, Shakespeare attended!—what a grave in which the pen of Shakespeare may be mouldering away!" (Stanley, *Historical Memorials*, 285–86).

20. This argument is most fully represented in the official organ of the Bacon Society in Eagle's "Is There a Shakespeare MS. Poem in Spenser's Tomb?" 263–264.

21. See Ibid., in which Eagle cheerfully admits that it was his letter to the *Daily News* that occasioned the paper to approach Dean Norris about opening the tomb.

22. WAM 61986A. 20 July 1937.

23. M.R., "Shakespeare Poem Discovery? Grave to be Opened," *The Era* 3103 (18 August 1938). Also WAM 61992.

24. Even if, somehow, he did not know when he agreed to open the tomb on 1 August. He must have known by 25 August when he received the letter (including the article from *The Era*) from the Bacon Society disavowing any connection to the *The Era* article (WAM 61992). Interestingly enough, the author of the essay (a certain Miss Rowlands) admitted only to speaking to the secretary of the dean.

25. "Is There a Shakespeare MS. Poem?" 263–264.

26. Collini, *Public Moralists,* 347.

27. Ibid., 369.

28. See Saler, *The Avant-Garde in Interwar England,* 76–77, 104.

29. London Transport Museum B2, "Art and Commerce," February 1916, 10, qtd. in Ibid., 27.

30. Patterson, *Negotiating the Past,* 9–18. Qtd. in Girouard, *The Return to Camelot,* 83.

31. The letter dated 24 August 1938 is from Valentine Smith and is addressed to the Secretary of the Dean. WAM 61992.

32. Hamer, "An Account of the Opening of a Grave," 18.

33. Tanner's account is found in his manuscript book of "Recollections," 126–127 in the Westminster Abbey Library.

34. The letter of 28 October 1938 can be found in Sir Charles Peers Papers Box III, folder XIII (12) kept in the Westminster Abbey Library.

35. WAM 62011*, 18.

36. WAM 62011*, 2.

37. Collini, *Public Moralists,* 370.

38. The letter from 7 October 1938 (WAM 62001) reads:

> "Dear Mr. Dean,
> Edmund Spenser's Tomb.
>
> I duly received your letter of 4th October in which you mention that you had opened the tomb to the extent of discovery of the Coffin, when work was stopped by the demands of A.R.P. [Air Raid Precautions].
>
> Naturally, I read this with great astonishment as I understood from our first interview that at least two representatives of The Bacon Society would be invited to witness the opening of the grave. No doubt it was your intention to do so at the point where work ceased and that the search will be completed in due course.
>
> Until the bottom level of the coffin is cleared, it cannot be regarded as conclusive as to whether or not Camden reported the truth. If the coffin is of wood, and in a fair state of preservation, the quills at least should have survived.
>
> In view of the importance of your letter, I immediately sent copies to Mr. Theobald and Mr. Valentine (p. 2) as there was a Council Meeting yesterday at which your letter was read and considered. In view of its importance to the Bacon Society generally, the Secretary was instructed to communicate with you and there is, for that reason, no necessity for me to go further into the matter myself.
>
> Yours very truly,
> (signed) R. L. Eagle"

39. WAM 62008, 8 November 1938. This letter had suffered quite a bit of damage from the Deanery fire in 1940. The parts of words in brackets are conjectural.

40. See his letters to F. C. Wellstood and the Duke of Rutland—both 28 October 1938 (Sir Charles Peers Papers Box III, folder XIII [12]).

41. Tanner, "Recollections," 126.

42. Tanner inserts the statement thus: "Later in the evening the Dean and myself drew up a statement which he telephoned to the Central News and B.B.C. (I insert the Dean's autograph M.S.)

[On 130v the statement reads thus]

"The search for the grave of Edmond (sic) Spenser took place in W.A. on Nov. 2 and 3. The space immediately in front of the Spenser monument was found to be taken up by solid foundations, and further search showed that the nearest grave was some 12 feet to the N.E. of the monument. It had been cut out of these foundations to a depth of 3 feet 8 inches from pavement level. This grave was carefully examined and was found to contain a lead coffin. There was no inscription or other means of identifying this, but there was reason to believe that it was post-Elizabethan. There were indications that two other interments had taken place in the same grave—but it was impossible to assign any definite date for these. The contents of the lead coffin were not disturbed, but the ground around was carefully sifted, and revealed no trace of any manuscripts or pens."

43. Hamer later changed his mind, but for his (and Peers's) initial impressions see his "An Account of the Opening of a Grave." See also Tanner, *Recollections of a Westminster Antiquary*, 101.

44. "We Have Now Lost Spenser," *Liverpool Daily Post* (22 November 1938).

45. William Spooner published at least thirty-seven of these views (ca. 1820s–1850s) that apparently could be used with the Polyorama Panoptique, an optical toy based on Daguerre's diorama. They often portrayed famous places such as the Thames tunnel. Spooner's most famous Protean View was of Mount Vesuvius in repose and then erupting when backlit.

46. Garber, "Shakespeare as Fetish," 247.

47. The anonymous *A Poetic Epistle from Shakespear in Elysium to Mr. Garrick at Drury-Lane Theatre* is quoted in Dobson, *The Making of the National Poet*, 167–168.

48. Davies, *Memoirs of the Life of David Garrick*, 2: 462.

49. Sheridan, *Verses to the Memory of Garrick*. Qtd. in Dobson, *The Making of the National Poet*, 183.

50. Pratt, *Miscellanies*, 2: 25.

CODA

1. Cathedral Archives, Memorandum (with four enclosures) for the board of trustees, the Cathedral Church of St. John the Divine, 1.

2. Ibid.

3. Anon, "Evermore."

4. Eagleton, "Having One's Kant," 9.

5. Cathedral Archives, Robert Gorham Davis to Mrs. Edward T. Chase, 16 July 1988.

6. Cathedral Archives, Mrs. Edward T. Chase to Robert Gorham Davis, 2 August 1988.

7. Smith, "Cathedral Bars Ezra Pound from Its Poets' Corner."

8. Ibid.

9. Ibid.

10. Ibid.

11. Ellison, "Jew-Hating Ezra Pound Barred from Poets' Corner."

12. S. "N.B." *Times Literary Supplement* (7 February 2007).

13. Ibid.

14. "The Dean of Westminster must give his permission for all burials and monuments in the Church. Ashes only are permitted. People who have served the Abbey in an official capacity, such as a Dean, a Canon, Organist or Surveyor of the Fabric may be buried here and eminent persons of British nationality from various fields may be considered. The last poet interred was John Masefield in 1967, and Laurence Olivier, actor, was buried here in 1991." www .westminster-abbey.org/.

15. McCrum, "Deptford Secrets."

16. "Marlowe Given Poets' Corner Tribute."

17. Ibid.

18. Ibid.

19. The accounts are virtually identical.

20. McCrum, "Deptford Secrets."

21. See for instance, Stanley Wells's comment: "It's quite obviously there because the Marlowe Society is in part dedicated to trying to prove that Marlowe wrote Shakespeare. It's absolute nonsense, of course" (qtd. in Reynolds, "Marlowe Tribute").

22. Caines, "Weeping on the Marge."

23. Ibid.

24. Howse, "Ted Hughes Memorial: Poets' Corner Is a White Elephants' Graveyard."

25. Ezard, "Poet's Own Words Say Goodbye." C. S. Lewis was memorialized in 2013, but probably less for his poetry than for his fiction and other writings.

26. Ibid. Both Caedmon and the War Poets are commemorated in Poets' Corner, and Hughes, in fact, unveiled the stone dedicated to the War Poets in 1985.

CHRONOLOGICAL LIST OF STONES AND MONUMENTS
IN THE SOUTH TRANSEPT

1. It is possible, however, that earlier testimony could tell us who was buried here. For instance, stones 13 and 18 might well be stones recorded by Brayley when they were still legible. Unfortunately, the inscriptions on the stones only recorded the initials of those buried beneath them (e.g., H.S.J. died 12 November, 1713; T. G. Ar. died 17 January 1713). See Brayley, *The History and Antiquities*, 268.

2. John Flete is our source for the original burial spot (Robinson, *The History of Westminster Abbey*, 122).

3. Thus says the official Abbey guidebook. Stanley claims he was buried here on the tenth (*Historical Memorials*, 307), but Brayley says that he lay in state for several days after his death (*The History and Antiquities*, 254).

4. Heather was also buried in the South Transept. For his monument (which is just in front of Camden's) see 1926.

5. Peter Heylyn, *Examen Historicum*, 69.

6. Aubrey, *Brief Lives*, 1: 239.

7. Stanley, *Historical Memorials*, 309–310.

8. Brayley, however, has it 18 September (*The History and Antiquities*, 267).

9. Whinney, *Sculpture in Britain*, 90.

10. Johnson, *Lives of the English Poets*, 1: 69.

11. Gunnis, *Dictionary of British Sculptors 1660–1851*.

12. The Chapter Book, March 17, 1790 contains an order for its erection. See Stanley, *Historical Memorials*, 317.

13. Brayley, *The History and Antiquities*, 2: 270.

14. See the funeral fee book.

15. John Physick, *Designs for English Sculpture 1680–1860* (London: Her Majesty's Stationery Office, 1969), 11.

16. *Gentleman's Magazine*, 1808, 1088. Stanley records the date of erection as 1808 (*Historical Memorials*, 301).

17. See the text from Dickens's publicly printed will in Matthews, *Poetical Remains*, 226.

18. Westminster Abbey, *Westminster Abbey: Official Guide*, 99.

19. See Stanley, *Historical Memorials*, 291n.

BIBLIOGRAPHY

Agamben, Giorgio. *Homo Sacer: Sovereign Power and Bare Life*. Trans. Daniel Heller-Roazen. Stanford: Stanford University Press, 1998.

————. *Stanzas: Word and Phantasm in Western Culture*. Trans. Ronald L. Martinez. Minneapolis: University of Minnesota Press, 1993.

Allen, Elizabeth. "'As mote in at a munster dor': Sanctuary and Love of This World." *Philological Quarterly* 87 (2008): 105–133.

Andrew, Malcom and Ronald Waldron, ed. *The Poems of the Pearl Manuscript*. Berkeley: University of California Press, 1978.

Aristotle, *Problems*. Trans. W. S. Hett. Cambridge: Harvard University Press, 1937.

Ascham, Roger. *Of Imitation*. In *Elizabethan Critical Essays*, ed. G. Gregory Smith. 1–45. Oxford: Clarendon Press, 1904.

Aston, Margaret. "English Ruins and English History: The Dissolution and the Sense of the Past." *Journal of the Warburg and Courtauld Institutes* 36 (1973): 231–255.

Aubrey, John. *Brief Lives*, ed. A. Clark. Oxford: Clarendon Press, 1898.

Baines, Paul and Pat Rogers. *Edmund Curll, Bookseller*. Oxford: Clarendon Press, 2007.

Baker, Emily Laurence. "Travel Advisory; Recovering the Calm at Westminster Abbey." *New York Times* (15 February 1998).

Barbaro, Francesco. *On Wifely Duties*. Trans. B. G. Kohl, in *The Early Republic: Italian Humanists on Government and Society*, ed. B. G. Kohl, R. E. Witt, with E. B. Welles. 189–230. Philadelphia: University of Pennsylvania Press, 1978.

Barlow, Frank, ed. *The Life of King Edward*. London: Thomas Nelson and Sons, 1962.

Barron, Oswald. "The Londoner." *Evening News*, 19 January, 1933.

Bate, Jonathan. *The Genius of Shakespeare*. Oxford: Oxford University Press, 1998.

————. "Shakespeare and Original Genius," in *Genius: The History of an Idea*, ed. Penelope Murray. 76–97. Oxford: Basil Blackwell: 1989.

Bayley, A. R. "Ben Jonson in Westminster." *Notes and Queries* 11 (5 February 1910): 112.

Benjamin, Walter. *One Way Street and Other Writings*. Trans. Edmund Jephcott and Kingsley Shorter. New York: Harcourt Brace Jovanovich, 1978.

Biddick, Kathleen. *The Shock of Medievalism*. Durham, NC: Duke University Press, 1998.

Bindman, David and Malcolm Baker. *Roubiliac and the Eighteenth-Century Monument: Sculpture as Theatre*. New Haven: Yale University Press, 1995.

Bloch, Marc, ed. *La Vie de S. Édouard Le Confesseur par Osbert de Clare* in *Analecta Bollandiana* 41. Paris: Libraire Auguste Picard, 1923, 4–131.

Bond, Donald F., ed. *The Spectator*. Oxford: Clarendon Press, 1965.

Bradley, M. C. and E. T. Bradley. *The Deanery Guide to Westminster Abbey*. London: Pall Mall Press, 1905.

Brayley, E. W. *The History and Antiquities of the Abbey Church of St. Peter, Westminster: including notices and biographical memoirs of the abbots and deans of that foundation.* London: J. P. Neale, 1818.

Brown, Peter. *The Cult of the Saints.* Chicago: University of Chicago Press, 1981.

Brown, Tom. *A Description of Mr. D—n's Funeral. A Poem.* 3rd ed. London: A. Baldwin, 1700.

———. "A Walk Around London and Westminster, Exposing the Vices and Follies of the Town," in *The Works of Thomas Brown.* 4th ed. London, 1720.

———. *The Works of Mr. Thomas Brown, serious and comical, in prose and verse.* London, 1745.

Browne, William. *Britannia's Pastorals, The Seconde Book* In *Poems,* ed. Gordon Goodwin. London, 1893–94.

Brownell, Morris R. *Alexander Pope and the Arts of Georgian England.* Oxford: Oxford University Press, 1978.

Burkert, Walter. *Greek Religion.* Trans. John Raffan. Cambridge: Cambridge University Press, 1988.

Butler, John. *The Quest for Becket's Bones.* New Haven: Yale University Press, 1995.

Caines, Michael. "Weeping on the Marge." *TLS* (17 October 2003).

Camden, William. *Reges, Reginae, Nobiles, & alij in Ecclesia Collegiata B. Petri Westmonasterij sepulti . . .* London, 1600.

———. *Tomus Alter Annalium Rerum Anglicarum, et Hibernicarum, Regnante Elizabetha, Qui nunc demum prodit: Sive Pars Quarta.* London, 1627.

Campkin, Henry. N.T. *Notes and Queries,* n.s. 5 (1852); 267–68.

Carlyle, Thomas. 1840. *On Heroes, Hero-Worship and the Heroic in History.* Ed. Michael K. Goldberg, Joel J. Brattin, and Mark Engel. Berkeley: University of California Press, 1993.

Castronovo, Russ. *Fathering the Nation: American Genealogies of Slavery and Freedom.* Berkeley: University of California Press, 1995.

Certeau, Michel de. *The Practice of Everyday Life.* Trans. Steven F. Rendall. Berkeley: University of California Press, 1984.

Chambers, E. K. *William Shakespeare: A Study of the Facts and Problems.* Oxford: Clarendon Press, 1930.

Chaucer, Geoffrey. *The Riverside Chaucer.* Ed. Larry Benson et al. Boston: Houghton Mifflin, 1987.

Cicero. *The Orations of Marcus Tullius Cicero.* Trans. C. D. Yonge. London: George Bell & Sons, 1902.

Coates, Reverend John. "On the Monument of the Honourable Lady Frances Nightingale," in *A Collection of Original Miscellaneous Poems and Translations, by the Reverend Mr. Coates.* 56–58. London, 1770.

Coleridge, Samuel Taylor. *Coleridge's Shakespearian Criticism,* ed. T. M. Raysor. Cambridge: Harvard University Press, 1930.

Collini, Stefan. *Public Moralists: Political Thought and Intellectual Life in Britain.* Oxford: Clarendon Press, 1991.

Connell, Philip. "Death and the Author: Westminster Abbey and the Meanings of the Literary Monument." *Eighteenth-Century Studies* 38 (2005): 556–585.

Craig, E. T. *Shakespeare's Portraits Phrenologically Considered.* Philadelphia: Printed for private circulation by J. Parker Norris, 1875.

Craske, Matthew. *The Silent Rhetoric of the Body: A History of Monumental Sculpture and Commemorative Art in England 1720–1770.* New Haven: Yale University Press, 2007.

————."Westminster Abbey 1720–70: A Public Pantheon Built upon Private Interest," in *Pantheons: Transformations of a Monumental Idea*, ed. Richard Wrigley and Matthew Craske. 57–89. Burlington, VT: Ashgate, 2004.

Crull, Jodocus. *The Antiquities of St. Peter's or the Abbey Church of Westminster.* 3rd ed. London, 1722.

Dahmus, Joseph H. *The Prosecution of John Wyclyf.* Hamden, CT: Archon Books, 1970.

Dart, John. *Westmonasterium, or the History and Antiquities of the Abbey Church of St. Peter's, Westminster.* London, 1723.

Davies, Thomas. *Memoirs of the Life of David Garrick*, 1808. New York: Benjamin Blom, 1969 (with notes by Stephen Jones).

Derrida, Jacques. *Spectres of Marx: The State of the Debt, the Work of Mourning, and the New International.* New York: Routledge, 1994.

Dictionary of National Biography. Oxford: Oxford University Press, 2004.

Dobson, Jessie. "Frank Buckland and Rare Ben Jonson." *Proceedings of the Royal Society of Medicine* 60 (1967): 296–298.

Dobson, Michael. *The Making of the National Poet: Shakespeare, Adaptation and Authorship 1660–1769.* Oxford: Clarendon Press, 1992.

Duffy, Eamon. *The Stripping of the Altars.* New Haven: Yale University Press, 1992.

Durandus, William. *Rationale Divinorum Officiorum.* 3rd edition. Trans. John Mason Neale and Benjamin Web. London: Gibbings and Co., 1906.

Eagle, R. L. "Is There a Shakespeare MS. Poem in Spenser's Tomb?" *Baconiana* 22, 3rd series (1938); 263–264.

Eagleton, Terry. "Having One's Kant and Eating It." *London Review of Books* (19 April 2001), 9.

Eliot, T. S. 1920. "Tradition and the Individual Talent" in *The Sacred Wood*, 30–40. London: Methuen, 1960.

Ellis, Havelock. "Genius and Stature." *Nineteenth Century* 41 (July 1897), 87–95.

————. *A Study of British Genius.* London: Constable, 1927.

Ellison, Michael. "Jew-Hating Ezra Pound Barred from Poets' Corner." *Guardian* (26 October 1999).

"Evermore." *New Yorker* (1 July 1985): 21–22.

Ezard, John. "Poet's Own Words Say Goodbye." *Guardian* (May 13, 1999).

Farmer, Jr., Norman K. "Fulke Greville and John Coke: An Exchange of Letters on a History Lecture and Certain Latin Verses on Sir Philip Sidney." *Huntington Library Quarterly* 33 (1970): 220–223.

Fellowes, E. H., ed. 1928. *Songs and Lyrics From the Plays of Beaumont and Fletcher.* New York: B. Blom, 1972.

Finnel, Andrew J. "The Poet as Sunday Man: The Complaint of Chaucer to His Purse." *Chaucer Review* 8 (1973): 147–158.

Fitzgerald, Thomas. "Upon the Poets' Corner in Westminster-Abbey," in *Poems on Several Occasions*, 24–25. London: J. Watts, 1733.

————. "Upon the Burning of the Cottonian Manuscripts at Ashburnham House" in *Poems on Several Occasions*, 71–74. Oxford: 1781.

Flacci, Horati. *Opera*, ed. D. R. Shackleton Bailey. Stuttgart: K.G. Saur Verlag, 1985.

Flatley, Jonathan. *Affective Mapping: Melancholia and the Politics of Modernism.* Cambridge: Harvard University Press, 2008.

Flete, John. *The History of Westminster Abbey*, ed. J. Armitage Robinson. Cambridge: Cambridge University Press, 1909.

Foucault, Michel. "Of Other Spaces." Trans. Jay Miskowiec. *Diacritics* 16.1 (1968): 22–27.

Fox, Adam. "Poetry Is the Great English Art," in Cecil Day-Lewis, *Guide to Poets' Corner: Westminster Abbey*, 3–7. Manchester: English Counties Periodical Limited, 1977.

Freccero, John. "The Fig Tree and the Laurel: Petrarch's Poetics." *Literary Theory/Renaissance Texts*, ed. Patricia Parker and David Quint, 20–32. Baltimore: Johns Hopkins University Press, 1986.

Freud, Sigmund. "Constructions in Analysis." *The Standard Edition of the Complete Psychological Works of Sigmund Freud*. Trans. ed. James Strachey. London: Hogarth Press, 1964. 23: 255–269.

———. "Mourning and Melancholia." Trans. Joan Rivière, in *Freud: General Psychological Theory*, ed. Philip Rieff, 163–179. New York: 1963.

Fuller, Thomas. *The Appeal of Iniured Innocence: Unto The Religious Learned and Ingenuous Reader. In a Controversie betwixt the Animadvertor Dr. Peter Heylyn and The Author Thomas Fuller*. London, 1659.

———. *The Church-History of Britain; From the Birth of Jesus Christ Until the Year M.DC. XLVIII*. London: Printed for John Williams at the Signe of the Crown in St. Paul's church-yard, 1655.

———. *The Histories of the Worthies of England*. London, 1662.

Fuss, Diana. "Corpse Poem." *Critical Inquiry* 30 (2003): 1–30.

Garber, Marjorie. "Shakespeare as Fetish." *Shakespeare Quarterly* 41 (Summer 1990), 242–250.

Gautier, Théophile. *Poésies Complètes de Théophile Gautier*. Paris, 1862.

Gay, John. *Poetical Works*, ed. G. C. Faber. London, 1926: repr. New York, 1969.

Geary, Patrick. *Living with the Dead in the Middle Ages*. Ithaca: Cornell University Press, 1994.

Girouard, Mark. *The Return to Camelot: Chivalry and the English Gentleman*. New Haven: Yale University Press, 1981.

Glancy, Jonathan. "Top 10 Buildings that Remain Just a Dream—or a Nightmare." *Guardian* (1 November 2001).

Goldgar, Bernard. *Walpole and the Wits: The Relation of Politics to Literature*. Lincoln: University of Nebraska Press, 1976.

Goldsmith, Oliver. *Persian and Chinese Letters*. Washington, D.C.: M. Walter Dunne, 1901.

Gunnis, Rupert Forbes. *Dictionary of British Sculptors 1660–1851*. London: Abbey Library, 1968.

Guthrie, William. "The Apotheosis of Milton." *Gentleman's Magazine* 8 (1738): 232–235; 469; 521–522; 9: 20–21; 73–75.

Haight, Gordon S. *George Eliot: A Biography*. New York: Oxford University Press, 1968.

Hamer, Douglas. "An Account of the Opening of a Grave in Westminster Abbey, November 2nd/3rd 1938, supposed at the time to be that of Edmund Spenser." WAM 62011*.

Hanna, Ralph. *London Literature 1300–1380*. Cambridge: Cambridge University Press, 2005.

Harrison, Robert Pogue. "Hic Jacet." *Critical Inquiry* 27 (2001): 393–407.

Harkin, Michael. "Modernist Anthropology and the Tourism of the Authentic." *Annals of Tourism Experience* 22 (1995): 650–670.

Harvey, Anthony and Richard Mortimer, ed., *The Funeral Effigies of Westminster Abbey*. Woodbridge, Suffolk: Boydell Press, 1994.

Harvey, Barbara. *Westminster Abbey and Its Estates in the Middle Ages*. Oxford: Oxford University Press, 1977.

Harvey, Gabriel. *Foure Letters and Certaine Sonnets*. London, 1592.

Hawthorne, Nathaniel. "Up the Thames." *Atlantic Monthly* 67 (1863): 598–614.

Haydon, Frank Scott, ed. *Eulogium (historiarum sive temporis): Chronicon ab orbe condito usque ad annum Domini M. CCC. LXVI, a monacho quodam Malmesburiensi exaratum. Accedunt continuationes duæ, quarum una ad annum M. CCCC. XIII., altera ad annum M. CCCC. XC. perducta est.* London, 1858–1863.

Hayes, Dawn Marie. *Body and Sacred Place in Medieval Europe 1100–1389.* New York: Routledge, 2003.

Helgerson, Richard. *Self-Crowned Laureates.* Berkeley: University of California Press, 1983.

Herford, C. H., Percy Simpson, and Evelyn Simpson, ed. *Works of Ben Jonson.* Oxford: Clarendon Press, 1954.

Herrick, Robert. *The Hesperides.* London, 1648.

Heylyn, Peter. *Examen Historicum: Or a Discovery and Examination of the Mistakes, Falsities, and Defects In Some Modern Histories. OCCASIONED By the Partiality and Inadvertencies of their Severall Authours.* London, 1659.

Hinman, Charlton. *The Norton Facsimile: The First Folio of Shakespeare.* New York: W. W. Norton, 1968.

Hobhouse, John Cam. *Recollections of a Long Life.* Cambridge: Cambridge University Press, 2011.

Hoock, Holger. "Nelson Entombed: The Military and Naval Pantheon in St. Paul's Cathedral," in *Admiral Lord Nelson: Context and Legacy*, ed. David Cannadine. 115–144. New York: Palgrave, 2005.

Horace. *Odes and Epodes*, ed. Trans. Niall Rudd. Cambridge: Harvard University Press, 2004.

Howse, Christopher. "Ted Hughes Memorial: Poets' Corner Is a White Elephants' Graveyard." *Telegraph* (5 December 2011).

Hughes, Paul L., and James F. Larkin, ed. *Tudor Royal Proclamations*, 3 vols. New Haven: Yale University Press, 1964–69.

Hutson, Lorna. "Fortunate Travelers: Reading for the Plot in Sixteenth-Century England." *Representations* 41 (1993): 83–103.

Huxley, Thomas Henry. *Life and Letters of Thomas Henry Huxley*, ed. Leonard Huxley. New York: Macmillan, 1900.

Huyssen, Andreas. *Present Pasts: Urban Palimpsests and the Politics of Memory.* Stanford: Stanford University Press, 2003.

Hyland, Anthony D. C. "Imperial Valhalla." *Journal of the Society of Architectural Historians* 2 (1962): 129–139.

Ingleby, Clement Mansfield. *Shakespeare's Bones: The proposal to disinter them, considered in relation to their possible bearing on his portraiture: illustrated by instances of visits of the living to the dead.* London: Trübner & Co., 1883.

Irving, Washington. 1819–20. *The Sketchbook of Geoffrey Crayon.* Reprinted with introduction by Susan Manning. Oxford: Oxford University Press, 1996.

Jackson, Alfred. "Pope's Epitaphs on Nicholas Rowe." *Review of English Studies* 7: 25 (1931): 76–79.

Jewel, John. *A Reply to Harding's Answer*, in *The Works of John Jewel, Bishop of Salisbury*, ed. Rev. John Ayre. Cambridge, 1845–50.

Johnson, Samuel. *Lives of the English Poets.* London, 1779–81.

———. *Lives of the English Poets: A Selection*, ed. John Wain. London: Dent, 1975.

Judson, Alexander. *The Life of Edmund Spenser.* Baltimore: John Hopkins University Press, 1945.

Kinney, Daniel with John Knapp and Genevieve McCarthy, ed. *The Abraham Cowley Text Archive*. At http://cowley.lib.virginia.edu/ (accessed 8 August 2014).

Keiser, Elizabeth B. *Courtly Desire and Medieval Homophobia*. New Haven: Yale University Press, 1997.

Lathem, Edward Connery. *England's Homage to Longfellow*. Portland: Maine Historical Society, 2007.

Leersen, Jeop. "Monument and Trauma: Varieties of Remembrance," in *History and Memory in Modern Ireland*, ed. Ian McBride. 204–222. Cambridge: Cambridge University Press, 2001.

Lefebvre, Henri. *The Production of Space*. Trans. Donald Nicholson-Smith. London: Blackwell, 1991.

Lefort, Claude. *Democracy and Political Theory*. Minneapolis: University of Minnesota Press, 1984.

Lerer, Seth. *Chaucer and His Readers*. Princeton: Princeton University Press, 1993.

Lethaby, W. R. "Chaucer's Tomb." *TLS* (21 February 1929), 137.

Levine, Joseph. *Humanism and History: Origins of Modern English Historiography*. Ithaca: Cornell University Press, 1987.

Libra. "Westminster Abbey, As It Is and As It Was." *Illuminated Magazine* 2 (1843): 21–25.

Loewald, Hans W. "Some Considerations on Repetition and Repetition Compulsion." *International Journal of Psychoanalysis* 52 (1971): 59–66.

Lombroso, Cesare. *The Man of Genius*. London: W. Scott, 1891.

Mack, Maynard. *Alexander Pope: A Life*. New York: W. W. Norton, 1986.

MacMichael, N. H. "Sanctuary at Westminster." *Westminster Abbey Occasional Papers* 27 (1971): 9–14.

Manningham, John. *The Diary of John Manningham*, ed, Robert Parker Sorlien. Hanover, University Press of New England, 1976.

"Marlowe Given Poets' Corner Tribute." At http://news.bbc.co.uk/2/hi/entertainment/2124844.stm (accessed 24 August 2014).

Mason, Emma. *Westminster Abbey and Its People, c. 1050–c. 1216*. Woodbridge: Boydell Press, 1996.

Matthews, Samantha. *Poetical Remains: Poets' Graves, Bodies, and Books in the Nineteenth Century*. Oxford: Oxford University Press, 2004.

McCoy, Richard. *Alterations of State: Sacred Kingship in the English Reformation*. New York: Columbia University Press, 2002.

McCrum, Robert. "Deptford Secrets." *Guardian Unlimited* (14 July 2002).

"Monuments in the Abbey." *Times* (London), 18 January 1933.

Moroney, Maryclaire. "Spenser's Dissolution: Monasticism and Ruins in *The Faerie Queene* and *The View of the Present State of Ireland*." *Spenser Studies* 12 (1998): 105–132.

Morris, William. 1884. *Architecture and History and Westminster Abbey*. Charleston, SC: BiblioBazaar, 2008.

M.R., "Shakespeare Poem Discovery? Grave to be Opened" *The Era* 3103 (18 August 1938).

Nashe, Thomas. *The Anatomie of Absurditie*. London, 1589. ·

Ng, David and David Kazanjian, ed. *Reading Loss: The Politics of Mourning*. Berkeley: University of California Press, 2003.

Nohrnberg, James. *The Analogy of "The Faerie Queene."* Princeton: Princeton University Press, 1980.

Nora, Pierre. "Between Memory and History: *Les Lieux de Mémoire*." *Representations* 26 (1989): 7–24.

"On the Old Bust, with a Sour Air, on Mr. Dryden's Monument, in Westminster Abbey." *Gentlemen's Magazine* 3 (1733): 95–96.

Patterson, Lee. *Negotiating the Past: The Historical Understanding of Medieval Literature*. Madison: University of Wisconsin Press, 1987.

Pearsall, Derek. "Chaucer's Tomb: The Politics of Reburial." *Medium Aevum* 64 (1995): 51–73.

———. *The Life of Geoffrey Chaucer*. Oxford: Blackwell, 1992.

Pepys, Samuel. *The Letters of Samuel Pepys 1656–1703*. Ed. Guy de la Bédoyère. Woodbridge, Suffolk: Boydell Press, 2006.

Perroy, Edouard. "Gras profits et rançons pendant la guerre de cent ans: l'affaire du Comte de Denia," in *Mélanges d'histoire du moyen âge dédiés à la mémoire de Louis Halphen*, 573–580. Paris: Presses universitaires, 1951.

Phillips, John. *Theatrum Poetarum: Or a complete Collection of the Poets*. London, 1675.

Physick, John. *Designs for English Sculpture 1680–1860*. London: Her Majesty's Stationery Office, 1969.

Playford, Henry and Abel Roper. *Luctus Britannici or the Tears of the British Muses for the Death of John Dryden, Esq . . . written by the most Eminent Hand in the two Famous Universities, and by several Others*. London, 1700.

Poole, Henry. "Westminster Abbey: A Study on Poets' Corner." *The Antiquary* 4 (1881): 137–139.

———. "Westminster Abbey, The Lost Chapel of St. Blaize." *The Antiquary* 3 (1881): 241–245.

Poole, Reginald Lane. "Review of *Johannis Wyclif, Tractatus de Ecclesia*." *English Historical Review* 3 (1888): 571–575.

Pope, Alexander. *The Twickenham Edition of the Poems of Alexander Pope*, ed. John Butt et al., 6 vols. in 7. London: Methuen: 1954–61.

Pratt, Samuel Jackson. *Miscellanies*. London, 1785.

Prendergast, Thomas A. *Chaucer's Dead Body: From Corpse to Corpus*. New York: Routledge, 2004.

———. "Politics, Prodigality, and the Reception of Chaucer's 'Purse.'" In *Reinventing the Middle Ages and the Renaissance: Constructions of the Medieval and Early Modern Periods*, ed. William R. Gentrup, 64–76. Turnhout, Belgium: Brepols, 1997.

———. "Spenser's Phantastic History: *The Ruines of Time* and the Invention of Medievalism." *Journal of Medieval and Early Modern Studies* 38 (2008): 175–196.

P.S. N.T. *Notes and Queries* 3 (10 May 1851): 381.

Rambuss, Richard. *Spenser's Secret Career*. Cambridge: Cambridge University Press, 1993.

Reynolds, Nigel. "Marlowe Tribute Puts Question Mark over Shakespeare." *Telegraph* (11 July 2002). At http://www.telegraph.co.uk/news/uknews/1401010/Marlowe–tribute–puts–question–mark–over–Shakespeare.html (accessed 24 August 2014).

Roach, Joseph. "Celebrity Erotics: Pepys, Performance, and Painted Ladies." *Yale Journal of Criticism* 16 (2003): 211–230.

Robinson, J. Armitage. "An Unrecognized Westminster Chronicler, 1381–1394." *Proceedings of the British Academy* 3 (1907–8), 61–92.

———. *Gilbert Crispin: Abbot of Westminster*. Cambridge: Cambridge University Press, 1911.

———, ed. *The History of Westminster Abbey*. Cambridge: Cambridge University Press, 1909.

Robinson, Eric, and David Powell, eds. *John Clare By Himself*. Routledge: New York, 2002.

Romano Alberti, *Trattato della nobiltà dell pittura* (Rome, 1585)

Ross, Trevor. "Just When Did 'British bards begin t'immortalize'?" *Studies in Eighteenth-Century Culture* 19 (1989): 383–398.

S. "N.B." *TLS* (7 February 2003). At www.the-tls.co.uk/tls/reviews/arts_and _commentary/article733615.ece (accessed August 24, 2014).

Saler, Michael. *The Avant-Garde in Interwar England: Medieval Modernism and the London Underground*. Oxford: Oxford University Press, 2001.

Schiesari, Judith. *The Gendering of Melancholia: Feminism, Psychoanalysis, and the Symbolics of Loss in Renaissance Literature*. Ithaca: Cornell University Press, 1992.

Scodel, Joshua. *The English Poetic Epitaph: Commemoration and Conflict from Jonson to Wordsworth*. Ithaca: Cornell University Press, 1991.

Shakespeare, William. *The Complete Works*, ed. Stanley Wells and Gary Taylor. Oxford: Clarendon Press, 1986.

———. *The First Folio of Shakespeare*, prepared by Charlton Hinman. New York: W. W. Norton, 1968.

Sherburn, George. *The Early Career of Alexander Pope*. Oxford: Clarendon Press, 1934.

Sheridan, Richard Brinsley. *Verses to the Memory of Garrick*. London, 1779.

Shoenbaum, Samuel. *Shakespeare's Lives*. Oxford: Oxford University Press, 1991.

Short, R. W. "Ben Jonson in Drayton's Poems." *Review of English Studies* 62 (1940): 149–158.

Sidney, Philip. *A Defense of Poetry*, ed. Jan Van Dorsten. Oxford: Oxford University Press, 1966.

Simpson, James. *The Oxford English Literary History, Volume 2, 1350–1547: Reform and Cultural Revolution*. Cambridge: Cambridge University Press, 2002.

Smiles, Samuel. *A Publisher and His Friends: Memoir and Correspondence of the late John Murray, with an Account of the Origin and Progress of his House, 1766–1843*. London, John Murray, 1891.

Smith, Dinitia. "Cathedral Bars Ezra Pound from Its Poets' Corner." *New York Times*, 23 October 1999. At http://www.nytimes.com/1999/10/23/books/cathedral–bars–ezra–pound–from–its–poets–corner.html (accessed 24 August 2014).

Spearing, A. C. *Readings in Medieval Poetry*. Cambridge: Cambridge University Press, 1987.

Spence, Joseph. *Observations, Anecdotes, and Characters of Books and Men: Collected from Conversation*. Oxford: Clarendon Press, 1966.

Spenser, Edmund. *Works of Spenser*, ed. John Payne Collier. London, 1845.

———. *The Works of Edmund Spenser: A Variorum Edition*, ed. Edwin Greenlaw, Charles Grosvenor Osgood, and Frederick Morgan Padelford. Baltimore: Johns Hopkins Press, 1932–1957.

———. *The Yale Edition of the Shorter Poems of Edmund Spenser*, ed. William A. Oram et al. New Haven: Yale University Press, 1989.

Spiers, W. L., ed. *Note-Book and Account Book of Nicholas Stone*. London: Walpole Society, 1919.

Sprat, Thomas. *An Account of the Life and Writings of Mr. Abraham Cowley* in *The Works of Mr. Abraham Cowley*, A1r–A12v. London, 1668.

Spurgeon, Caroline F. E. *Five Hundred Years of Chaucer Criticism and Allusion 1357–1900*. Cambridge: Cambridge University Press, 1925.

Stafford, Barbara. *Body Criticism: Imaging the Unseen in Enlightenment Art and Medicine*. Cambridge: MIT Press, 1991.

———. *Good Looking*. Cambridge: MIT Press, 1999.

Stallybrass, Peter. "Patriarchal Territories: The Body Enclosed," in *Rewriting the Renaissance*, ed. Margaret W. Ferguson, Maureen Quilligan, and Nancy J. Vickers. 123–142. Chicago: University of Chicago Press, 1986.

Stanley, Arthur Penrhyn. *Historical Memorials of Westminster Abbey.* London: John Murray, 1868.

———. *Letters and Verses of Arthur Penrhyn Stanley D. D.*, ed. Rowland Prothero. New York: Scribners' Sons, 1895.

———. "Recollections." WAM 64918.

Strachey, J, ed. *Rotuli parliamentorum; ut et petitiones, et placita in parliamento.* Collected and arranged by R. Blyke, P. Morant, T. Astle, & J. Topham. London, 1767–1777.

Strohm, Paul. *Chaucer's Tale: 1386 and the Road to Canterbury.* New York: Viking, 2014.

———. "The Trouble with Richard: The Reburial of Richard II and Lancastrian Strategy." *Speculum* 71 (1996): 87–111.

Summit, Jennifer. "Monuments and Ruins: Spenser and the Problem of the English Library." *English Literary History* 70 (2003): 1–34.

Sydney. *Sydney's Letters to the Editor of the Courier, on the Reported Exclusion of Lord Byron's Monument From Westminster Abbey.* London: James Cawthorne, 1828.

Tanner, Lawrence. "We Have Now Lost Spenser." *Liverpool Daily Post* (22 November 1938).

———. "Recollections." Unpublished, Westminster Abbey Library.

———. *Recollections of a Westminster Antiquary.* London: J. Baker, 1969.

Thompson, Edward Maunde, ed. *Chronicon Angliae, ab anno domini 1328 usque ad annum 1388, auctore monacho quodam Sancti Albani.* London: Longman, 1874.

Thynne, Francis. *Emblemes and epigrammes*, ed. F. J. Furnivall. *EETS* o.s. 64. London: N. Trübner & Co., 1876.

Trigg, Stephanie. *Congenial Souls: Reading Chaucer from Medieval to Postmodern.* Minneapolis: University of Minnesota Press, 2001.

———. "Walking Through Cathedrals: Scholars, Pilgrims, and Medieval Tourists." *New Medieval Literatures* 7 (2005): 9–34.

Troutbeck, Henry. N.T. *The Nineteenth Century* 42 (August 1897): 336.

Verdery, Katherine. *The Political Lives of Dead Bodies.* New York: Columbia University Press, 1999.

Walsingham, Thomas. *Historia Anglicana.* Ed. Henry Thomas Riley, Rolls Series 23, Stationery Office, London, 1863.

———. *The Saint Albans Chronicle: The Chronica Maiora of Thomas Walsingham*, ed. John Taylor, Wendy R. Childs, and Leslie Watkiss. Oxford: Oxford University Press, 2003.

Warner, William. "To the Reader," in *A Continuance of Albions England*, A2r-A3r, London, 1606.

Watson, Nicola J. *The Literary Tourist: Readers and Places in Romantic and Victorian Britain.* New York: Palgrave, 2006.

Watt, Ian. "Publishers and Sinners: The Augustan View." *Studies in Bibliography* 12 (1959): 3–20.

Weever, John. 1599. *Epigrammes in the oldest cut, and newest fashion*, ed. R. B. McKerrow. London: Sidgwick & Jackson, 1911.

Wells, Stanley and Gary Taylor. *William Shakespeare: A Textual Companion.* Oxford: Oxford University Press, 1987.

Westminster Abbey. *Westminster Abbey: Official Guide.* Norwich: Jarrold Publishing, 1988.

Whinney, Margaret. *Sculpture in Britain: 1530–1830.* Baltimore: Penguin Books, 1964.

Wilson, Jean. "The Patron of the Monument to Michael Drayton in Westminster Abbey."
    Church Monuments Society Newsletter 9.1 (1993): 16–17.
Workman, Herbert B. *John Wyclif: A Study of the English Medieval Church.* Hamden, CT:
    Archon Books, 1966.
Young, Edward. *Conjectures on Original Composition.* London, 1759.
Žižek, Slavoj. *For They Know Not What They Do: Enjoyment as a Political Factor.* New York:
    Verso, 1991.

INDEX

Saints are indexed by their first name followed by St. Nobility are indexed by place followed by (first, last name) title.

English identity: cultural patriotism, 99;
defining, 130; literature's role in, 2, 131,
136; monuments in creating and
maintaining, 5–6, 13, 15, 44, 46,
105–106; the Valhalla of, 62, 113, 116–118
Epistle to Arbuthnot (Pope), 93, 102
Epistle to Paul Methuen (Gay), 96–97
epitaphs, truthfulness of, 65–66
Epithalamion (Spenser), 50
Essex, Earl of. *See* Devereux, Robert
Euripides, 61
exhumations and reburials: Chaucer,
Geoffrey, 126–127, 130–131; critics of,
127–129; Edward the Confessor, 22; to
establish authenticity, 15–16, 127–128,
131–142; to gain intelligence about
genius or virtue, 128–131; May, Thomas,
4, 127; monuments marking, 179;
politics of, 4, 69, 127, 190n9, 201n9;
public interest in, 137–142; rationales
for, 127, 129–130; to reinstitutionalize
Catholicism, 5, 126–127; Shakespeare,
advocates of, 60, 131; Spenser, attempted,
15–16, 131–142, 197n48; support for,
134–138. *See also* burials; translation

Faerie Queene (Spenser), 45, 46, 53
fame: by association, 85, 92; monumental vs.
literary, 104; monuments in ensuring,
56–57, 116; of rulers vs. poets, 71, 85
feast of St. Edward, 24
feast of the Conception of the Blessed
Virgin, 34
Feckenham, John, 12
Fergusson, James, 117–119
festival of St. Edward, 24
First Folio (Shakespeare), 60, 62
Fitzgerald, F. Scott, 150
Fitzgerald, Thomas, 4, 29, 83–87, 92–93, 97
Flatley, Jonathan, 12
Fletcher, John, 57
Flete, John, 35
Fonteyn, Margot (Royal Ballet), 163, 186
Forbes-Robertson, Johnston, 135
Ford, Edward Onslow, 181
Foucault, Michel, xiii

Founders of the Royal Ballet, 163, 186
four-fold tomb, 57–58, 61–62, 64
Fox, Adam, 161, 184
Frecerro, John, 12
Freud, Sigmund, 18, 48
Fulham Churchyard, 177
Fuller, Thomas, 4, 52, 56, 64–67, 78
funerals, commemorative function of, 15
furniture, funereal, 43–44
Fuss, Diana, 38

Garber, Marjorie, 143–146
Garrick, David, 146–147, 161, 174, 176
Garrick, Eva, 174, 176
Gascoigne, Joseph, 74
Gaskell, Elizabeth, 125
Gay, John, 92, 97, 162, 170, 172
Geary, Patrick, 20
genius, 15–16, 66, 128–131
"Genius and Stature" (Ellis), 130
Gentleman's Magazine, 121–122
George II, 173
George III, 173, 174
Gibbs, James, 86
Gibson, Wilfrid (War Poets memorial),
164, 184
Gielgud, John, 185
Gifford, William, 162, 177
Gilbert, lord abbot, 22
Glasnevin Cemetery, Dublin, 184
Gloucester Cathedral, 167
Goldsmith, Oliver, 63, 90–91, 102–103, 116,
162, 174
Gordon, Adam Lindsay, 162, 182
Gordon, George (Lord Byron), 15, 106–110,
112–119, 125, 143, 162, 183
Gower, John, 196n1
Grabe, John Ernest, 162, 171
Grasmere, Cumbria, 115, 178
graveplan: chronological list of stones and
monuments based on, 165–187; Poets'
Corner, 19, 159
Graves, Robert (War Poets memorial), 164,
184
graves, sharing of: by families, 167–172, 174,
175, 181; by friends, 177, 179; leveling

iconoclasm, 5–6, 43–46, 179
idolatry, 4, 11–12, 43–45
Iliad (Homer), 59
immortality, poetic vs. monumental, x–xii,
    6–9, 11–12, 43, 49–50, 59–63, 68,
    79–80, 84–86
Imperial Hall and Tower, 117
Imperial Monumental Hall, 118
Ingleby, C. M., 126–129
Inglis, Robert H., 177
Innocent II, 24
inspiration, 46–49
Ireland, John, 107, 162, 177
Irving, Henry, 162
Irving, Washington, vi, ix–xi, 1, 11–12,
    157, 181

James, Henry, 162, 184
James, P. D., 153
James, St., 4
James I, 135, 166
James II, 85, 96, 168
James VI, 40
Jesus, son of Mary, 4, 34
Jewel, John, 48–49
John of Gaunt, 13, 30
Johnson, Samuel, 81, 92, 121, 162, 173, 174
Jones, David (War Poets memorial), 164, 185
Jonson, Ben, 6, 14–15, 43, 51–52, 60–64,
    67–72, 78–80, 83, 90, 146, 162, 168, 171
Jowett, Benjamin, 124

Kantorowicz, Ernest, 26
Keats, John, 162, 182–183
Keats-Shelley Memorial Association, 183
Keble, John, 112–114, 162, 178–179
Kensal Green Cemetery, London, 178, 185
Keynes, Geoffrey, 183
Kilwardby, Robert, 23
kings: burial in Westminster Abbey,
    justifying, 85; fame of vs. poets, 71, 85;
    inviolate nature of, 104; kingly
    corpse-body politic connection, 12;
    power, post-death, 26–27
Kingsley, Charles, 112–113
Kipling, Rudyard, 162, 182

Kirchstetten, Lower Austria, 184
Kyd, Thomas, 61

Laleham, Middlesex, 180
Lamb, Edward Beckitt, 118
Lambert, Constant (Royal Ballet), 163, 186
Lane, John, 51
Lanfranc, Archbishop of Canterbury, 192n17
Langton, Archbishop, 23
Las Palmas English cemetery, 185
Laugharne, South Wales, 184
Lawrence, D. H., 162, 184
Lazarus, George, 184
Lear, Edward, 162, 185
Lechmere, Elizabeth, 181
Leeson, Jeop, 105–106
Lefort, Claude, 26–27
Leicester (Robert Dudley), Earl of, 53
Leo (*sic*, surname is Loe), William, 162, 167
Lethaby, W. R., 43, 136
Lewes, George Henry, 124
Lewis, C. S., 162, 186
lies of poets and painters, 48–49, 65
Life (Aelred), 192n17
Life (Osbert of Clare), 22–23
Lind-Goldschmidt, Jenny, 162, 174, 181
Lintot, Bernard, 98
literary culture: American, 150; contempo-
    rary, 155–156; corporeal presence and,
    148; primary claims of, xi; relevance of,
    11, 15–16, 142
literary marketplace, 98–99, 101–103
literature: English identity and, 2, 131, 136;
    reader-author relationship, x, xiii, 3,
    7–9, 11–12, 142; religion and, separat-
    ing, 150
Litlyngton, Nicholas, 163, 179
Little Poets' Corner, 112–114, 116
Lives of the Poets (Johnson), 81
Lofft, Capel, 127–129
Lombroso, Cesare, 131
Longfellow, Henry Wadsworth, 163, 180
Lord Byron. *See* Gordon, George (Lord
    Byron)
loss: melancholia and, 46–48; memorial
    recuperation of, x–xi, 45

14–15, 15, 50; of poets, 85–86; of Poets'
Corner, xi, 7, 13; politics and, 85–86;
of the public, 137–142; of the sovereign,
post-death, 26
Pratt, Samuel Jackson, 146
Primrose, Archibald Philip, Earl of Rosebery
180
Pringle, James, 174
Pringle, John, 163, 174
printing, invention of, 74, 98, 103
Prior, Matthew, 86, 89–90, 103, 122, 155, 163,
171
Prior monument, 86
Pritchard, Hannah, 163, 173, 177
Problems (pseudo-Aristotle), 46–49
production (manufacturing), 20
Protestant Cemetery, Rome, 182
Protestants, 5, 13–14, 43–45, 49
Psalm 45, 149
the public: monument funding, 99–101, 177,
178, 180–184; poetry and, 15, 72; Poets'
Corner as a space for, 1–2, 28–29, 72,
74; power of, 137–142; as readers, x, xiii,
3, 7–9, 11–12, 74, 98–99, 142, 156. *See
also* society; visitors
public love, 14, 156

Quarles, Francis, 63
Queensbury (Catherine Hyde), Duchess of,
172
Queensbury (Charles Douglas), Duke of, 172

Ra, Marsha, 151
Raphael Sanzio da Urbino, 127
Rationale (Durandus), 34
Ravis, Thomas, 196n11
Read, Herbert (War Poets memorial), 164, 185
reader-author relationship, x, xiii, 3, 7–9,
11–12, 142, 156
reading public, x, xiii, 3, 7–9, 11–12, 98–99,
142, 156
"Recollections" (Tanner), 140
reconsecration, politics of, 32–34
Reformation, 5, 13, 27, 43–45, 49
Reges, Reginae, Nobiles et alij (Camden), 35–36
relics, 4–5, 20, 23–24, 78

religion: art as a replacement for, 136; and
literature, separating, 150; national, 21,
40, 149–151; politics linked to through
the body, 12–13
Reply to Harding's Answer (Jewel), 48–49
Reynolds, Christine, 165
Richard de Kedyngton (alias Sudbury), 161,
165–166
Richard II, 13, 26, 27, 30
Richard III, 26
Richard of Chichester, St., 23
Richmond Parish Church, Surrey, 173
Riddell, George James, 163, 174
Riddell, James, 174
Riddell, Sarah, 174
Roach, Joseph, 100
Roberts, Dorothy, 173
Roberts, John, 163, 173
Roberts, Rebecca, 173
Roberts, Susannah, 173
Robinson, Elizabeth, 163
Robinson, Thomas, 163, 174, 181
romance, planning in, 19
romance writing, 49
Romantic writers, 106, 120
Rosebery, Earl of. *See* Primrose, Archibald
Philip
Rosenberg, Isaac (War Poets memorial), 164,
185
Roubiliac, Louis-François, 74, 173
Rowe, Charlotte, 172
Rowe, Nicholas, 80, 93, 155, 163, 172
Rowlands, Miss, 136–137
Royal Ballet, The Founders, 163, 186
Rudolph, abbot of St. Trond, 34
The Ruines of Time (Spenser), 46–47, 50–51,
56, 71
rulers. *See* kings; monarchy
Ruskin, John, 136, 140, 163, 178, 181
Rysbrack, John Michael, 74, 86

Sacrarium, 169, 170
sacred space: the body as, 4–5, 12–13, 20, 113;
boundaries of, 13; Poets' Corner as,
13–15; South Transept, 113; Westminster
Abbey, 20

Stafford, Barbara, 129

Stallybrass, Peter, 122

St. Andrew's churchyard, Coniston, 181

Stanley, Arthur Penrhyn, 9–10, 20, 27, 35, 58, 70, 103–104, 106–107, 109–110, 112–114, 116–117, 120, 123, 125, 149, 168, 178

Stapleton, Robert, 78, 187

the state: kingly corpse-body politic connection, 12; poetry and the, 91–92, 96–97, 99; sanctuary principle and, 30–34

St. Benedict's Chapel, 35–36, 38–39, 54, 80, 159, 166, 167, 180, 186

St. Blaize's Chapel, 86, 89, 169, 179, 202n32

St. Edmund's Chapel, 26

Steele, Mary (Prue), 164, 170

Steele, Richard, 170

St. Enodoc's, Trebetherick, 185

St. Faith's Chapel, 76, 159

St. George's Chapel, 112, 180

St. Giles's, Cripplegate, 172

St. Helen of Athyra, 20

Stinsford, Dorset, 182

St. James, Westminster, 174

St. John's Chapel, 103

St. John the Divine, 1, 16

St. Margaret's Church, Westminster Abbey, 4

St. Margaret's Churchyard, 179

St.-Martin-in-the-Fields, 175

St. Mary's the Virgin gallery, 91

St. Michael and All Angels, Haworth, 182

St. Michael's, Highgate, 180

Stoke Poges, 174

Stone, Nicholas, 53

stones marking burial places, 165–187

Stoney, Andrew Robinson, 119

St. Pancras parish church, 171

St. Paul's Church, 71

St. Paul's Church, Covent Garden, 116, 170

Stratford upon Avon, 114, 115, 172

Strathmore, Countess. See Bowes, Mary Eleanor

Strong, William, 164, 179, 201n9

St. Swithins, Bath, 176

Sudbury, Archbishop, 30

Sulcard, 22

Swedenborg, Emanuel, 127

Tait, Archibald Campbell, 164, 180

Tale of Sir Thopas (Chaucer), 46

Tanner, Lawrence, 137–138, 140–141

Taylor, Robert, 164, 175

Teddington, 173

The Tempest (Shakespeare), 2

Temple Churchyard, London, 174

Tennyson, Alfred Lord, 155, 164, 180, 181

Tennyson Society, 155

Thackeray, William Makepeace, 119, 164, 176, 178

Theatrum Poetarum (Phillips), 53

Theobald, B. G., 137

Thirwall, Connop, 164, 179

Thomas, Dylan, 164, 184

Thomas, Edward (War Poets memorial), 164, 185

Thomas of Woodstock, 176

Thomson, James, 164, 173

Thorndike, Sybil, 135

time, poetry's ability to defeat, x–xii, 6–9, 11–12, 43, 49–50, 59–63, 68, 79–80, 84–86

Tityrus, 46

tombs, functions of, 75

"On the Tombs in Westminster Abbey" (Beaumont), 58

tourist attraction, Westminster Abbey as, 1, 3, 40, 74, 115, 140, 155. *See also* visitors

"Tradition and the Individual Talent" (Eliot), 10

tragedy, genre of, 31–32

translations: Becket, Thomas, 25; Catholicizing space through, 5, 12, 43–44; Chaucer, Geoffrey, 5, 126–127, 130–131; Edward the Confessor, 23–25; Shakespeare, William, 14, 127–128. *See also* exhumations and reburials

Trigg, Stephanie, 190n8, 215n22

Triplett, Thomas, 164, 168, 180

Trollope, Anthony, 164, 185

Troutbeck, Henry, 130–131

Trowles, Tony, 165

ACKNOWLEDGMENTS

This book is about the dead, but it is the living who have helped it come to be. Terry Prendergast has read this book many times, in many different forms, and in many different places. Her love, encouragement, and insight made this book possible. Stephanie Trigg's intellectual companionship and warmth have been inspiring. Elizabeth Allen, Russ Castronovo, and Tassie Gwilliam, have read various versions of the manuscript, and their comments made the book much better than it would have been. Jeffrey Cohen and Peter Travis offered encouragement and advice at fraught moments in the book's long journey. Tom Goodmann's friendship, conversation, and wisdom helped sustain me over the years it took to understand Poets' Corner. Terry Rowden's camaraderie and theoretical acumen have meant more to me than he probably knows. Ana Hill's technical expertise, care, and enthusiasm made producing the graveplan a joy. Elizabeth Allen and Bobby Meyer-Lee graciously shared forthcoming work on the problem of sanctuary. Jerry Singerman's patience, understanding, and good humor make him *the* editor you want to work with. Thanks to David Blake and another (anonymous) reader for the University of Pennsylvania Press for their well-considered suggestions. Thanks to those at Westminster Abbey and the Abbey Library (particularly Tony Trowles and Christine Reynolds), without whose help this book would be a pale shadow of itself. Thanks also to Leslie Bow, Carolyn Dinshaw, John Ganim, Frank Grady, Patty Ingham, Sarah Kelen, David Matthews, Myra Seaman, David Wallace, Lawrence Warner, Michelle Warren, the staff at the Cathedral Church of St. John the Divine, the Folger Shakespeare Library, and my friends and colleagues at the College of Wooster who have listened to me talk about dead bodies for longer than they probably can remember.

I begin this book talking about that important word—home. And so I dedicate this book to those who make up my own—beloved Terry and Charles.

A portion of Chapter 2 appeared previously in "Spenser's Phantastic History: *The Ruines of Time* and the Invention of Medievalism," *Journal of Medieval and Early Modern Studies* 38 (Spring 2008): 175–196.